T H E
WEIGHT-LOSS
BIBLE

BETSY A. HORNICK, M.S., R.D.

Publications International, Ltd.

Betsy A. Hornick, M.S., R.D., is a registered dietitian specializing in nutrition education and communications. She has written and edited numerous nutrition and health education publications for both consumers and health professionals, including materials published by the American Dietetic Association. She is a regular contributor to *Diabetic Cooking* magazine and a consultant for *Easy Home Cooking* magazine.

Additional contributing writers: Joan Horbiak, M.Ph., R.D.; Elizabeth M. Ward, M.S., R.D.; Densie Webb, Ph.D., R.D.

Nutritional Analysis: Linda R. Yoakam, M.S., R.D., L.D.

The nutritional information that appears with each recipe was submitted in part by the participating companies and associations. Every effort has been made to check the accuracy of these numbers. However, because numerous variables account for a wide range of values for certain foods, nutritive analyses in this book should be considered approximate.

ISBN: 1-4127-1024-3

Library of Congress Control Number: 2004106045

Pictured on the front cover *(left to right):* Stuffed French Toast with Fresh Berry Topping *(page 130),* Spiced Turkey with Fruit Salsa *(page 234),* and Spaghetti Squash Primavera *(page 208).* Please note: The Spiced Turkey with Fruit Salsa pictured on the front cover is one standard serving of poultry (approximately 3 ounces).
Pictured on the back cover *(left to right):* Stanley Sandwich *(page 242)* and Blackberry Sorbet *(page 300).*

Microwave Cooking: Microwave ovens vary in wattage. Use the cooking times as guidelines and check for doneness before adding more time.

Preparation/Cooking Times: Preparation times are based on the approximate amount of time required to assemble the recipe before cooking, baking, chilling, or serving. These times include preparation steps such as measuring, chopping, and mixing. The fact that some preparation and cooking can be done simultaneously is taken into account. Preparation of optional ingredients and serving suggestions is not included.

contents

introduction

If you want to lose weight but don't know where or how to begin, you've come to the right source. *The Weight-Loss Bible* will help you choose the weight-loss route that's right for you. You'll not only find honest and reliable information on dieting, but you'll get advice about how to choose the best diet for your personality and lifestyle.

Your first stop on The Road to Weight Loss, the first section of the book, is for a guided tour of healthful eating. You'll learn how the body uses nutrients so you can choose foods that will assist your weight-loss efforts and keep you from straying off the path. Then, to demystify diet labels such as "low carb" or "food combining," you'll take a short trip through the basic types of diet plans. We'll give you a simple explanation of each, as well as the pros and cons. As you continue on the first leg of your journey, you'll also learn just how important physical activity is to your weight-loss efforts and how to get your calorie-burning engine revved up.

The end of section one offers you side trips through reviews of 20 different popular diet plans, including Atkins, Jenny Craig, South Beach, and Weight Watchers. These reviews will help you determine if a weight-loss book or program is your best route to taking off pounds. For a quick comparison of features, use the Diets-at-a-Glance chart that follows the reviews.

The second section, Personalize Your Weight-Loss Plan, helps you assess your current weight and physical fitness and gives you the tools you need to plot a course to your weight-loss goals. If you prefer a do-it-yourself approach to weight loss, we offer practical, easy-to-implement suggestions for building your own diet plan. The nutrient counter, at the end of the section, will help you choose foods that will keep you satisfied while losing weight.

In the last section, Winning Weight-Loss Recipes, there are scrumptious recipes galore that fit your calorie budget while tantalizing your taste buds. You'll find recipes that work with any diet plan.

Weight loss is all about making the right choices—whether it's choosing a diet plan, a method for increasing physical activity, or a technique to manage your cravings. *The Weight-Loss Bible* will help you weigh the options and get you to your weight-loss destination safely, comfortably, and deliciously!

the road to weight loss

You've decided to embark on a journey—a trip to a healthier, slimmer you. But there is more than one way to reach your destination: Which road should you take? This section will give you the information you need about nutrition, diet plans, and physical activity to map out the fastest and safest route. You'll also learn which rare situations call for serious roadside assistance in the form of weight-loss drugs or surgery.

before you embark: what you need to know

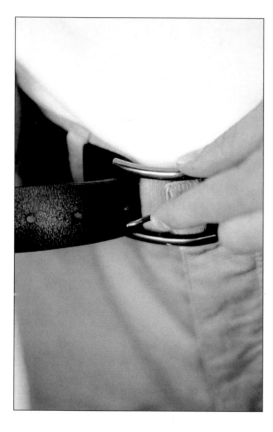

There is something you need to get under your belt before you embark on any weight-loss program. Don't worry—it won't make your clothing fit more tightly. But it will help you lose weight effectively and safely. And it may help you keep the weight off.

Basic nutrition information—that's what you need under your belt. And it's calorie free! Whether you want to lose 5 pounds or 50 pounds, it's easy to be led astray and ultimately become disappointed by diets that make outrageous promises. That's why it is important to learn about the role of nutrients in food and how these nutrients are used in your body. Armed with this knowledge, you can resist the siren call of unhealthy diets and make an informed decision about a weight-loss plan that's right for you.

nutrition fundamentals

Most foods contain a combination of three energy-producing nutrients—protein, fat, and carbohydrate. These nutrients are responsible for providing the energy that your body's engine needs to run well, and they are essential to your health. Your body requires all three, as well as vitamins, minerals, and water. Fiber, a type of carbohydrate, and fluids both play important roles in managing your weight, too.

If you're trying to lose weight, you've certainly heard the word calorie. Basically, calorie is another word for energy. There are four sources of calories: the three energy-producing nutrients mentioned above (protein, fat, and carbohydrate) and alcohol. Fiber, although it's a carbohydrate, is not processed by the body and is calorie free.

calorie basics

Weight loss (and weight gain, for that matter) is primarily an issue of calories:

how many you consume and how many you expend. If the number of calories you eat and the number of calories you use each day are approximately the same, your weight won't budge. It's only when you consume fewer calories than you use over a period of time that you will lose weight. And it's only when you eat more calories than you use that you will gain weight.

So what numbers of calories are we talking about? This is the crucial equation: One pound of body weight is equal to 3,500 calories. This means that to lose one pound, you must create a 3,500-calorie shortage by eating fewer calories, burning more calories through physical activity, or a combination of both. The exact opposite is true for weight gain. Sounds like a lot, doesn't it? But it's not really. Gaining a pound is as easy as eating an extra 250 calories a day (for instance, any of these: three chocolate chip cookies, one milk chocolate bar, two ounces cheddar cheese, or a medium-size bagel) for two weeks or skipping a daily workout without cutting back on eating.

And despite claims from popular diet plans, a calorie is a calorie, whether it comes from protein, fat, or carbohydrate. Any calories eaten that your body doesn't burn for energy are stored as body fat, no matter what kind of food package they came in.

There are a few other factors, in addition to calories, that influence your weight. They are your age, your gender, and your genetic blueprint. Unfortunately, these factors are out of your control. So focus on food intake and physical activity, the areas in which you can have an impact.

protein

Although some popular diet books maintain that high-protein diets have the power to build muscle and melt away fat, the truth is that most of us already get plenty of protein in our diets and still have to battle the bulge. Physical activity, not a high-protein diet, builds muscle. You do need some protein to build, repair, and maintain your body's tissues, including muscles, skin, and internal organs. But you don't need a lot of it.

Protein is supplied by both animal and plant foods, including meat, poultry, fish, eggs, dairy products, legumes, nuts, and grain products. A key difference between animal and plant sources of protein is the amount and type of fat. Animal sources

Calorie counts

Here's where the calories you eat come from. All are nutrients except alcohol, which provides only calories.

- 1 gram of protein provides 4 calories
- 1 gram of fat provides 9 calories
- 1 gram of carbohydrate provides 4 calories
- 1 gram of alcohol provides 7 calories

The power of 100 calories

Gradual weight gain is caused, on average, by an excess of only about 100 calories per day. So eliminating 100 calories by eating a little less and getting more physical activity may be all it takes to manage your weight. Losing 10 pounds over a year can be as simple as eating 100 calories less each day for a year. Try these tips to get started.

Five ways to trim 100 calories from food:
- Swap a 12-ounce regular soft drink for a diet soft drink or water.
- Drink 2 cups of fat-free milk instead of 2 cups of whole milk.
- Use 1 teaspoon of mustard or ketchup or 1 tablespoon of fat-free mayonnaise in place of 1 tablespoon of regular mayonnaise.
- Split a small order of french fries with a friend.
- Slice a typical piece of pie or cake about one-third smaller.

Five ways to burn 100 calories through physical activity:*
- Pedal an exercise bike for 13 minutes.
- Practice some fast dance steps for 16 minutes.
- Work in the garden for 18 minutes.
- Walk briskly for 23 minutes (3.5 mph).
- Clean the house for 25 minutes.

Five food and foot power combos to cut 100 calories:*
- Eat 5 fewer potato chips, and walk for 6 minutes.
- Eat one-quarter cup less of spaghetti with tomato sauce, and walk for 11 minutes.
- Top toast with 2 teaspoons apple butter instead of 2 teaspoons butter, and walk for 11 minutes.
- Spoon out 3 tablespoons less mashed potatoes, and walk for 13 minutes.
- Skip 2 half-and-half creamers in coffee, and walk for 15 minutes.

* Physical activity and walking estimates based on calories burned by a 150-pound person. Calories burned will increase with higher body weights and decrease with lower body weights.

Tips are reprinted with permission of Food Insight, *a publication of the International Food Information Council Foundation, 2003.*

of protein tend to have more fat and often have more saturated fat, the type of fat that can increase blood cholesterol levels. When you eat more protein than you need, it is converted and stored as body fat. Protein, no matter what its source, provides four calories per gram.

fat

Though fat has been blamed for America's growing weight problems, the truth is, fat is only a problem when you eat too much of it. In fact, fat is an essential component of every cell in your body—not just fat cells. Your body can't function without it. Fat promotes healthy skin, and it acts as a partner with certain vitamins, carrying these nutrients to wherever your body needs them. And the fat stored in your body provides insulation against extreme temperatures and helps cushion and protect vital organs, such as your heart and liver.

Fat also plays an important role in satisfying hunger. This is one reason that you may feel hungry within an hour or two after eating a very low-fat meal. Just remember that it takes some time for fat to send satiety signals to your brain (longer than protein and carbohydrate), which is why it can be easy to overeat fatty foods, such as fries and chips.

Fat occurs naturally in meat, poultry, fish, dairy products, and nuts. Vegetable oil, butter, margarine, cream, and mayonnaise are almost all fat. All types of fat provide nine calories per gram—more than twice as much as carbohydrate and protein—making them a double threat if you eat too much. Most health experts suggest that your fat intake should not exceed 30 percent of your daily calorie intake and that most of it should be from

monounsaturated (for example, olive oil and canola oil) and polyunsaturated (for example, soybean, safflower, corn, and cottonseed oils) fats. However, dietary fat intake recommendations vary substantially from one diet plan to the next, ranging from 10 to 45 percent of total calories.

carbohydrate

Carbohydrate, which includes both sugars and starches, is the body's primary source of fuel. But this energy-producing nutrient has been getting a bum rap lately. Just like fat, which for generations was the fall guy when it came to weight gain, carbohydrate is now taking the brunt of the blame. But you can't generalize about carbohydrate any more than you can about fat. We now know that some kinds of fat are better for you than others; in fact, some kinds of fat actually help protect against heart disease. The same is true of carbohydrate. Some carbs are loaded with vitamins, minerals, fiber, and disease-fighting antioxidants and phytonutrients. Others simply are high in calories and low in nutritional value. And some fall in the middle, providing some calories and some nutrients. In general, the more processed or refined the carbohydrate is, the fewer nutrients and the more calories it has.

All plant foods, including fruits, vegetables, grains, and legumes (dried beans and peas), naturally contain carbohydrate, which is converted by the body into glucose and used as fuel. The brain especially depends on this glucose to stay sharp. Although you may benefit from cutting back on the kind of carbohydrate that provides "empty calories" (calories with little or no nutritional value), most nutritionists recommend a diet that obtains 45 to 65 percent of its calories from carbohydrate. So carbohydrates are a very important part of your diet. You just have to know how to choose them. There are two basic types:

complex carbohydrates. These are found mostly in grains, legumes, and vegetables. These foods are often rich in fiber, vitamins, minerals, and other nutrients, and they may help lower the risk of cancer and other diseases. Complex carbohydrates that have been refined, such as white flour and white rice, have had most of the fiber removed and are generally not as nutritious.

simple carbohydrates. These are found in sugar, syrup, milk, fruits, and some vegetables. Table sugar and syrups such as high-fructose corn syrup are short on nutrients. However, some foods with simple sugars, such as milk, fruit, and vegetables, also deliver other healthful nutrients, including vitamins and minerals.

Regardless of the type, all carbohydrates provide four calories per gram. Fiber, which is part of the carbohydrate family, is the exception: It's calorie free.

fiber

Fiber is the indigestible part of plant foods, including legumes, whole grains, fruits, and vegetables. A no-calorie nutrient, fiber is essential to good health. Among fiber's many positive attributes is its ability to keep you feeling full longer, which can help you stick to your diet.

Fiber also softens and adds bulk to stools, stimulating your intestines to pass them faster and with greater ease. A high-fiber, low-fat eating plan also helps keep cholesterol levels down and decreases your risk for colon cancer. Fiber helps regulate blood sugar so levels don't rise too quickly or too high after eating carbohydrate-rich meals.

But how does fiber help control weight? It sops up fluid like a sponge, expanding in your stomach so that it takes less food to satisfy your hunger. Fiber also can help keep you from overeating and make you feel full longer. Experts recommend that you consume about 20 to 35 grams of fiber every day, whether or not weight loss is your goal. That's the amount of fiber that will help prevent disease. Unfortu-

nately, most people typically take in much less than that amount because they don't eat enough produce and whole grains. Fresh produce and whole-grain breads, pasta, and cereals are the best and cheapest fiber-filled choices.

To benefit from fiber to the fullest, make sure you drink enough fluid.(See next column for fluid requirements.) Fiber can't do its job filling you up without it.

water

Water is often shortchanged as a nutrient. But like other nutrients, it's essential to life. It helps regulate your body temperature so your body stays at a near-constant 98.6°F. Water transports nutrients to your body cells, and it carries waste products away. It also aids in digestion; moistens body tissues such as your eyes, mouth, and nose; and helps cushion your joints and protect your body organs and tissues.

Each day, your body loses about two to three quarts of water. It's important to replace them by drinking water and other fluids throughout the day. Aim to drink about eight cups of fluid each day. Choose liquids such as unflavored water, fruit juices, milk, and soups. Beverages with caffeine, such as coffee, tea, and soda, also count. Caffeine in these drinks may make your body lose some water, but the amount is quite small. Many foods also supply your body with water. Depending on your food choices, you can obtain about three to four cups of fluid a day from foods.

Water is a plus for dieters because it's filling. That's especially true when your diet's rich in fiber, because fluid and fiber work together to provide a sense of fullness. It has also been shown that foods with a high water content help you feel more satisfied sooner. Foods that are naturally rich in water include fruits, vegetables, low-fat milk, and cooked grains, as well as lean meats, poultry, fish, beans, and water-rich dishes, such as soups, stews, casseroles, pasta with vegetables, and

Calcium delivers weight-loss results

Calcium does more than just keep your bones healthy. There's new evidence that getting plenty of calcium may make it easier to lose weight and body fat. A calcium-rich eating plan, especially one that includes milk and other dairy foods, has been found to curb weight gain by cranking up your body's fat-burning ability. When combined with a reduced-calorie diet, calcium can help make your weight-loss plan more effective. To get results, aim to eat at least 3 to 4 servings of calcium-rich foods per day (milk, yogurt, cheese, or leafy green vegetables), enough to provide at least 1,000 milligrams of calcium.

fruit-based desserts. Be sure to include a variety of these foods along with your other fluids.

vitamins and minerals

Vitamins play a significant role in virtually all the important events in the body, including the production of energy, hormones, enzymes, immune cells, and neurotransmitters (chemical messengers in the brain), to name a few. Minerals are just as critical. For example, they are essential for building bones and teeth, keeping your heart beating regularly, and helping your blood to clot.

Unlike the three main nutrients, vitamins and minerals do not supply calories. Instead, they help your body digest, absorb, metabolize, and transport the energy-producing nutrients—protein, fat, and carbohydrate. Ironically, your vitamin and mineral needs do not change when you cut back on these three nutrients. That's why a restrictive eating plan is often lacking in vitamins and minerals. Whenever you're on a diet, be sure to meet your daily vitamin and mineral needs; they are crucial to your overall health.

Food should be your primary source of vitamins and minerals.

Food provides a "package" of nutrients that work together to maintain health. Eat a diet with a variety of foods—whole grains, fruits, vegetables, nuts, seeds, legumes, low-fat dairy foods, lean meat, poultry, and fish—and you're most likely to get the vitamins and minerals you need. That's one good reason why you should be wary of diets that are very restrictive: You can wind up with a deficiency in one or more vitamins and minerals. Yes, you can also take a multivitamin and mineral supplement, but it's not a good idea to rely on supplements for meeting your vitamin and mineral needs. Supplements cannot "fix" a poor diet.

Now that you know what makes up a good diet from a nutritional standpoint, make it your goal to find a weight-loss plan that will allow you to eat foods that will keep you satisfied and healthy. And always listen to your body. You can read more about the various types of diets in the next chapter.

the many routes to weight loss

Diet plans are like various routes that can take you to the same destination: a more svelte version of you! But how do you know which is the best route to take? Well, your top priority is to get to your destination safely, so first you need to weigh each plan on a basic nutritional scale. A diet plan that compromises your health is definitely the wrong route to weight loss.

Before you review the specific diet plans beginning on page 29 or attempt to devise your own personal route to weight loss, familiarize yourself with the various types of diets and the pros and cons of each. Most diet plans fall into one of the categories described in this chapter.

which way to go?

Certain diet plans, including those that are very restrictive and some fad diets, can be considered "shortest route" diets. They may result in quick weight loss, but they aren't likely to deliver lasting results. Short-term weight loss is not the best measure of a diet's ultimate value. A better measure is whether you can enjoy the pleasures of eating while you're losing weight. A diet like that is one you're more likely to be able to live with, which means you're more likely to keep the weight off for good. The "scenic route" to slimming down is one that promotes gradual and safe weight loss and is often the best way to go.

As you review the basic types of diets, consider your goals, your lifestyle, your food likes and dislikes, and your activity level. All these factors will influence the success of your weight-loss plan. Just keep in mind that some types of diets are difficult to stick with over time, and for certain diets,

Separating the good from the fad

Diets that promise quick, effortless weight loss are seldom effective over the long run. Fad diets may result in short-term weight loss, but they are often unrealistic and take the fun out of eating. It's probably a fad diet if it

- promotes or bans a specific food or food group
- promises incredible results
- blames specific nutrients or foods for weight problems
- presents rigid rules for eating
- relies on testimonials, anecdotal support, or unpublished studies

You're more likely to lose weight and keep it off when your weight-loss plan

- does not restrict calories to fewer than 1,200 calories per day
- includes foods from all of the food groups
- does not make any foods forbidden
- encourages lifelong, healthful eating habits
- advocates regular physical activity

long-term effects on health may not be known. If following a popular fad diet is the jump start you need, go ahead and give it a try (with your health care professional's approval). But be sure to have a backup plan for when you grow tired of the restrictive eating regimens common in these diets. Most people who successfully lose weight change their lifestyle and eating patterns along the way, and these changes become habits. This is the key to maintaining weight loss.

types of diets
food-specific diets

premise: Individual foods, such as cabbage or grapefruit, are touted as having special properties that promote weight loss by melting

away fat, boosting metabolism, or blocking the digestion of certain nutrients. These diets require you to eat large amounts of certain foods and limit many other foods.

reality check: No food can live up to the claims; still, some people swear by these diets. If you can stick with one of the plans, weight loss will likely occur. But it won't be because of a "magical" quality to any one food. When so many foods are off-limits, you simply eat fewer calories. These diets are nutritionally unbalanced. Besides getting bored with the limited choices, you may feel hungry and less energetic.

high-fiber, low-calorie diets

premise: These diets suggest that eating high-fiber foods will fill you up faster, so it's easier to eat fewer calories. Some diets that rely on this approach are vegetarian and very low in fat as well.

reality check: The thinking behind these diets is correct: Fiber is not digested so it is calorie free, and it takes up more room in your stomach so you feel full sooner. On the flip side, eating too much fiber (more than 50 to 60 grams per day) can cause bloating, cramping, and diarrhea, as can increasing your fiber intake suddenly. If the diet is very low in fat, meals may not provide enough lasting satisfaction. And if the diet is very stringent, it may be difficult to stick with over time.

Certainly, adopting some of the low-fat, high-fiber strategies can lead to positive health changes. Fiber supplements are an option for boosting fiber intake, but remember that these supplements do not supply the vitamins, minerals, and phytochemicals found in fiber-rich foods. Also, your body can come to rely on fiber supplements for regularity, so if you quit suddenly (or don't drink enough fluids), you may have problems with constipation.

low-carbohydrate, high-protein diets

premise: These diet plans are based on the premise that carbohydrate causes weight gain. Eliminating or severely limiting carbohydrate is believed to force your body to use the fat it already has in storage for energy.

reality check: The initial rapid weight loss commonly experienced on this type of diet is mostly water, not fat. After that, the high-protein foods promoted, which are typically also high in fat, help to keep hunger at bay so it's easier to eat fewer calories. Some low-carbohydrate diet plans require you to give up or limit many fruits, vegetables, grain products, legumes, and milk products—foods with many healthful qualities. Critics of these diets are most concerned about eliminating these healthful foods and eating large amounts of protein and high-fat foods, which can increase the risk for other

health problems, such as heart disease and kidney problems. As far as burning fat on these diets, if you keep your carbohydrate intake very low, your body will eventually turn to burning fat, but not without some unpleasant side effects, such as fatigue, nausea, constipation, and bad breath. Part of the weight lost on these plans is also water and lean muscle tissue. And there is often a rebound effect. When you grow tired of the restrictive eating plan, you may return to your old eating habits and regain the lost weight, replacing some of the lost muscle with fat. Keep in mind that there is no standard amount that defines a low-carbohydrate diet. Some plans recommend carbohydrate intake of 40 percent of total calories, while others go as low as 10 percent or less. Lower-carbohydrate diets that are less restrictive do offer ways to cut back on refined carbohydrates, which are commonly overeaten, without missing out on healthier carbs, such as fruits, vegetables, and whole grains.

liquid diets

premise: A liquid shake, either prepackaged or made from powdered mix and milk, replaces one or two meals a day. These shakes provide sugar, protein, fiber, vitamins, and minerals. They claim to fill you up on fewer calories.

reality check: The first problem with these diets is that your hunger may not be satisfied by the shakes. Second, these liquid "meals" can't begin to substitute for the array of valuable nutrients found in whole foods, including phytonutrients and other components, that work together in powerful ways to provide health benefits. If you have only a few pounds to lose and you stick with it, you can take off the weight. However, you may reach your boredom limit before you reach your weight-loss goal.

food-combining diets

premise: These diets suggest that certain foods should not be eaten together or at specific times of the day. For instance, some plans recommend eating carbohydrate and protein at different meals or eating fruit only in the morning. Some even suggest that foods of varying textures should not be eaten together. Promoters contend that certain food combinations do not digest well, slow down metabolism, or produce toxins that prevent elimination of the body's waste.

reality check: There is simply no evidence to support food combining. All foods, even when eaten individually, are a combination of protein, fat, and carbohydrate. Fruit is nutritious at any time of the day, and the food-texture theory has no scientific basis.

fasting

premise: Fasting is believed to cleanse the body of toxins that can contribute to weight gain. Periodic fasting is suggested to help keep calorie intake low and to get a head start on weight loss.

reality check: Fasting does little more than cause your body to lose water weight. Starvation diets are not recommended, even if you are very overweight. One-day fasting is unlikely to contribute to weight loss. Longer fasting deprives your body of nutrients—and makes you feel lousy. There is no evidence that fasting removes toxins from your body.

being active: getting better mileage from your diet

No matter what type of diet you follow, when you add physical activity to it, your diet becomes more powerful. You get more mileage, or results, from your dieting efforts when regular physical activity is part of your daily routine.

According to the National Institutes of Health, regular physical activity is as essential to your weight-loss efforts as a healthy reduced-calorie diet. Neither cutting calories nor physical activity alone can get you to your goal as effectively or as quickly as they can together. And the results don't stop there. Physical activity is also key to maintaining your weight once you've lost the extra pounds.

Notice that the operative words here are "physical activity," not "exercise." While exercise is certainly a type of physical activity, one that helps to boost your weight-loss efforts, it's not necessary to do power aerobics or to lift heavy weights at the gym to win the weight-loss game. Physical activity encompasses all types of movement, including household chores, recreational activities, exercise classes, and sports. All require energy and produce progressive health benefits.

This chapter will give you the incentive to add more physical activity into your daily life. We'll explain the various types of physical activity and the many ways each will help you lose weight and feel better. When you're ready to create your personal activity program, go to Part 2 on page 74, where you'll find the tools to help you get started.

physical activity payoffs

Besides burning calories to help you lose weight, being physically active offers an abundance of other benefits. As you reduce your waistline, regular physical activity also reduces your risk

Take steps to be more active

One of the easiest ways to get physically active is to walk. If you just can't squeeze in a 30-minute walk each day, experts say you can stay fit by walking about 10,000 steps a day (the equivalent of about five miles) while doing your normal activities. Chances are you haven't a clue how much walking that is. An easy way to find out is to use a pedometer. It's a small device you attach to your waistband that tracks the number of steps you take each day. You can easily see how far you've gone and how far you have yet to go to reach your goal. Pedometers can be purchased at a local sports equipment store.

of developing many serious health problems, including heart disease, some types of cancer, high blood pressure, osteoporosis, diabetes, and arthritis.

The rewards don't stop there. Physical activity helps you manage your weight—and look and feel better—in ways you probably never imagined. Consider these additional reasons to make physical activity a part of your daily routine.

boost your metabolism

Because physical activity preserves and builds muscle, it also increases your metabolism (the rate at which you burn calories). That's because muscle tissue burns more calories than fat tissue, even at rest. So when you have more muscle, you can eat more calories without gaining weight. Having more muscle also makes it easier to lose weight, even if you're eating the same number of calories. And if you're consuming fewer calories, having muscle makes weight loss even easier. Ironically, the more active you are, the more energetic you often feel. This energizing boost comes when you make movement a part of your daily life.

improve your body composition

When you cut calories alone, you tend to lose muscle tissue along with body fat. But you don't want to lose muscle; it supports your body in all of its activities—and it helps you burn more calories. That's where exercise comes in. It keeps you from losing muscle as you lose weight, and it actually builds muscle, too. Muscle takes up less space, so your body will appear trimmer even if you don't lose weight. As you age, the amount of lean tissue in your body naturally declines—and it's replaced by fat. Being active helps to slow down, and even reverse, this exchange.

curb your appetite

You may be surprised to find that when you're physically active, you're just not as hungry. In addition, as you feel the positive effects of physical activity on your body, you may be more motivated to make healthy food choices. Participating in regular physical activity also means that you're less likely to be munching, which can help control eating binges that make weight control more difficult.

relieve stress

Regular physical activity helps reduce feelings of stress, anxiety, and depression. It helps brighten your mood, improving your outlook on life and making everyday problems seem less daunting. Physical activity also allows you to think more clearly by releasing tension and increasing circulation. And if you replace stress-induced nibbling with physical activity, you'll save yourself from taking in extra calories and putting on extra pounds.

get better rest

When you are physically active, you sleep more soundly and awaken feeling rested and ready to start your day. And getting enough sleep turns out to be important for weight loss, too. Studies suggest that the lack of sufficient sleep may alter your body's metabolism, making weight control more challenging. As you feel your energy dropping throughout the day, you are more likely to turn to food for a pick-me-up. Your body doesn't usually need these extra calories, and they wind up being added to your fat stores. When you haven't had enough

sleep, you're likely to be too tired to be physically active, or if you do manage to exercise, you'll work out less intensely. Sleep experts recommend at least eight hours of sleep a night for adults.

feel good about yourself

Physical activity helps boost your self-confidence by improving your strength, stamina, flexibility, and appearance. A stronger, more fit body will make everyday activities, such as picking up a small child or bringing the groceries in from the car, easier to accomplish.

on your "weigh" to being more active

No matter what your age or stage of life, it's never too late to start being more active. Experts recommend being physically active every single day. Adults should aim for at least 30 minutes daily. To help slim down, it's even better if you can work up to a total of 60 minutes of moderate-intensity activity each day. The 60 min-

Everyday ways to move

There are lots of ways to burn calories—and the more you do, the more you burn.

Lifestyle Activities:
• Gardening
• Pushing a vacuum cleaner or stroller
• Taking the stairs instead of the elevator
• Carrying groceries
• Washing and waxing a car
• Washing windows or floors
• Raking leaves
• Shoveling snow
• Playing actively with children

Exercise or Recreational Activities:
• Walking or jogging
• Bicycling
• Swimming laps or water aerobics
• Golfing (pulling or carrying clubs)
• Basketball
• Dancing
• Cross-country skiing
• Tennis or racquetball
• Volleyball
• Exercise classes

Play at losing

Being active with kids is a fun way to get up and move—and it's great for the kids, too.

- Play tag, hopscotch, or hide-and-seek
- Fly a kite
- Jump rope
- Hop on a pogo stick
- Ride a bicycle, scooter, or tricycle
- Roller or in-line skate
- Dance
- Go bowling
- Play charades
- Play a game of backyard soccer, baseball, basketball, flag football, or hockey

utes are cumulative, so don't be daunted by the number. You can divide your physical activity into shorter sessions, and it will still be effective.

Any type of physical activity you choose will increase the number of calories your body uses. But to burn the most fat and get the maximum health benefits from your activity program, strive to include different types of activities. Each of the following three types of physical activity offers different benefits. It's best to vary your routine so you spend time doing all three over the course of a week.

aerobic activities. These are the ones that get you huffing and puffing. Your heart rate and breathing speed up as you use the large muscles in your arms and legs at an increased pace for an extended period of time. These activities help improve your circulation, strengthen your heart, lower blood pressure, and burn the most calories, which is why aerobic activities are especially good for losing weight. Examples include brisk walking, dancing, and playing basketball.

strength-building activities. These are stop-and-go activities, such as weight training, calisthenics, and yoga, and help build and strengthen

muscles. These activities burn some calories, but not nearly as many as those burned during the same amount of aerobic activity. Strength training, also called weight training or resistance training, helps to tone and strengthen certain muscle groups, enhancing your ability to do aerobic exercise and increasing support for your bones. This type of physical activity can be done in a gym or at home. You can even use simple household items to provide the resistance.

stretching. Stretching helps your muscles and joints stay flexible. Stretching before and after aerobic and strength-building activities keeps your muscles from tightening and helps prevent injury.

choose to move

There are many ways to make physical activity a regular part of your lifestyle.

You can schedule structured activities into your day, such as exercise classes or recreational activities. Or you can focus on adding short segments of moderate-intensity physical activity throughout your day. This includes activities that you may already be doing, such as gardening or housework. Other examples of moderate-intensity activities include swimming laps, bicycling, and raking leaves. The more vigorous your activity, the shorter the workout time necessary to reap the same health benefits.

If you can talk but not sing while doing the activity, you are exercising at moderate intensity. During vigorous activity, such as hiking uphill, steady cycling, aerobic or ballroom dancing, racquetball, jogging, or a brisk game of tennis, talking should be possible but only in short phrases, not conversations.

prudent precautions

Most healthy people can start a sensible activity program without medical testing. However, if you have or are at risk for a chronic health problem such as heart disease, hypertension, diabetes, or osteoporosis, or if you are pregnant or are greatly overweight, you need to consult a doctor before you start. And men older than age 40 and women older than age 50 should also speak to a doctor before beginning a new program of vigorous activity.

If you haven't been active in the past, start slowly to give your heart and muscles time to adjust. Start each activity session with stretching, then a few minutes of activity at a slower pace. Then end the session with a few minutes of cooldown at that slower pace. If the activity hurts at any time, slow down or stop. You should feel challenged during physical activity, but it should not be painful.

Work up to your goals gradually, no matter what shape you are in. To progress, slowly increase the intensity of the movement or the heaviness of the weight over time. You can also increase the time you spend being active. Just don't try to advance too quickly. You are more likely to get injured if you don't give your body the chance to build strength and stamina.

the road less traveled: weight-loss drugs and surgery

Have you been traveling the road to weight loss but never even get close to your destination? If so, you're not the only dieter for whom weight loss remains a tantalizing mirage. Sometimes people who are seriously overweight need more help than diet and exercise can provide.

Even being moderately overweight can put you at risk for such life-threatening conditions as diabetes, cardiovascular disease, hypertension, orthopedic problems, gallbladder disease, and sleep apnea. But the risks are even greater if you are seriously or severely overweight (at least 100 pounds overweight or twice your ideal weight). If you are desperate to shed weight to reduce health risks, weight-loss drugs or surgery may be options to consider. But before you decide to take one of these routes, there is much to learn.

weight-loss drugs

First, talk to your doctor about your interest in using medication to lose weight. The doctor will determine whether you are a good candidate for the medication route and whether prescription medication or an over-the-counter product would be more appropriate. Weight-loss drugs work best when combined with a healthy diet and regular physical activity, and the doctor will help you work out a beneficial eating and activity plan.

prescription medications

Your doctor will consider a number of factors, including your current weight, your weight history, your medical history, and the methods you have used to lose weight in the past, to determine if you are a good candidate for prescription weight-loss medication.

If you have obesity-related health problems or are at high risk for such problems, and if you have been unable to lose weight or maintain weight using traditional methods, the doctor may decide that a weight-loss medication is right for you. These medications are not intended for people who are only mildly overweight. And they are not to be used only to improve appearance.

Weight-loss medications work by either suppressing your appetite (such as sibutramine), creating a feeling of fullness (such as phendimetrazine), or reducing the body's ability to absorb fat from food (such as orlistat). Other medications used to treat conditions such as depression or diabetes may have an "off-label" use for weight loss. This means that while they have not been approved for the treatment of obesity, they may have a side effect that promotes weight reduction and are prescribed by a doctor for that purpose. Talk with your doctor about the different types of medications available and which fits best with your medical and personal history. Be sure to ask about the following:

effectiveness. How effective a weight-loss medication will be is difficult to predict because it depends on how your body responds. Some people lose more than 10 percent of their starting body weight, while others may lose less. Your doctor may need to adjust the dosage of your medication based on your medical condition and response to the drug. Most studies of weight-loss medications show that maximum weight loss usually occurs in the first six months.

side effects. While most side effects reported are mild, a serious heart problem was linked to two popular medications (fenfluramine and dexfenfluramine) that have since been withdrawn from the market. Side effects will vary depending on the medication and may include restlessness, insomnia, dizziness, dry mouth, diarrhea, constipation, and elevated blood pressure. Side effects often decrease with continued treatment.

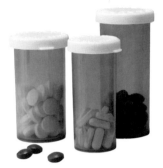

post-treatment experiences. Many people are concerned that they will regain weight after stopping a weight-loss medication. Although this is certainly possible, maintaining healthy eating and physical activity habits will increase your chances of keeping the weight off.

over-the-counter pills and supplements

There is a crucial difference between prescription and over-the-counter weight-loss medications. Prescription weight-loss drugs must go through rigorous research before being released, while over-the-counter diet pills and supplements may not be tested at all. Nonprescription diet pills and supplements are loosely regulated, and manufacturers do not have to prove that their products are safe or effective for weight loss.

This is not to say that there are no over-the-counter diet pills or supple-

Buyer beware

When it comes to weight-loss products, be wary of claims that sound too good to be true. Be on the lookout for claims containing words and phrases that are clues to fraud, such as

- Ancient
- Breakthrough
- Easy
- Effortless
- Exclusive
- Exotic
- Guaranteed
- Magical
- Miraculous
- Mysterious
- New discovery
- Secret

ments that aid weight loss. But you have to be extremely careful. Some products are simply worthless, while others may interact dangerously with prescription or over-the-counter drugs that you may be taking. And some have very unpleasant side effects.

The Federal Trade Commission has taken steps to prevent marketers of bogus weight-loss pills, potions, and powders from selling their products. And the Food and Drug Administration has banned certain ingredients from over-the-counter diet products, including alcohol, caffeine, dextrose, guar gum, phenylpropanolamine (PPA), and ephedra, because they have proved ineffective or unsafe. However, their efforts have not completely prevented the sale of products that are useless, dangerous, or both. If you want to try an over-the-counter diet product, first check with your doctor or a pharmacist. They can advise you about the benefits and risks of various products and warn you about potential interactions with any other medications or supplements that you are taking.

the magic bullet myth. Everyone is looking for the "magic bullet" when it comes to weight loss. Dieters spend loads of time and money on diet pills and supplements that promise to "burn," "block," "flush," or otherwise eliminate fat from your body. The truth is that science has yet to come up with

a "magic bullet" for weight loss, and none of these diet pills and supplements *cause* weight loss on their own. When combined with a healthful diet and physical activity plan, you *may* see results. Don't expect instant results or tremendous weight loss. Side effects, you should know, can be unpleasant.

Here are just a few examples of products that claim to promote weight loss but simply do not work:

- Fat blockers claim to absorb fat and interfere with its digestion so the fat you eat doesn't supply calories.
- "Magnet" diet pills allegedly attract fat and flush it out of the body.
- Diet patches, which are worn on the skin, purportedly to suppress your appetite.
- Chitosan diet pills claim to assist weight loss by binding dietary fat before it is digested.
- Blue-green algae, also known as spirulina, promises to help control your appetite.

In addition to being a waste of time and money, the following products and ingredients can be harmful to your health:

- "Bulk" or "filler" products, such as fiber-based products, absorb liquid and swell in your stomach, making you feel full. Some products can cause blockages in the esophagus, stomach, or intestines.
- Starch blockers promise to impede digestion of starches, or complex

carbohydrates. Users have reported nausea, vomiting, diarrhea, and stomach pains.

- Pyruvate-containing products claim to boost metabolism and promote weight loss. Taking large amounts can cause intestinal distress, bloating, and diarrhea.

weight-loss surgery

Surgery to promote weight loss is a drastic measure. It is a permanent procedure, and to be successful, it requires a lifetime commitment to changes in how and what you eat. Weight-loss surgery, also called bariatric surgery, is for people who are severely overweight and cannot lose weight by traditional means or who suffer from serious, life-threatening, weight-related health problems. If you fit this profile and are determined to lose weight and improve your health, surgery may be the answer.

You may be a candidate for weight-loss surgery if you meet these criteria:

- You have tried and failed with dieting, exercise, and lifestyle changes.
- Your Body Mass Index (BMI) is 40 or greater, or your BMI is between 35 and 40 and you have a life-threatening, weight-related health problem such as diabetes, severe sleep apnea, or heart disease. (See Taking Stock, page 76, for more on BMI, including the formula to calculate your own.)

- You are more than 100 pounds over ideal weight.

how it works

There are two main categories of surgery that promote weight loss. Restrictive procedures, which include gastric banding, gastric bypass, and vertical banded gastroplasty, limit the amount of food the stomach can hold by closing off or removing parts of the stomach. This type of surgery does not interfere with the normal digestive process; it prevents you from eating large amounts of food at one time.

Malabsorptive procedures, such as the biliopancreatic diversion and the Roux-en-Y gastric bypass (RGB), limit the calories and the amount of nutrients that can be absorbed by the intestine in addition to reducing the size of the stomach. In the RGB procedure, a surgeon first creates a small stomach pouch, then makes a direct connection from the stomach to a lower segment of the small intestine, bypassing the portions of the digestive tract that absorb calories and nutrients.

Depending on your weight and medical history, your surgeon may be able to use laparoscopic technology. Instead of making a large incision, a surgeon using laparoscopic techniques makes one or more small incisions through which slender surgical instruments are passed. A laparoscopic procedure usually reduces the length of the hospital stay, diminishes discomfort, limits surgical scarring, and shortens recovery time.

benefits vs. risks

Weight-loss surgery is a serious undertaking. You'll need to clearly understand what the surgery involves and the potential benefits and risks before you make your decision. As with any surgery, there are some risks, but for many people the health risks of remaining at their current weight are greater than the risks of surgery.

benefits. Most people lose weight fairly rapidly in the first few weeks after surgery and continue to lose for 18 to 24 months afterward. Regaining some weight is common, but most people maintain a long-term weight loss of around 100 pounds or more. Weight-related health conditions, including diabetes, heart disease, joint problems, and sleep apnea, often improve dramatically with weight loss. Emotional benefits may include a better self-image, higher self-esteem, and the reversal of depression.

risks. Risks of any surgery can include bleeding, infections, and respiratory problems. Follow-up surgery to correct complications is necessary in about 10 to 20 percent of people who have weight-loss surgery. In addition, some people develop gallstones after surgery as well as nutritional deficiencies such as anemia, osteoporosis, and meta-bolic bone disease. These deficiences can usually be avoided if you get a enough vitamins and minerals from a combination of food and supplements.

life after surgery

You will need to follow strict eating instructions provided by your health-care team after weight-loss surgery. In the early weeks, it may be difficult to eat anything without feeling uncomfortably full, and your stomach may still be very tender. Depending on the type of surgery, you may be on a liquid diet for several weeks. Gradually, you will work up to eating soft, easily chewable foods and then progress to frequent, small meals (about two ounces each). The actual number of meals may vary from four to six a day. Not only do you need to adjust to eating more frequently and consuming smaller amounts of food, but you will also need to eat slowly and chew your food thoroughly. Initially, you won't be able to drink fluid with meals because it can cause discomfort. Instead, you'll drink fluids $\frac{1}{2}$ to 1 hour after meals. You will receive lists of suggested foods to eat and foods to avoid. In general, you will need to eat foods higher in protein and low in fat.

Depending on the type of surgery you have, you may need to take a multivitamin with iron every day and a calcium supplement. You may also need intramuscular shots of vitamin B_{12}.

deciphering the diet reviews

There used to be just a few diet plans to choose from if you were looking to lose weight. Today, there are dozens. You can't turn on the radio or TV or open a magazine or newspaper without hearing about the most well-known ones. In The Many Routes to Weight Loss, we explained the pros and cons of the main types of diet programs available. In this section, we'll give you the nitty gritty on 20 of the most popular plans, all of which fit into one of the categories we covered earlier.

Each diet review will describe the main ideas and rationale behind the diet's guidelines and philosophies, including what differentiates it from other diet plans. You'll read what nutrition experts have to say about each plan and learn what results you can expect as well as what potential dangers there are in following it. You'll find out what kinds of foods you can

eat and how they are managed during a day of meals and snacks. Each review also lists other similar diets, so you can check those out, too. Finally, look for our "stick-to-it-ability" rating in the upper right corner of the first page of every review. This will give you an idea of how easy—or hard—it is to stay on the diet. The higher the number, the easier the diet is to stick with for the long haul.

When you're looking through the plans, try to think about choosing a new way to eat rather than a short-term solution to dropping a few pounds. Picking a healthy, practical diet can be challenging, especially considering all the choices out there. Just remember that diets have their unique personalities and characteristics, and so do you. The trick is finding one that feels comfortable.

For a quick comparison, you can check out the Diets at a Glance chart that follows the reviews. It compares the most important features of the 20 diet plans.

dr. atkins

Quick take

- Very low-carb, high-protein, high-fat diet
- Causes body to burn fat for fuel
- Claims to stabilize blood sugar levels
- Can cause fatigue, headaches, nausea, and constipation

the premise

Dr. Robert Atkins is still the king of low-carb diets, even though he passed away in 2003. He began his reign almost 35 years ago with his first diet book, *Dr. Atkins' Diet Revolution*. His empire includes the updated and renamed *Dr. Atkins' New Diet Revolution*, a cookbook, a Web site, a line of supplements and food products, and The Atkins Center for Complementary Medicine in New York City. Follow his diet plan, says Atkins, and you'll remove toxins from your body's cells, stabilize blood sugar, and rid yourself of fatigue, irritability, depression, headaches, and joint pain.

the rationale

Dr. Atkins believes that if you severely restrict carbohydrate intake, your body will be forced to use extra fat deposits for energy. During the process of converting fat to energy, the body produces an abundance of substances called ketones, which are believed to suppress appetite. The fat calories are said to be flushed out in urine, resulting in rapid weight loss. This is called ketosis and is central to the Atkins weight-loss plan. You are expected to check your urine for ketones. If it's negative, you haven't cut back enough on carbohydrate.

what's for breakfast, lunch, and dinner?

The Atkins diet consists mostly of protein and fat in the form of meat, oils, butter, and cream. During the two-week "induction" period, only 20 grams of carbohydrate a day are allowed; that's less than the amount in one slice of whole-grain bread. Atkins recommends that the carbohydrates come from salads and vegetables. After the two-week induction period, the dieter can increase carbohydrate consumption to 25 to 90 grams a day, depending on total daily calorie intake (that's equal to 100 to 360 calories, which is less than 10 percent of calories). Even that increase is still a tiny daily carbohydrate allowance. A healthy diet usually obtains 50 to 60 percent of calories from carbohydrate, which amounts to at least 250 grams a day.

fact or fiction: what the experts say

Does the diet work? There are plenty of followers who swear by the diet's effectiveness. But according to Keith Ayoob, Ed.D., R.D., director of nutrition at the Rose F. Kennedy Center at Albert Einstein College of Medicine, the fact that people generally lose weight on the Atkins plan isn't necessarily a good thing. Sure, ketosis may help you lose weight, but it's also what happens when people starve. Despite Atkins' claim that the body is flushing out a lot of extra calories in the urine, one study published in the *Journal of the American Medical Association* found that only about 100 calories a day make their way into urine.

Bottom-line: There's no metabolic magic about the Atkins diet. Weight loss is inevitable when you're cutting out major food categories, thus reducing your calories. You may profit initially from the diet, but you may regain weight when you grow weary of the limited food choices and return to your previous eating habits, says Ayoob.

gains and losses/ what's the damage?

Since the diet does not supply enough of the body's preferred source of fuel— carbohydrate—your body breaks down its own muscle for energy. You lose more water as it breaks down muscle. Thus, much of the weight lost in the early weeks is the result of an unhealthy loss of muscle tissue and water.

The side effects of a low-carb, high-protein diet plan may include fatigue, nausea, headaches, constipation, and bad breath, which are caused by the buildup of ketones in the body.

People who follow a low-carbohydrate diet typically see initial improvements in blood cholesterol and glucose levels even though the diet is often high in fat, saturated fat, and cholesterol. Experts believe those reductions are associated with the weight loss. However, studies looking at long-term effects of the diet on heart health have not been conducted. Plenty of evidence points to an increased risk for heart disease and some forms of cancer from a diet high in fat and saturated fat. Recently the Atkins program has revised its thinking on meats, bacon, eggs, and other saturated fats, saying that people should limit the amount of fatty meats and saturated fat they eat.

The Atkins diet is shy on vital nutrients supplied by fruits, vegetables, whole grains, and dairy products, including B vitamins; vitamins A, C, and D; antioxidants and phytochemicals; and calcium. Over time, a diet high in protein can draw calcium from the bones, increasing the risk of osteoporosis and hip fractures. High intake of protein can also put an added burden on the kidneys and liver.

Other similar diets

The Zone, Sugar-Busters!, The Carbohydrate Addict's Diet

the carbohydrate addict's lifespan program

Quick take

- Maintains that excessive production of insulin triggers carbohydrate cravings that make you overeat
- Advises restricting carbohydrate intake to control your cravings and, therefore, lose weight
- Less restrictive than Atkins diet
- Requires that you eat foods in particular proportions to each other

the premise

This is one of the latest in a series of diet books written by the husband-and-wife team of Richard and Rachael Heller. Most of these books are follow-ups to their original 1991 book, *The Carbohydrate Addict's Diet*. This updated version was written with the over-40 reader in mind, but it is basically the same song with some different verses. The Hellers believe that 75 percent of overweight people—and many people of normal weight—are addicted to carbohydrate and that dealing with that addiction is the key to successful weight loss. They define carbohydrate addiction as a compelling hunger, craving, or desire for carbohydrate-rich foods: an escalating, recurring need or drive for starches, snack foods, junk food, or sweets. The Hellers maintain that for some people eating carbohydrate is like doing drugs. Their diet plan greatly restricts carbohydrate intake, distributing it in measured amounts at a single meal. There is a Carbohydrate Addict's plan for just about everyone, including carbohydrate-addicted kids.

the rationale

According to the Hellers, overproduction of insulin is what triggers hunger and drives the carbohydrate addiction. Eating too many carbohydrates, they say, causes a spike in insulin production, triggering carbohydrate cravings. This drives you to eat even more carbohydrate, which creates a never-ending cycle of craving, overconsumption of carbohydrate, and overproduction of insulin. An overindulgence in carbohydrate-rich foods, then, leads to weight gain and out-of-control eating. Carbohydrate addiction is not a matter of willpower, they say; it is a matter of biology. Their answer is to regulate and restrict carbohydrate intake, especially eliminating foods that contain refined carbs such as sugar and flour.

what's for breakfast, lunch, and dinner?

Though the Hellers' plan is basically a low-carb diet, it doesn't restrict carbohydrate to the extent that the Atkins diet does (see Dr. Atkins, p. 30). In fact, it allows for a single carbohydrate-rich meal each day. Their diet prescription calls for two no-carb meals (called "craving-reducing" meals) and one controlled-carbohydrate meal (called a reward meal) each day. The daily reward meal consists of one-third protein-rich foods, one-third carbohydrate-rich foods, and one-third non-starchy vegetables. If you want second helpings, you have to dish up the same one-third, one-third, one-third distribution on your plate—and eat everything. You can eat as much as you want, but you must eat it all within a one-hour time limit. The Hellers recommend eating complex carbohydrates such as pasta, bread, and potatoes. Sugar is not on the menu. Once you've lost the weight, you can add carbohydrate to your reward meal a little at a time if you're maintaining your weight.

fact or fiction: what the experts say

While the "insulin-makes-you-fat" theory is a popular one and sounds reasonable enough, there's no proof that it's true. In fact, researchers have actually found that managing insulin levels does not help you lose weight. However, the reverse has been proved to be true: Losing weight can help control insulin levels. According to Gerald Reaven, M.D., professor of medicine at Stanford University School of Medicine and an expert on insulin metabolism, "The whole thing is mumbo-jumbo. A calorie is a calorie; if you take in more than you need, you gain weight."

Moreover, the quiz that's supposed to diagnose the extent of your carbohydrate addiction is very general, including questions like, "Does the sight, smell, or even the thought of food sometimes stimulate you to eat?" Almost everyone could answer yes to these questions.

gains and losses/ what's the damage?

Though not as extreme as the Atkins diet, the Hellers' diet plan is just as likely to be low in calcium and fiber and high in cholesterol-raising saturated fat. The symptoms, such as weakness, irritability, and dizziness that the Hellers attribute to carbohydrate craving could be due to any number of medical conditions and should be checked out by your health care provider, not treated with a diet book. And, ironically, the lack of concentration that they attribute to overindulging on carbohydrate is actually a symptom of not getting enough carbohydrate. That's because glucose, the sugar the body manufactures from the carbohydrate you eat, is the brain's primary fuel. Like the Atkins plan and other low-carb diets, the Hellers' plan is likely to result in weight loss, at least in the beginning. But limiting all carbohydrate intake to one meal a day is not realistic, and it's unlikely that most people would be able to stick to that regimen for a lifetime.

Other similar diets

Dr. Atkins, The Zone, SugarBusters!

choose to lose

Quick take

- A balanced diet that includes a wide variety of foods
- Encourages fresh foods but makes great allowances for convenience foods
- Allows occasional splurges
- Encourages exercise
- Not just a weight-loss diet but a healthy eating plan for life

the premise

Nancy and Ronald Goor have been writing and rewriting their *Choose to Lose* series for the past 15 years. Billed as a "food lover's guide to permanent weight loss," this 500+ page volume tells you everything you need to know, and more, about eating healthy and losing weight. Taking the opposite tact of many diet books, *Choose to Lose* encourages carbohydrate consumption, as long as most of it comes from fruits, vegetables, and whole grains. The focus of the diet is fat: finding it, counting it, and budgeting it. It explains how to plan your own personal fat budget, read food labels, ferret out the fat in the foods you eat, fat-proof your home, eat out healthfully, and switch to healthy fats. They encourage dieters to keep a food diary, at least in the beginning, to learn about their own food habits and to reveal their weaknesses. One of the reasons the book is so long is that it provides a comprehensive food table with the nutrient content of each food, plus discussions of everything, literally, from soup to nuts. The information tells dieters what's good (low-fat, high-fiber, and most nutritious), what's bad (high-fat, low-fiber, empty calories) and how you can plan your new diet to keep some of your favorite foods on your weight-loss menus.

the rationale

While some diets focus on limiting carbohydrate intake, the Goors' plan focuses on limiting fat intake, especially saturated fat, since fat is the most concentrated source of calories in the diet and saturated fat is linked to heart disease. The diet plan has no gimmicks or hooks; it's a no-nonsense approach to good nutrition that has withstood the test of time. Fat intake is limited but not excessively restricted, and the diet even allows for an occasional high-fat splurge. The goal, say the Goors, is not to think of *Choose to Lose* as a diet but as an eating plan for life. Foods are clearly divided into groups according to how much of them you can eat. The diet also provides examples of "before" menus and then shows better "after" alternatives. Follow the guidelines of their plan, say the Goors, and over time you will adjust your taste buds to a lower-fat diet without having to greatly restrict your food choices.

what's for breakfast, lunch, and dinner?

The Goors' diet provides more information about specific foods than most other diets, and it gives a week's worth of sample menus and recipes. More than 250 of the book's pages are devoted to food tables that give the calorie, fat, and saturated fat content of foods. You'll find brief, informative sections on such foods as bread, potatoes, cereals, chicken, seafood, popcorn, and pretzels, just to name a few. A typical day's menus might include oatmeal and whole-wheat toast with jelly, cottage cheese, strawberries, and skim milk for breakfast; chickpeas, whole-wheat pita, tangerine, carrot sticks, and orange juice for lunch; tortilla soup, chicken, green beans, rice, squash, cauliflower, nonfat yogurt, and blueberries for dinner; and nonfat yogurt and popcorn for snacks during the day. Total calories: 2,300. Guidelines are provided for cutting calories to 1,500 to 1,600—the minimum they recommend. Supplements are not recommended. Follow a balanced diet, they say, and supplements shouldn't be necessary.

fact or fiction: what the experts say

Information is power, and the Goors' plan provides dieters with power over their diets and, ultimately, their health. The diet plan goes hand-in-hand with what most experts currently recommend, and it basically follows the USDA Food Guide Pyramid and meets the needs of seniors as well. It's a diet high in complex carbohydrate—mostly from whole grains, fruits, vegetables, and legumes—with limited fat intake, most of it from healthy fats such as olive oil. Though it's not billed as such, the diet is in line with dietary recommendations for reducing the risk of heart disease, diabetes, high blood pressure, and cancer.

gains and losses/ what's the damage?

If you follow the Goors' plan, using the recommended calorie adjustments, it should allow you to lose weight successfully. You get a lot of variety and choices on this diet, which also offers much-needed guidance for keeping the diet balanced and realistic. One chapter is devoted to exercise, which they sum up as "Eating Right + Exercise = Perfection."

Other similar diets

Richard Simmons, Weight Watchers

curves

Quick take

- Strong emphasis on the exercise component
- Limits total amount of carbohydrate
- Claims to reset your metabolism
- Recommends nutritional supplements

the premise

The Curves diet is a component of the Curves Weight-Loss and Fitness Program, a franchise of health clubs for women that provides a 30-minute workout including resistance training, aerobics, and stretching. The Curves program includes a meal plan, a workout, and a supplement regimen. Gary Heavin, founder of Curves International, is a health and nutrition counselor specializing in women's fitness. Heavin maintains that following the Curves diet and fitness program will help you slim down and tone your body while resetting your metabolism at a faster calorie-burning rate.

the rationale

Many weight-loss programs fail, says Heavin, because they don't consider the effect of dieting on metabolism. According to Heavin, dieting turns on "starvation hormones" that enable the body to survive on less food and burn less energy. This sabotages weight loss. The key, says Heavin, is to increase your metabolism. He advocates a fitness program that includes strength training to build more muscle because the more muscle you have, the more calories your body burns, even at rest. And Heavin contends that the Curves meal plans will also help correct the effects of years of yo-yo dieting. He offers a method for resetting your metabolism so you can maintain your weight loss. Once you reach your goal weight, you are instructed to increase your calorie intake to 2,500 to 3,000 calories a day. Within a day or two, you will probably gain about 3 to 5 pounds. At this point, you go back to the Phase 1 diet for one to two days to "burn off the fat." When you lose the weight again, you return to Phase 3. This cycle continues for two to three months until you do not gain weight. At this point, your metabolism is supposedly reset at a higher level. Still, Heavin suggests that you may have to return to Phase 1 for one or two days a month to maintain your weight over the long term.

what's for breakfast, lunch, and dinner?

The Curves diet plans recommend six *small* meals a day, such as a meal of strawberries and cottage cheese; cooked carrots and a ground beef patty; an ounce of nuts; or sautéed shrimp, cauliflower, and a salad. Both the carbohydrate-sensitive and the calorie-sensitive meal plans are fairly high in protein and both limit carbohydrate, including bread, rice, pasta, and potatoes, as well as sweets. The meal plans are divided into three phases. Phase 1 of both plans lasts one or two weeks and allows no more than 20 grams of carbohydrate a day. During Phase 2, certain fruits and vegetables and some whole grains are allowed. Once you reach your desired weight, you progress to Phase 3 and no longer follow specific meal plans.

The book provides seven weeks of sample meal plans for both diet types, weekly shopping lists, recipes, and charts for tracking progress. The meal plans include a Curves shake or similar protein shake on most days.

fact or fiction: what the experts say

Phases 1 and 2 of the diet are basically low-calorie, low-carbohydrate eating plans that, when combined with the exercise component, are likely to promote weight loss. The "Phase 3 miracle," a technique Heavin claims will raise your metabolic rate so you can eat a normal amount of food without gaining weight, is complicated and tiresome, and it's likely to turn off

dieters. It also has no scientific basis. And the Phase 3 calorie prescription of 2,500 to 3,000 calories a day is quite high. If weight loss occurs on this diet, it's because you are burning more calories than you are taking in, which becomes easier when you have more muscle. Heavin also claims that nutrient deficiencies can sabotage your weight-loss efforts by promoting food cravings. This is false and a fairly transparent tactic to sell the Curves nutritional supplements.

gains and losses/ what's the damage?

The cornerstone of the Curves program is the workout. The program is commended for its strong emphasis on fitness and muscle building. Building more muscle and exercising aerobically will make you stronger and healthier, boosting your weight-loss efforts by burning more calories. Helpful illustrations and instructions for a Curves at-home workout are included in the book. The complicated process of alternating between the different phases based on weight fluctuations is not a realistic, long-term solution for achieving and maintaining a "permanent" healthy weight. The meal plans are also inadequate for meeting daily vitamin and mineral requirements. Keep the workout; consider another diet plan.

Other similar diets

South Beach Diet, Dr. Atkins

eat, drink, and be healthy

the premise

Dr. Walter Willett, a well-known Harvard researcher, believes that the USDA Food Guide Pyramid is not only wrong, it's dangerous to your health. In its place he offers his own new and improved pyramid that focuses more on plant foods and de-emphasizes dairy. He even incorporates daily exercise and weight control into the pyramid. Willett falls somewhere between the pro-dairy and the anti-dairy camps that are duking it out these days. He's not totally against dairy products but doesn't believe there's a "calcium crisis," as many experts do. In fact, he says that drinking too much milk can actually make your body lose calcium because milk is high in protein, which causes the body to excrete calcium. He advocates getting calcium from other food sources and from supplements, if necessary. Other than that bit of controversy, Willett's diet offers up a healthy dose of good nutrition that's free of gimmicks and exaggerated promises. While the overall theme of the book is good

nutrition, Willett calls weight control the number one nutritional factor for good health.

the rationale

Control your weight; eat a plant-based diet with lots of fruits, vegetables, and whole grains; limit dairy foods; exercise every day; and take a multivitamin for insurance: That's pretty much Willett's philosophy in a nutshell. He also says that drinking alcohol in moderation is probably healthy for most people, though he doesn't advise people to start drinking if they don't already. To back up his diet advice, he cites a lot of studies (he's been involved in much of the research himself) that suggest that these dietary changes are a boon to your health, reducing the risk of heart disease, cancer, diabetes, and stroke. By eating a plant-based diet, Willett points out that you increase your intake of phytonutrients, many of which are antioxidants that prevent disease-causing damage to the body's cells. It's not about deprivation or counting calories; it's about eating more of the right foods and much, much less of the wrong ones. While

Quick take

- A plant-based diet with lots of fruits, vegetables, and whole grains
- Makes physical activity and weight control an integral part of the diet
- Dairy products are not considered an essential part of the diet
- Glycemic load, rather than glycemic index, dictates which foods should be included

many diets admonish people to avoid foods with a high glycemic index (foods that cause a sudden rise in blood sugar), *Eat, Drink, and Be Healthy* offers a slightly modified version, called the glycemic load, that factors in a food's carbohydrate content, which Willett says is a more accurate representation of the impact specific foods have on blood sugar levels.

what's for breakfast, lunch, and dinner?

Though there is no strict diet plan per se, the book provides a week's worth of sample menus and about 50 recipes in keeping with Willett's pyramid. But you're pretty much on your own in devising your menus and tracking your calorie intake. A typical day's menu might include fresh-squeezed orange juice and multigrain hotcakes for breakfast; grilled chicken, salad, cantaloupe, and strawberries for lunch; and mushroom meat loaf, roasted vegetables, green salad, and a spiced poached pear for dinner. Some of the sample menus have made allowances for a snack, and one even lays out the day's intake over six small meals. Coffee is allowed but sugar is not. A few sweet treats such as orange juice sorbet and rum-glazed pineapple are allowed, but there is no allowance for an occasional indulgence in fudge ice cream or cheesecake.

fact or fiction: what the experts say

Though Willett's advice about dairy foods is controversial and his diet won't provide the amount of calcium currently recommended for most people, the rest of his philosophy about how you should eat and control your weight is sound. He lays out a nutritious plan that will improve your health over the long term and fend off chronic diseases, such as diabetes, high blood pressure, and heart disease, that become increasingly common with age.

gains and losses/ what's the damage?

Eat, Drink, and Be Healthy is not a plan for rapid weight loss. It's a diet designed to help you change your eating habits for good and improve your health. However, if you follow Willett's guidelines and adjust your calorie intake for weight control, you should lose weight while reaping the health benefits he promises.

Other similar diets

The Origin Diet; Eat More, Weigh Less

eat more, weigh less

Quick take

- A very low-fat diet (10 percent of total calories)
- Includes lots of fruits, vegetables, whole grains, and legumes
- Prohibits sweeteners and refined carbohydrates
- Requires meal preparation to ensure variety in the diet
- Encourages meditation and exercise

the premise

Dr. Dean Ornish is famous for his strict low-fat diet program that reduces heart disease risk and even reverses arterial damage. The findings from his now-famous "Lifestyle Heart Trial" research, which show that major lifestyle changes can significantly reduce the risk of developing atherosclerosis and heart disease, are so well accepted that participation in one of the lifestyle program's hospital sites is even covered by some health insurance companies. His program restricts fat intake to 10 percent or less of daily calories and prohibits animal products, oils, and sugar. The Ornish plan calls for eating a very low-fat vegetarian diet, relaxation, and exercise. A side benefit of the program, he discovered, is weight loss. How much the diet benefits you is not a matter of age but how well you follow the program. This book is already a classic; it was one of the first to advocate such a major cutback in fat while increasing the intake of complex carbohydrate foods. Here Ornish translates the Lifestyle Heart Trial program for people focusing on weight loss.

the rationale

Ornish believes that it's better to make broad, comprehensive changes in your diet all at once rather than to make small, moderate changes. Thus, he advocates dropping your fat intake from the typical 30 to 40 percent of calories to 10 percent and switching from a diet high in sugar to one that contains virtually none. The rationale for the drastic reduction in fat, Ornish says, is that fat calories are more easily converted to fat in the body. A diet high in complex carbohydrate, on the other hand, is inefficient at converting the calories to fat. In fact, some calories are wasted during the conversion, allowing you to eat more calories than you could on a higher-fat diet. Moreover, a diet low in fat is by default low in calories and reduces the body's production of free radicals, which are destructive compounds that are believed to contribute to the aging process.

what's for breakfast, lunch, and dinner?

Eat More, Weigh Less provides more recipes than most diet books—and with good reason. It's tough to buy and prepare foods with such a low fat content. In fact, more than half the book's pages are devoted to recipes. A typical day's menu might include Scrambled Mexican Tofu, salsa, whole-wheat toast, and orange juice for breakfast; Black Pepper Polenta with Bell Pepper Sauce and Shiitake Mushrooms, Italian Bean Salad, tossed green salad, and Melon Sorbet for lunch; Roasted Tomato Sandwiches, Anasazi Bean Soup with Corn and Chili, Oven-Roasted Potatoes with Fresh Herbs, green salad, fresh fruit, and Apples and Raspberries in Apple-Ginger Consommé for dinner. A table of some common foods and their nutrient content is also provided at the end of the book.

fact or fiction: what the experts say

Most experts acknowledge Ornish's body of research showing the dramatic opening of clogged arteries experienced by most people following his program. However, the biggest problem most experts have with Ornish's diet is that it's just not realistic for most people. The real test of any diet program is how easy it is to stick with over the long haul. Regardless of how healthful a diet may be, it's useless if you can't stay on it. That lack of stick-to-it-ability may be the downfall of Ornish's plan for most people.

gains and losses/ what's the damage?

There's no doubt that if you're able to stick with it, Ornish's diet works. The question is whether you're willing to go that far with your dietary changes. Though exercise is encouraged, especially walking, few specifics are provided about how to get started and keep going. And because the diet is so low in fat, you'll need to do some special food preparation every day if you want to avoid meal monotony. While the diet should help lower your risk of cardiovascular disease, it could be low in some fat-soluble vitamins, such as vitamins D and E, if you don't supplement them. The same is true of calcium. While calcium-rich, fat-free dairy products are allowed on the diet, the sample menus provide only about one serving a day—not enough to meet your calcium needs.

Other similar diet

The Pritikin Weight-Loss Breakthrough

jenny craig

Quick take

- Offers a variety of prepared, packaged meals and snacks that are required during the initial phase of dieting
- Safe and nutritionally balanced
- Weekly, one-on-one counseling sessions required
- Gradual weight loss encouraged
- Can be expensive, depending on how long it takes to lose the weight and how slowly you make the transition to real food

the premise

The Jenny Craig program was founded more than 15 years ago by a woman who was struggling with her own weight. At the time, the program was unique because it offered frozen or shelf-stable prepared meals to help with portion management and calorie-intake control. Today Jenny Craig has nearly 800 centers, making it one of the largest weight-management programs in the world. Jenny Craig offers weekly one-on-one counseling that provides both information and motivation. Developed by registered dietitians and psychologists, the program focuses on lifestyle changes, such as incorporating exercise into your daily life and diverting your attention away from food. If you don't have a Jenny Craig Weight Loss Centre near you or if you prefer to go it alone, you can try Jenny Direct, her at-home program. Jenny Direct offers a personalized weight-loss program, delivery of materials to your home, and weekly support consultations over the phone. With Jenny Direct you can order a minimum of two-weeks supply of Jenny Craig foods.

the rationale

With individual counseling and prepackaged meals, the program leaves little to chance—or the dieter's discretion. Jenny Craig helps you set a realistic weight-loss goal and then helps you craft a plan to successfully achieve that goal. The program teaches you "how to manage food, feelings, and fitness." Jenny Craig believes that the combination of complete support, step-by-step instruction about what to eat, and controlled portions during the initial dieting stage together help dieters win at weight loss.

what's for breakfast, lunch, and dinner?

The diet consists of three meals and three snacks per day. About 20 percent of the daily calories are from protein, 20 percent from fat, and 60 percent from carbohydrate. During the initial phase, and as long as it takes to knock off the first half of the total number of pounds you want to lose, Jenny Craig requires that you purchase and eat Jenny Craig prepared entrées and snacks at every meal. There is a wide variety of dishes to choose from, including sweet-and-sour chicken, beef sirloin dinner, pancakes and vegetarian sausage, raspberry swirl cheesecake, and double chocolate cake. Written materials and your diet counselor will help you add fruits, vegetables, dairy foods, and whole grains to your meals. The number of calories you should consume every day is calculated according to your height and weight, but you are not allowed to go below the minimum of 1,000 calories. Diet plans are available for vegetarians, people with diabetes, and those who observe kosher dietary laws.

Once the first half of your extra weight is lost, you can begin the transition to supermarket food, using a food diary to record everything you eat. Counselors guide dieters with their new food choices, and during the weekly counseling sessions, the dieter and counselor together decide how rapidly or how slowly the transition to supermarket foods should be.

fact or fiction: what the experts say

If you follow the prescribed diet, you'll eat a balanced, nutritious, reduced-calorie diet. However, like most commercial weight-loss programs, there is no research to show that Jenny Craig's program is effective over the long haul. "It may be a good way to get started, but for the dieter, very little thought is going into what they're doing in the beginning. The dieter has no control over what they're eating," says Liz Ward, M.S., R.D., nutrition counselor in Reading, Massachusetts. And, while the counselors are trained to be Jenny Craig counselors, they are not nutritionists. Keep in mind that it's almost impossible to get all the nutrients you need from 1,000 calories a day. It's healthier if you set 1,200 or 1,500 calories as your personal minimum intake.

gains and losses/what's the damage?

If you follow the program and exercise as recommended, you can expect to lose one to two pounds a week. Though the diet is a safe one, it doesn't come cheap. Prices vary depending on your individual choices, but the company says the average cost is about $65 a week, including entrées and snacks. There are generally three membership options. Depending on which membership level you choose and which meals and snacks you choose, it can cost you about $400 during the first month of the program. Vitamin and mineral supplements aren't required, but Jenny Craig does offer and encourage members to purchase its brand of supplements (about $18 for a month's supply). Jenny Craig also sells audiocassettes for walkers and a fitness video series.

Other similar diets

Nutri/System, Weight Watchers

the 90/10 weight-loss plan

Quick take

- Low-calorie, mostly balanced diet
- Relatively low in fruits and vegetables
- Allows a once-a-day controlled splurge on junk food
- Limits refined carbohydrates, aside from the "fun food" daily splurge

the premise

Registered dietitian Joy Bauer, the author of the 90/10 plan, says that years of developing nutrition plans for clients have convinced her that there is no diet that will magically melt fat away. The key to weight loss, she says, is to sensibly cut calories, and that's why she developed the 90/10 plan. The "90" in her title stands for "90 percent sensible choice" and the "10" for "10 percent fun food choices," which allows for some flexibility and indulgence. Bauer believes that no matter what the diet, you won't stick with it for long if you're not already used to eating that way. She asserts that carbohydrates will not make you fat—disputing the claims of low-carbohydrate diets—and that including them in your diet will, in fact, make weight loss easier while keeping your energy level up. While her diet discourages eating refined carbohydrates such as sugar and candy, the 10 percent rule allows for what she calls "soul-soothing" foods that aren't exactly healthful. The diet is a realistic food strategy, not exact math. The program places more of an emphasis on exercise than do most diet plans.

the rationale

Bauer says the reason her plan works is because it's realistic. Any diet that forbids favorite foods is an invitation to "cheat," which is followed by guilt and surrender to old eating habits. By allowing 10 percent leeway in choosing some typically forbidden foods, it gives dieters freedom of choice. Exercise is also an integral part of the plan. Bauer acknowledges that heredity, age, frame, and metabolism are factors that impact your weight although you have no control over them. But her diet focuses on the factors that you can control, such as food intake, exercise, and your metabolism. While you can't control the inherited part of your basic metabolism, she says, you can increase your metabolic rate through exercise. Her suggestions for physical activity range from walking to weight training. The point, she says, is to exercise regularly. She provides lots of tips for warming up and even provides forms for keeping track of your activities.

'Y NEWSPAPERS

'URES &

Paul G. Donohue, M.D.

Medical Columnist

DEAR DR. DONOHUE: A few months ago, my healthy, 43-year-old son died suddenly of a ruptured brain aneurysm. He passed out and was put on life support right away. He had tubes inserted all over his body. Five days later he was taken off life support and was gone. What a nightmare: I was told he was born with this. At the time I was too distraught to ask questions, but I would like to know how someone could live 43 years and never know he had a brain aneurysm. He never complained of anything — not even a headache. Can you please

son. When they wake, they complain of a terrible headache, and their necks are usually stiff. Vomiting is another common sign.

Even when people with a ruptured aneurysm are brought to the hospital alive, 45 percent die within a month and, of those who survive, half are left with serious disability. When it's possible to do so, doctors place a clip around

and people can inhale them. Many people are infected with the fungus. Few come down with illness because most have a natural immunity to it.

In the few who do become ill, the fungus can travel from the lungs to the brain and infect the

Directions & Recipes

Other similar diet

Weight Watchers

nutri/system

Quick take

- Online weight-loss support program offering almost round-the-clock counseling and support
- Menus feature low glycemic-index carbs balanced with protein and fiber-containing foods
- Offers prepackaged, shelf-stable entrées and snacks, but they are not required to follow the program
- Encourages physical activity and helps to set up an exercise plan based on your lifestyle and goals

the premise

Nutri/System began 30 years ago as just another diet program offering prepackaged meals and dietary counseling. But two years ago, it morphed into an almost exclusively online weight-loss program, complete with online counseling and menu planning. More recently, Nutri/System introduced its new Nutri/System Nourish program, a meal plan featuring low glycemic-index (GI) foods and optimal amounts of protein, fat, and fiber to "help keep your blood sugar levels stable and your metabolism burning strong, so you can burn more fat." The new program also includes MindNourish, a series of mental exercises to help you create a healthy mindset for losing weight, and BodyNourish, an exercise program to help you incorporate physical activity into your weight-loss plan. Membership in the online weight-loss community is free of charge. Newcomers are assigned to a personal weight-loss counselor, who will track their progress and give advice as long as they follow the program. New members also receive a menu plan, a catalog of products, a food diary, a weight chart, an online weekly newsletter, and a few other goodies to get them started. Other services include online bulletin boards, chat room support groups, and a free diet analysis. You can purchase prepackaged entrées and snacks, but unlike Jenny Craig, they are not mandatory for you to be enrolled in the program. However, Nutri/System's menus incorporate its Nourish foods throughout, making it difficult to follow the plan without buying the products.

the rationale

Like Jenny Craig, the rationale is that preplanned menus incorporating prepackaged, preportioned foods make it easier to stick with a weight-loss program. Nutri/System's shift to an online dieting service offers more flexibility to people with irregular schedules and little free time to attend meetings. Most areas of the Web site are available round-the-clock so dieters are never more than a few clicks away from information and support. You can make an appointment with your assigned counselor or log on anytime for help from any counselor who is available. Members also have the option of talking to fellow Nutri/System dieters.

what's for breakfast, lunch, and dinner?

The diet plan allows for three meals, two snacks, and one dessert each day. There are more than 100 different prepackaged, shelf-stable, microwavable entrées and snacks to choose from. You can make your own menus from the prepackaged foods or you can choose from a 28-day meal package. The meal plans are based on low GI, low-fat food choices from the USDA Food Guide Pyramid. You add a specific number of servings of fruits, vegetables, and dairy products to them. The products don't have to be stored in the refrigerator or freezer, a definite plus as long as you have access to a microwave oven. But shelf-stable foods never taste as good as frozen, and certainly not as good as fresh.

fact or fiction: what the experts say

The claim that "bad" carbs, those with a high GI, break down too quickly and cause your insulin levels to spike and your body to store fat is not exactly the full story. While experts believe that GI scores can be helpful for guiding food choices, there is no evidence that eating mainly low GI foods will promote weight loss. In fact, GI scores are based on single foods eaten by themselves, which doesn't happen in real life. When you eat a combination of foods, the fat, fiber, and protein in them all affect the GI score, usually lowering it. Other factors, such as how the food is cooked, also affect the GI value. Another concern is that all the preplanned menus with packaged foods may be too much of a crutch. But the program does offer some advantages. Chat rooms and online counseling may be useful weight-loss aids for some people. And, as with any prepackaged plan, it offers the no-brainer approach as a kick-start to a long-term goal of weight loss.

gains and losses/ what's the damage?

Anyone who follows the Nutri/System diet plan will get a well-balanced, reduced-calorie diet that, combined with regular physical activity, should result in weight loss of one to two pounds per week. Despite the focus on the glycemic index rating of foods, the diet provides a sensible approach to eating with emphasis on lowering overall fat intake and increasing fiber. One small study of the Nutri/System program by the Obesity Research Center at St. Luke's Roosevelt Hospital in New York found that postmenopausal women who followed a 1,200-calorie plan for 16 weeks lost an average of 21 pounds. The Nutri/System Nourish foods cost about $60 a week, so you need to examine your budget before signing on to the program.

Other similar diets

Jenny Craig, Weight Watchers

overeaters anonymous

the premise

Overeaters Anonymous describes itself as a "fellowship of individuals who, through shared experience, strength, and hope, are recovering from compulsive overeating." It is an international, nonprofit organization that operates through a network of volunteers. Its main function is to offer a support system for people trying to overcome compulsive overeating and to spread the message of hope and recovery to those who are suffering in silence. The organization has no diet plan or diet book, and as a result, there is no calorie counting or recipe exchanging, no sharing of dieting tips, and no membership dues or fees. There currently are about 7,000 groups meeting in more than 52 countries around the world. Overeaters Anonymous (OA) is completely self-supported through contributions and the sale of publications, one of which is an international monthly magazine called *Lifeline,* which includes true stories by OA members.

the rationale

Compulsive overeating is viewed by OA as an addiction, just like drinking or gambling, and it is treated as such. In fact, the OA program is modeled after the 12-step program for Alcoholics Anonymous, which addresses physical, emotional, and spiritual recovery. The only requirement for becoming a member of OA is a desire to stop eating compulsively. Each member has a sponsor, someone who is already a recovering member of OA. There is a strong spiritual component to the group, and members must be willing to "surrender" themselves to

God (not a particular god, but their personal concept of a higher power), as the ultimate authority over their destiny.

what's for breakfast, lunch, and dinner?

There is no diet plan or calorie counting. In fact, no diet recommendations are made at all, except for the encouragement to stop compulsive overeating and to develop a personal eating plan based on your own likes, dislikes, and lifestyle. The organization says that "individual plans of eating are as varied as our members." Though every chapter is different, the organization recommends that all members consult a qualified professional for help in creating an individual diet plan.

fact or fiction: what the experts say

Some experts have reservations about the loosely knit organization and the rule-free atmosphere OA offers. And some argue that while it may make a person feel less guilty about their compulsive eating, it does nothing to address and "fix" the underlying problems. Others, however, say that if it offers much needed support, that alone may make membership in OA worthwhile.

gains and losses/ what's the damage?

Because there is no diet plan, there's no way to assess if attending OA meetings will result in weight loss. However, for people who have serious issues with food and a history of compulsive overeating, the group meetings may offer additional support during recovery.

Other similar diets

Since OA is not really a diet plan, there are no other similar programs. However, it is modeled after the 12-step programs of Alcoholics Anonymous and Gamblers Anonymous.

richard simmons

Quick take

- Personality-driven diet that provides the energy and motivation to keep dieters going
- A philosophy of inclusion, offering hope to even the most overweight and sedentary who want to succeed at weight loss
- A well-balanced diet that offers both flexibility and variety
- Emphasizes physical activity
- A diet plan that can be followed indefinitely and altered to maintain weight loss

the premise

Richard Simmons is hard to miss, so chances are you've heard about or seen him even if you weren't thinking about losing weight. He's been the star of several television shows, infomercials, and videos, and he has written an autobiography. For some, his explosive enthusiasm is hard to take. His diet is a healthful one, but there is little that's unique about Richard Simmons' diet plan other than Simmons himself. He is indeed the main attraction. His diet plan is updated regularly and repackaged; the latest version is called SlimAway Everyday. The program, which is available from TV infomercials and his Web site (www.richardsimmons.com), includes 3 exercise videos, 12 recipe cards, a dietary instruction booklet, a resistance-exercise firming cord, a sample introductory pack of Simmons' energy-boosting supplements, and the Food-Mover, a useful little handheld plastic device that allows you to keep track of your daily food allowances, water intake, and exercise expenditures. The exercise videos are unique in that they feature people of all sizes and shapes.

Having been extremely overweight himself, Simmons obviously empathizes with anyone who's unhappy about their weight.

the rationale

With Richard Simmons as your personal cheerleader, you may find the motivation you need to get with the program and to stick with it. His overriding philosophy is one of inclusiveness. No matter how overweight you are or how miserable you feel because of your weight, Simmons reassuringly offers hope to even the most hopeless among us. Register as a member on his Web site (it's $9.95 a month), and you can join dieters' chat rooms and an occasional live chat with Simmons himself. There are lots of extras, including grocery lists, an online FoodMover, and many more recipes than those provided in the original kit. Simmons places considerable emphasis on physical activity, and this is the one trait of his weight-loss program that stands out and puts it a notch above the rest. In fact, Simmons was, and probably still is, best known for his exercise videos that include aerobic activity to the beat of a wide variety of music, from disco to Broadway. Though some of his advice smacks of pop psychology, for some people it may be just what the doctor ordered.

what's for breakfast, lunch, and dinner?

SlimAway Everyday lays out a well-balanced and varied diet that admirably includes a minimum of seven servings of fruits and vegetables and two servings of low-fat dairy foods a day. He also wisely recommends not going below 1,200 calories and drinking eight glasses of water each day. It's a no-nonsense program that sets clear guidelines but leaves individual food choices up to the dieter. There are no prepackaged foods, and he encourages you to choose from fresh foods, such as fish, strawberries, greens, oranges, and whole-grain breads. The foods are grouped according to categories, and the diet is set up much like the exchange system used by people with diabetes. For example, one slice of bread equals one bread exchange, 8 ounces of skim milk equals one milk exchange, etc. You're allowed a certain number of exchanges from each group, depending on your daily calorie quota. The FoodMover Exchange booklets also include exchanges for international cuisine and restaurant meals.

fact or fiction: what the experts say

Bonnie Taub-Dix, R.D., a nutrition consultant in private practice in New York City, says she believes the Richard Simmons program makes sense and is not extreme. Plus, she gives him extra points because he acknowledges and accommodates the needs of even the most overweight people. Few experts take real issue with any of Richard Simmons' programs, with the exception of the inclusion and marketing of his own brand of supplements.

gains and losses/ what's the damage?

Those who follow Simmons' diet could run a little low on calcium and vitamin D, even though it includes more dairy than many other weight-loss programs. As admirable as the program is overall, Simmons loses face over the addition of his own brand of supposedly energy-boosting supplements, which are hawked by a telemarketer soon after you place your order for the program. Still, if you ignore the hype and just buy any over-the-counter multivitamin, there's little bad to say about the Simmons plan. If you follow his recommended calorie intakes, you should expect to lose about one to two pounds per week. It is a diet and exercise plan that's designed for long-term success.

Other similar diet

Weight Watchers

the schwarzbein principle

the premise

As suggested by the subtitle, *The Truth About Weight Loss, Health and Aging,* this book is about adjusting your diet to curb disease, turn back the biological clock, and lose weight. Endocrinologist Diana Schwarzbein offers her own version of a low-carbohydrate, high-protein diet that she says will help control insulin. High insulin levels, the result of a high-carbohydrate, low-fat diet, are responsible for a wide variety of ills, accelerate the aging process, turn off your metabolism, and cause weight gain, food cravings, depression, and mood swings, according to Schwarzbein. Instead of using a food pyramid model, she has developed a food box representing four food groups—proteins, fats, nonstarchy vegetables, and carbohydrates—that need to be eaten together in the proper amounts to balance the body's hormone systems. Sugar, says Schwarzbein, is addictive. To complement her diet plan, she recommends a variety of supplements, including a multivitamin, magnesium, calcium, 5-hydroxytryptophan, and essential fatty acids.

the rationale

The basic principle behind Schwarzbein's "healing" diet plan is using a diet that's high in protein and healthy fats and low in carbohydrates to control insulin and glucagon levels. Glucagon is a hormone that causes blood sugar to rise, and insulin is a hormone that brings blood sugar levels back down. She says that you can balance and control hormones in the body that affect food cravings and metabolism by eating right. You can lower insulin levels by exercising and eating "good" oils and fats and fiber. Levels of serotonin (a chemical produced by the body that controls nerve impulses in the brain) can be regulated by avoiding alcohol, caffeine, refined carbohydrates, chocolate, and sugar. The result, she says, is reduced cravings. Carbohydrate calories are limited because she believes that it's impossible to overeat protein and "good" fats. Only carbohydrates cause insulin levels to rise too much, which triggers weight gain. Sugar is blamed for interfering with the body's use of nutrients and keeping insulin levels high.

Quick take

- A high-protein, high-fat diet
- Prohibits refined carbohydrates and other high glycemic-index foods
- Claims to regulate hormone levels in the body
- Recommends choosing foods that you could, in theory, pick, gather, milk, or hunt or fish for

what's for breakfast, lunch, and dinner?

The diet provides four weeks' worth of sample menus for the "healing program," which Schwarzbein says reverses insulin resistance and repairs your metabolism. She also provides four weeks' worth of menus and recipes for vegetarians. The menus are designed to keep your insulin-to-glucagon ratio and your glycemic index balanced by providing only 15 grams of carbohydrates per meal and by including foods from the four designated food groups in the proper proportions. A typical day's menu might include scrambled eggs and sausage, oatmeal with butter and cream, and sliced tomatoes for breakfast; Cobb salad with olive oil and vinegar dressing and an apple for lunch; and roast pork loin, brown rice with butter, asparagus with butter, and a mixed-greens salad with olive oil and vinegar dressing for dinner. Two snacks are allowed, one of sunflower seeds and another of almonds and string cheese.

fact or fiction: what the experts say

The Schwarzbein Principle is basically a variation on several other high-protein, low-carb diets. If weight loss results it's due to a reduced-calorie intake, not a dietary manipulation of hormones. Carbohydrate intake is so restricted that it could be energy draining. And the levels of cholesterol and saturated fat in the diet far exceed what almost all experts recommend for a heart-healthy diet. There is no proof, say experts, that following this diet will exert some sort of hormonal control over your body that will speed weight loss and ultimately slow the aging process.

gains and losses/ what's the damage?

Whether or not weight loss would actually result is unclear from the menu plans, since recommended serving sizes for many foods, including high-calorie foods, are not provided. Despite what Schwarzbein says about not focusing on calorie counts, if you eat too many calories, you'll gain weight. With the menus provided and the limited information on portion sizes, it would be easy to actually gain weight on this diet. Don't expect to lose weight fast, even if you're keeping your total calorie intake in check. Because of the limitations placed on several nutrient-rich foods, the diet could easily fall short of several nutrients, including calcium, vitamin D, folic acid, and fiber.

Other similar diets

Dr. Atkins,
Enter the Zone

dr. shapiro's picture perfect weight loss

Quick take

- Raises your awareness of food so you can make better choices
- Uses photographs to help you visualize your options
- Says there are no "bad" foods
- Has no calorie counting

the premise

Dr. Howard M. Shapiro, a weight-loss doctor to the rich and famous in New York City, has developed a weight-loss strategy that helps dieters develop "food awareness." By visually demonstrating the choices you can make in your diet (for instance, 1 fat-free, sugar-free muffin has the same number of calories as 1 whole pineapple, ½ cantaloupe, 2 pears, ½ papaya, 5 ounces grapes, ½ kiwifruit, and 2 whole-wheat rolls together), Shapiro says you'll be able to make better food choices— choices that will allow you to eat any food you want and yet lose weight. In more than 100 pages of photographs, he shows you how to get more food for fewer calories. In his 20 years of counseling people about losing weight, Shapiro says he has learned that there is no single weight-loss program that can work for everyone.

the rationale

The rationale behind Shapiro's diet is one found in several other diet plans— it's the calorie concentration of foods that is the key to controlling weight.

You can eat more of foods that have a lower calorie concentration than you can of those with a higher calorie concentration. Through clear explanations and graphic illustrations, Shapiro shows you which kinds of foods are more concentrated. And he dispels a lot of myths about low-calorie choices. Think you're being virtuous by having a dry bagel? Well, it turns out that only one-third of that dry bagel provides the same number of calories as a vegetarian "ham" sandwich on light bread with lettuce, tomato, mustard, and a pickle. The sandwich will fill you up more, and it also is more nutritious. Shapiro frowns upon deprivation because it leads to cravings, which lead to overeating. Instead he recommends that you understand the choices you make and adjust your diet accordingly. He considers portion cutting an "ill-advised exercise in a false kind of willpower." You don't need to have smaller portions but rather larger portions of lower-calorie food. He doesn't discourage eating carbohydrates— either sugar or starch, asserting that a calorie is a calorie, no matter what it is made of or when you eat it. Shapiro encourages dieters to keep a food diary to increase their food awareness.

what's for breakfast, lunch, and dinner?

The diet allows anything your heart desires, as long as you keep your calorie count under control. While it gives no guidelines for daily calorie intakes, it encourages dieters to stick with low-calorie foods that are high in volume. He doesn't offer any menu plans, recipes, or food exchanges. According to Shapiro, there are no bad foods and there are no correct portions. It's all up to your ability to visualize the calorie counts and portion sizes of foods and make the right choices.

fact or fiction: what the experts say

If you can trust the calorie comparisons in the photographs, then his idea makes some sense. Eating more for less (fewer calories) is a concept all nutritionists try to teach. But, according to Kathleen Zelman, R.D., nutrition consultant in Atlanta, Georgia, dieters should double-check the portions, since some of the photographs appear to underestimate the serving size of high-calorie foods and overestimate the serving size of low-calorie foods. In addition, Shapiro's complete focus on caloric density seems to overlook the

nutrient density of foods. Choosing foods that offer the most nutrients for the fewest calories is also an important weight-loss strategy.

gains and losses/ what's the damage?

Although Shapiro's basic idea is a good one, he seems to have side-stepped nutrition. Almost no consideration is given to making sure you get enough calcium, vitamin D, vitamin B_{12}, folic acid, or any of the other nutrients that are so important for your continued good health. Neither does he mention the possibility of getting too much of some nutrients, such as sodium. If you follow his concept carefully, you should lose weight and feel more satisfied, but there's no guarantee that you'll be getting all the nutrients you need. One chapter of the book is devoted to exercise and gives a broad overview of how to get fit. While it's more information than some diets offer, there is very little in terms of day-to-day guidelines on what kind of exercise to do and how much of it to do.

Other similar diets

Volumetrics, The Pritikin Principle

slim-fast

Quick take

- Liquid diet plan that centers around Slim-Fast meal replacements and snacks
- Incorporates three servings of fruits and at least four servings of vegetables into the daily diet plan
- Two calorie levels are available: 1,200- and 1,500- calories per day
- Online Slim-Fast Club offers additional information, recipes, chat rooms, and more after a free sign-in

the premise

All liquid diet plans basically offer quick weight loss by substituting a sweet-tasting nutritionally fortified shake or bar for a meal. In the past, liquid diets developed a bad reputation because dieters were restricting their intake to only 500 to 800 calories a day and getting sick—even dying—as a result of their weight-loss efforts. But the liquid-diet industry has cleaned up its act, and now companies like Slim-Fast, which has been around for more than 20 years, offer a safer program. Like many other diet programs, today Slim-Fast offers an online dieting community complete with an online weight-charting tool, a personal food and exercise diary, chat sessions with registered dieticians, a weekly newsletter, and the ability to "converse" with an online Slim-Fast Buddy. There is no one-on-one counseling, however. Slim-Fast boasts almost 400,000 members. It now offers low-carb products, too.

the rationale

Most liquid diets imply, if not promise, quick weight loss, suggesting you can satisfy your sweet tooth and curb your appetite at the same time with liquid meal replacements. Slim-Fast falls into that category, though as liquid diets go, it's one of the more responsible plans. Total calories don't go below 1,200 per day, and the plan includes lots of fruits and vegetables in addition to the Slim-Fast foods and snacks. Liquid diets, such as Slim-Fast, are appealing because of their simplicity and convenience. There's minimal meal planning, and the meal replacements in a can or in a bar can be carried and consumed almost anywhere with no muss or fuss. For some people, that simplicity and convenience spell success.

what's for breakfast, lunch, and dinner?

The Slim-Fast diet plan is centered around Slim-Fast's meal replacements, which make up two meals a day during the weight-loss phase of the plan. Buying the company's products, which include ready-to-eat shakes, snack and meal bars, and powders, then, is mandatory. You can find the products for sale online as well as in most supermarkets and drugstores. The 11-ounce shakes are the main attraction and cost about $1.25 each. The meal replacement bars cost about $1.00 each. Though dairy products are not a part of the basic diet plan, the meal replacements are fortified with calcium, vitamin D, and riboflavin, three of the chief nutrients in milk, as well as fiber. The products are low in fat (only about 1 to 3 grams per shake), but they are also high in sugar.

The one "real meal" a day allowed during the weight-loss phase consists of 4 to 6 ounces of poultry, fish, or lean meat; 1/2 baked potato; 1 1/2 cups of steamed vegetables; a large salad; and a piece of fruit. In addition to a Slim-Fast snack, two pieces of fruit are also allowed as snacks each day.

As the dieter reaches goal weight, the plan allows regular foods at two meals a day. However, there is no instruction for weaning yourself away from Slim-Fast products, leaving dieters dependent on the products forever.

fact or fiction: what the experts say

Though the Slim-Fast diet and other liquid diet plans should result in weight loss, dieticians question whether any liquid diet can train people to eat right. But eating right is what changing your eating habits should be all about, says Keith Ayoob, Ed.D, R.D., director of nutrition at the Rose F. Kennedy Center at Albert Einstein College of Medicine in New York City. Losing weight is simply a benefit of eating right, he maintains. Slim-Fast has recently begun to tout the results of research studies

using meal replacements. In one study, people who followed the Slim-Fast plan routinely to lose and manage their weight were, on average, 33 pounds lighter after 10 years as compared to a matched group from the same community not using Slim-Fast. Experts argue that incorporating meal replacements is generally a short-term solution to weight loss and not a realistic way to eat over the long term.

gains and losses/ what's the damage?

If you follow the plan as suggested, a 1,200- to 1,500-calorie diet should result in a gradual weight loss for most people. However, 1,200 to 1,500 calories may be too low to begin with for those who are extremely overweight, and no formula is given for increasing the calorie level beyond that point. Some medically supervised programs, such as Optifast, offer much lower calorie levels, but because they are medically supervised, the dieter is being closely monitored for any potential complications. Slim-Fast's informational brochures do mention physical activity, but they don't emphasize it enough. Slim-Fast's diet may be a useful starting point for some people who need a gimmick to get them going, but it offers very little education or advice about entering the real world.

Other similar diet

Cambridge Diet

south beach diet

Quick take

- No set calorie, carbohydrate, protein, or fat allowances
- Claims to correct body chemistry that will decrease disease risk
- Encourages high-fiber vegetables and whole grains

the premise

The *South Beach Diet* was developed by Dr. Arthur Agatston, a cardiologist, out of frustration with his patients' lack of results when they followed high-carbohydrate, low-fat diets. His plan is neither low carb nor low fat. Instead, Agatston concentrates on teaching you how to eat the right carbs and the right fats to help you lose weight and reverse health problems associated with being overweight. He blames highly processed carbohydrates for creating food cravings and says that learning to control the cravings will lead to weight loss. Considered by some to be a relaxed version of the Atkins diet, the South Beach Diet starts with a two-week phase that eliminates most carbohydrates. After this, the diet gradually reintroduces "good carbs," including fruits, vegetables, and high-fiber grains, and healthier unsaturated fats.

the rationale

Eating may put an end to your immediate hunger, but certain foods, particularly white bread, potatoes, rice, and other highly

processed carbs, can cause an infusion of insulin into the blood, which leads to cravings for more carbohydrates, says Agatston. When you eat carbohydrates that are more slowly metabolized, such as unprocessed whole grains and high-fiber vegetables, insulin release is gradual. As a result, he says, food cravings and blood levels of glucose and insulin are better controlled, making it easier to lose weight and keep it off. Agatston claims that you will not only lose weight on the South Beach Diet, but you can correct the way your body responds to "bad carbs" and alter your body chemistry to decrease your risk of weight-related health problems, including diabetes and heart disease.

what's for breakfast, lunch, and dinner?

Agatston believes that hunger undermines weight-loss plans, so he doesn't require you to count calories, carbohydrate, protein, or fat. If you follow his eating plan, he says, your hunger will be under control. In the first two weeks of the plan, you cleanse your body by eliminating carbs altogether. There are no limits on allowed foods, but meals should be just enough to relieve your

hunger. In Phase 2 you liberalize your carb intake gradually while watching your weight and how you feel. Preferred carbohydrates during this phase are those with a low glycemic-index score (a measure of the degree to which a certain food increases blood glucose levels), such as whole grains, some fruits, and plain yogurt). But you should not go overboard on the good carbs, either, because large portions of these foods can still increase your blood glucose and insulin levels. Once you reach your goal weight, you can move into Phase 3, the maintenance phase. At this point, any food is allowed, including desserts on occasion, but if you begin to gain weight, you are directed to go back to Phase 1 or 2 to get back on track. Two weeks of sample meal plans and dozens of recipes are provided for each phase of the diet.

fact or fiction: what the experts say

After the first phase, the diet is much more moderate than the Atkins diet. However, there are no limits on any of the allowed foods during Phase 2 and 3, which could be a concern. While Agatston instructs dieters to eat normal-size meals, this could be a problem for those who have problems interpreting their feelings of hunger and fullness. On the flip side, the plan does encourage snacking and desserts, which can help keep hunger at bay and reduce

feelings of deprivation. Many experts contend that making food choices based on glycemic index is a limited way of looking at foods. Doing away with carbs such as carrots, potatoes, pasta, bananas, pineapple, and watermelon during the early phases of the diet simply because of their higher glycemic score ignores the fact that these foods contain essential nutrients.

gains and losses/ what's the damage?

Overall, the diet recommended in Phases 2 and 3 is fairly well-balanced and moderate. You can expect to have lower glucose, insulin, and cholesterol levels, though more likely as a consequence of weight loss rather than the diet itself. Agatston recommends exercise but says it's not necessary to lose weight; rather, it's key for faster weight loss and for reducing insulin and glucose levels. The recommendation to go back to Phase 1 or 2 any time you start gaining weight could cause nutrient shortfalls if you stay on the restrictive Phase 1 diet too long. Since weight loss will slow during Phase 2 and pounds may creep back on during Phase 3, dieters may get frustrated and want to return to, or stay on, Phase 1. With more guidelines for personalizing the diet, this eating plan could have even more potential for lasting and healthy results.

Other similar diet

The Zone

sugarbusters!

Quick take

- Based on the belief that foods with high glycemic indexes stimulate the overproduction of insulin, which results in excess fat storage
- Lots of unprocessed, whole foods
- Eliminates sugar and foods high in sugar, while restricting foods that have high glycemic indexes

the premise

This diet program, described most recently in *The New SugarBusters! Cut Sugar to Trim Fat,* has become a virtual classic among calorie counters. The message is straightforward and clear: Sugar makes you fat; only by avoiding it, as well as foods that cause blood sugar to rise, can you hope to lose weight and keep it off. The diet doesn't restrict your total carbohydrate intake, but it prohibits or severely restricts certain carbohydrate foods such as refined sugar, honey, white potatoes, white bread, beer, rice, pasta, and corn. SugarBusters! also includes a little bit of food-combining theory in the mix, recommending that you eat fruits by themselves. You don't need to count calories, weigh foods, or calculate grams of carbohydrates on this plan, but you are expected to balance the portions on your plate and "eyeball" your portion sizes. And no going back for seconds or thirds.

the rationale

Some experts believe that much of America's problems with weight stem from the fact that we eat too many sugary foods. Too much sugar, they say, causes the body to overproduce insulin, a hormone that regulates blood sugar levels and fat storage. It's not the excess calories we eat but the types of foods and how we eat them that are the problem. The authors of the Sugar-Busters! diet go so far as to claim that fat, in and of itself, is not necessarily the cause of weight gain. The theory is that by balancing the insulin-glucagon relationship in the body (insulin is a hormone produced by the body to lower blood sugar when it gets too high, and glucagon is a hormone produced by the body to raise blood sugar when it gets too low), you'll lose body fat regardless of your calorie intake.

what's for breakfast, lunch, and dinner?

The SugarBusters! diet is based on low glycemic-index (GI) carbohydrates (those with the least effect on blood sugar levels), including high-fiber fruits, vegetables, and whole grains; lean meats; and fats. The book has several charts showing the GI of foods, as well as lists of acceptable foods and foods to avoid. According to the SugarBusters!

theory, the lower a food's GI, the less effect it has on blood sugar levels and the better it is for weight loss. Because you'll be eating more fruits, vegetables, and whole grains, you'll be taking in lots more vitamins, minerals, and phytochemicals (disease-preventing compounds found in plant foods). The book provides two weeks of sample menus; about one-fourth of the book is devoted to SugarBusters!-friendly recipes. Although you don't have to count carbohydrate grams on this diet, by avoiding refined sugar and processed grain products, you'll likely eat fewer carbohydrates than you do now.

fact or fiction: what the experts say

This is an area of controversy. Proponents of the insulin theory say that eating a diet full of high glycemic-index foods causes the body to overproduce insulin, prevents the breakdown of fat, and encourages fat storage. Opponents believe that overproduction of insulin is caused by insulin resistance in which fat, liver, and muscle cells become insensitive to normal levels of insulin. With insulin resistance, larger and larger amounts of insulin are pumped into the blood in an effort to lower blood sugar. This, they say, is caused by obesity. Insulin-theory proponents, on the other hand, say that overproduction of insulin is the cause, rather than the effect, of weight gain.

There's research to back up both points of view. According to Hope Warshaw, M.MSc., R.D., a certified diabetes educator and author of *Diabetes and Meal Planning Made Easy*, eating too much of any kind of carbohydrate can cause too much insulin to be produced, and it can result in weight gain because of the extra calories. The general recommendation today, even for people with diabetes, is to tightly control the total number of carbohydrate grams you eat each day rather than worry about their source.

gains and losses/ what's the damage?

If you set aside some unproven explanations as to why the diet works, SugarBusters! offers up a healthful diet plan that encourages dieters to eat lots of fruits, vegetables, and whole grains while avoiding junk foods and sweet desserts. However, physical activity is all but dismissed as a waste of time in the battle of the bulge, something that research strongly contradicts. A change in diet combined with an increase in regular physical activity is the best formula for weight loss and weight-loss maintenance. Very little dairy is included in the SugarBusters! diet plan, so it's likely to be low in calcium and vitamin D. But a multivitamin plus a calcium supplement should be more than enough to make up the difference.

Other similar diet

Carbohydrate Addict's LifeSpan Program

Stick-To-It-Ability Rating

1 2 **3** 4 5

TOPS

Quick take

- Offers a loosely knit support system of TOPS chapters
- No official diet plan is provided
- Dieters are on their own to develop the approach that works best for them
- Weekly meetings offer the only real consistent component of TOPS
- Local, national, and international contests offer weight-loss incentives to members

the premise

TOPS, which stands for Take Off Pounds Sensibly, is a no-frills, low-cost diet plan. Actually, it's not a diet at all but rather a loosely knit support system for people trying to lose weight. Founded in Milwaukee more than 50 years ago, the nonprofit organization has none of the traditional diet-plan offerings: There's no official diet, no prepackaged foods, no supplements, and no counseling. But for $21.50 a year plus local chapter dues of about $5 a month, members can attend weekly support meetings at one of about 9,000 local TOPS chapters (there are 235,000 members), where they will weigh themselves, discuss problems, and even exchange recipes. Chapter leaders are volunteers from the TOPS membership. In addition to weekly support meetings, the national organization offers incentives for weight loss and even crowns a new weight-loss king and queen each year. Once you become a member, you'll receive a monthly magazine called *TOPS News* that offers contests, weight-loss incentive plans, self-help articles, and recipes. The magazine also chroni-

cles TOPS success stories from around the world (there are about 2,000 chapters in other countries). TOPS members who reach their goal weight, which is supposed to be set with the help of a health care professional when you join, are eligible for membership in KOPS (Keep Off Pounds Sensibly). Little is different with the maintenance membership; KOPS members still attend meetings with TOPS members and have weigh-ins, etc. TOPS also offers motivational rallies, workshops, and retreats. Kids and teens are welcome in the program, too.

TOPS now has online help, too, at www.tops.org. You can find most of the material from *TOPS News* and read TOPS success stories. As a TOPS member, you can also access chat rooms, e-cards, message boards, and other support materials.

the rationale

For people who feel more comfortable figuring out their own path to weight loss, TOPS offers a loose system of support but little more. Exactly what kind of support you'll get from your local chapter is impossible to predict, since chapters vary quite a bit from one to another. In fact, the organization prides itself on the individuality of its chapters, which cater to the needs of the group. Weekly TOPS meetings always begin with a confidential weigh-in, which is followed by a program that sometimes includes presentations by health professionals who volunteer their time to speak. Through group support and some weight-loss competitions, TOPS provides incentives for weight loss. The competitions are set up so that you compete only within your own age category and weight class.

what's for breakfast, lunch, and dinner?

Because there is no official diet plan or even preset calorie intakes, there are no typical meals. However, TOPS recommends that its members go to a health care professional for personalized diets and physical activity plans. In addition, the organization does offer an optional diet planning book called *The Choice Is Yours,* which contains simple guidelines for planning low-calorie diets of 1,200- 1,500- and 1,800-calories a day, based on the USDA Food Guide Pyramid and the diabetic exchange list, and it offers a sample 28-day menu guide.

fact or fiction: what the experts say

Because there is no single TOPS program or diet plan, experts say it's hard to make any kind of judgment as to its safety or effectiveness. However, there's nothing to indicate it's unsafe, and for some people, it could be helpful. Just keep in mind that no counseling is offered and group leaders are untrained volunteers who are also TOPS members.

gains and losses/ what's the damage?

With no set TOPS diet and everyone pretty much on their own to plan their diets, it's hard to say how much you might lose or how quickly you can expect to lose it. Neither the TOPS organization nor the individual chapters make any claims about an expected rate of weight loss. The organization leaves this up to the discretion of each dieter and his or her physician. While this freedom may work well for some people, it carries some risks, too. It could lead some ill-informed dieters to unwittingly cut back too far on calories or to follow an unbalanced diet. Though physical activity is recommended, and some local chapters incorporate group walks into their weekly meetings, it could be emphasized more as an essential part of weight loss. *The Choice Is Yours* does offer step-by-step instructions for beginner, intermediate, and advanced exercise programs.

Other similar diets

Overeaters Anonymous

volumetrics

Quick take

- Diet based on the energy density of foods
- Large servings of low-density foods are allowed
- Encourages drinking lots of water and eating foods that have a high water content
- Allows three meals and a snack each day

the premise

This diet is all about losing weight without feeling hungry. It's based on the concept of "energy density," which means how concentrated the calories are in a portion of food. High energy-density foods provide a large number of calories in a small serving, while low energy-density foods provide a small number of calories in a large serving. Authors Barbara Rolls, Ph.D., a nutrition researcher at Pennsylvania State University, and journalist Robert Barnett maintain that if you eat mostly low energy-density foods, you can eat more, satisfy your hunger, and still lose weight. For example, you can eat 3 chocolate chip cookies (53 calories each) or, for the same 160 calories, you can eat 1½ bananas or 2 apples. The fruit will satisfy you more not just because you can eat more of it but because it's high in fiber. Fiber and water both fill you up, while water dilutes calories per portion. The higher the water content and/or the higher the fiber content, the lower the energy density of the food and the more volume the food has, which affects how full you feel. Keep fiber intake high, drink a lot of water, and eat a lot of foods high in water content and low in energy density and you will lose weight, promise the authors.

the rationale

The principle behind the Volumetrics diet is simple: Eat more foods that have low caloric density and you'll be able to eat more, satisfy your hunger, and still cut back on calories. According to the authors' research, we all tend to eat the same average weight in food every day, no matter how many calories the food contains. The Volumetrics approach is to eat the same volume of food but lower the number of calories by eating foods that are higher in fiber and water. If you do, you'll consume fewer calories and lose weight without that empty feeling in your gut. Once you learn to think about the energy density of foods, you'll be surprised by how much food you can eat. Volumetrics' message: Eat more fruits, vegetables, whole grains, legumes, and beans, and eat less high-fat, low-nutrient junk foods.

what's for breakfast, lunch, and dinner?

There are no menus that you have to follow and no mandates as to how or when certain foods should be eaten. Instead, Volumetrics contains extensive charts of the energy density (E.D.) and caloric content of one serving of dozens of foods. One set of charts is broken down by the USDA Food Guide Pyramid food group; the other set provides listings for beverages, mixed dishes (such as stew with vegetables), fast food, and desserts. The charts are arranged from lowest to highest energy density, making it easy to make good low-cal, low-density choices. Though the charts are extensive, you can calculate the E.D. of any food by dividing the number of calories per serving by the weight in grams per serving. A low E.D. means you can eat more of the food; a high E.D. means you should restrict your intake. The authors provide a collection of breakfast, lunch, and dinner menus from which to choose, plus a list of 200-calorie snacks. You'll also find more than 60 pages of recipes for dishes that have low E.D.s. Soup is promoted as an appetite controller, and research is cited showing that eating soup before meals may help control calorie intake due to its high volume, high water content, and low calorie count.

Overall, the diet provides about 20 to 30 percent of calories from fat, 55 percent from carbohydrate, and 15 percent from protein. It also includes 20 to 30 grams of fiber and lots of water—9 cups a day for women and 12 cups a day for men.

fact or fiction: what the experts say

Rolls, one of the authors of Volumetrics, is an expert in appetite and appetite control and has been researching the topic for years. She has published dozens of scientific papers on the topic and has translated them into a practical diet. According to Liz Ward, M.S., R.D., nutrition counselor in Reading, Massachusetts, "Volumetrics is all about a dieting philosophy that nutritionists have been preaching for years—choose foods wisely and you can eat more." The authors also make exercise an integral part of the Volumetrics plan, a recommendation about which all experts agree.

gains and losses/ what's the damage?

The diet is a healthful one that encourages the consumption of more plant foods—fruits, vegetables, whole grains, legumes. The sample menus and recipes are helpful in following the guidelines. If you are true to the Volumetrics formula for eating, you should feel satisfied and still lose weight.

Other similar diets

The Picture Perfect Diet, The Pritikin Principle

weight watchers

Quick take

- Well-balanced diet of at least 1,200 calories a day
- Encourages regular exercise
- Weekly group support meetings
- Moderately priced
- Requires keeping a food diary and tallying your daily food points

the premise

Probably the most recognized of the organized weight-loss programs, Weight Watchers has been around since 1963. Its goals still are to offer weight-loss guidance and support, emphasize a balanced diet, and encourage exercise. The diet plan is based on a simple, straightforward point system. Foods are assigned a certain number of points according to their calorie count, the number of fat grams they contain, and their fiber content. Dieters are allotted a certain number of points they can consume daily, which is determined by their body weight and the number of pounds they want to lose. This system allows dieters to eat any food they want and still lose weight as long as they don't exceed their daily point allotment. To encourage exercise, dieters can trade physical activity for points. (The idea being, the more active you are, the more you can eat.)

Support is essential to the Weight Watchers approach, and so dieters are expected to attend local weekly meetings, which are led by a trained member (not a nutritionist). The meetings

include a private, confidential weigh-in, and they give dieters a chance to exchange suggestions, ideas, and strategies. Those who don't have a local Weight Watchers group or don't have time to attend one can receive online support at the Weight Watchers Web site: www.weightwatchers.com.

the rationale

Weight Watchers claims it has helped millions of people worldwide lose weight with its easy-to-follow, no-frills diet plan and integrated support system. Part of its great appeal is that no foods are forbidden. Working within your allotted number of points per day—which can range from 18 to 35, depending on your starting weight and your weight-loss goals—you are free to eat any foods you like whenever you want each day. The choices you make determine the amount of food you can eat. For example, one cup of grapes counts as one point, one scoop of ice cream as four points, and one slice of pizza as nine points. The more points you use on a single item, the fewer foods you'll be able to eat during the day. Although the choices are left to the dieter, Weight Watchers offers considerable guidance for choosing a healthy and nutritious diet. The program's success can also be attributed to its insistence on record keeping: Dieters must record all foods eaten and their point value every day to make sure they're staying within their assigned points.

what's for breakfast, lunch, and dinner?

Nothing is forbidden on the Weight Watchers diet, though high-fat, high-calorie foods do "cost" a lot of points, and tradeoffs must be made during the rest of the day to accommodate such indulgences. Weight Watchers materials help dieters avoid the temptation to use all the day's points on pizza and ice cream by explaining how to distribute the points during the day and among the food groups. Menu plans typically include lots of fruits, vegetables, whole grains, and low-fat dairy products. Once you've lost the weight and have begun maintenance, your points are adjusted upward as necessary and you continue to attend the same group meetings for support.

fact or fiction: what the experts say

Research out of the University of Colorado and Saint Luke's Roosevelt Hospital in New York City has found that about half of Weight Watchers' lifetime members (those who have stayed

within two pounds of their goal weight for six weeks and weigh at least five pounds less than when they started the program) had still kept the weight off two years after completing the maintenance part of the program. Whether or not this relatively short-term success translates into long-term weight control, however, has not been studied. Still, most weight-loss experts regard Weight Watchers as the standard against which all other weight-loss programs are measured.

gains and losses/ what's the damage?

Weight Watchers is not the most expensive diet plan, but it's not the least expensive either. Membership is $20 a year. Meetings generally cost about $10 to $15 a week, but there are frequent special discount packages and prepayment plans that can decrease the cost considerably. The online version costs $14.95 per month plus an initial $29.95 sign-up fee. You'll get a personalized Web site, an online journal, message boards, access to more than 1,000 recipes with point values, and meal plans. There's a search function within the recipes that allows you to plug in the number of points you have left and the type of food you're hungry for. Some of the site, including a "panic button" to click for advice, is free to anyone who wants to log on.

Other similar diets

Nutri/System, Jenny Craig

enter the zone

Quick take

- Meals must adhere to a strict ratio of carbohydrate, fat, and protein (40/30/30), which will put you in "the Zone"
- Foods eaten in "blocks" made up of a certain amount of either a protein, carbohydrate, or fat
- Low in calories
- Meal planning can be tricky, but another book by Sears, *A Week in the Zone*, provides more specifics about meal planning
- Includes large servings of approved vegetables

the premise

The Zone is basically a high-protein diet plan for better health, with weight loss as an added bonus. Dr. Barry Sears (a Ph.D., not an M.D.), founder of the Zone, advocates eating more protein and large amounts of low glycemic-index vegetables (those that do not raise blood sugar levels too much) to lose weight and stay healthy. In that way, his diet is much like Dr. Atkins' plan (see p. 30). Sears believes that it's too many carbohydrates, especially high glycemic-index carbs, that cause you to put on pounds, not extra calories. Still, his rendition of the high-protein diet allows for considerably more carbohydrate than the Atkins diet, and he has devised his own dietary proportions: 40 percent carbohydrate, 30 percent protein, and 30 percent fat (40/30/30). Sears insists that his diet is better at alleviating hunger and generating mental and physical energy. He claims that the diet not only burns fat, but it helps fight heart disease, diabetes, PMS, chronic fatigue, depression, and cancer, and that it helps alleviate the symptoms of multiple sclerosis and AIDS.

the rationale

By adhering to his dietary formula—what he calls "entering the Zone"—Sears promises dieters a reduced risk of several diseases as well as easy weight loss. Like some other weight-loss diets, which have very little in common with the Zone, Sears' plan is supposed to do this by controlling and bringing into balance the body's hormones, particularly insulin. Sears goes so far as to say, "Food is the most powerful drug you will ever encounter. Learning how to control hormonal responses to food is your passport to entering and staying in the Zone." Though Sears has little good to say about most carbohydrates (they take you out of the Zone and are stored as excess fat), the diet allows for 40 percent of calories from high-fiber, carbohydrate-rich foods such as broccoli, cauliflower, kiwi, cherries, chickpeas, and black beans.

what's for breakfast, lunch, and dinner?

Sears insists that the 40/30/30 ratio is the secret to good health and must be adhered to at every meal, not just over the course of the day. Food is dished up in "blocks," which are divided up into protein, fat, and carbohydrate. A meal could consist of 2 to 4 blocks of protein, carbohydrate, and fat, but it must be consistent. In other words, if you have 2 blocks of protein, 2 blocks of carbohydrate, and 2 blocks of fat at breakfast, you must eat the same number of each type of block at lunch and dinner, too. The diet generally ends up providing about 800 to 1,200 calories a day. The guidelines about the number of blocks each of us needs are fairly strict, and the book guides readers in determining protein needs based on body size, age, and activity level. Once you know what your protein needs are, you'll also be able to set limits for the amount of fat and carbohydrate you can eat. But it's difficult to plan and follow the ratio, making sure to choose the right food and stick to the prescribed number and proportion of food blocks at each meal. Because the carbohydrate foods allowed generally provide so few calories per serving, the dieter is required to consume large quantities from the "favorable carbohydrates" list. To avoid hunger and maintain your energy, you should never let more than five hours pass without eating a Zone-favorable meal or snack. Several packaged Zone-friendly foods, such as snack bars, microwavable meals, and drinks, as well as Zone-friendly supplements, are available for purchase online at www.zoneperfect.com. (By

joining the ZonePerfect Club, you get discounts on the Zone products.)

fact or fiction: what the experts say

Chris Rosenbloom, Ph.D., R.D., associate professor of nutrition at Georgia State University, has analyzed and even followed the diet herself and says it's hard to plan and stick with Sears' recommendations. And all his talk about "carbohydrate hell"—the physical problems that eating too many high glycemic-index foods cause—has little basis in fact. The diet may work for some people, but it's no magic formula for weight loss, Rosenbloom says.

gains and losses/ what's the damage?

Rosenbloom's analysis of the Zone found it came up short in B vitamins, magnesium, and zinc. The restrictions to only low glycemic-index foods leave some super-nutritious foods, which happen to be high glycemic, out of the plan. Moreover, the diet advises against dairy foods and wheat and therefore could come up low in calcium, vitamin D, and fiber. Ironically, though Sears promises dieters increased energy, sticking with the diet too long could end up making you feel dragged down. That's because the calorie levels can be far too low to keep you going or provide all the nutrients necessary for good health.

Other similar diet

Dr. Atkins

diets at a glance

Diet	Diet type	Calories	Risks	Nutritionally balanced?	Stick-to-it-ability rating
Dr. Atkins	High-protein, low-carb	Calories aren't counted but may be about 1,400 a day	High choles-terol, bad breath, low blood sugar	No	2
The Carbohy-drate Addict's LifeSpan Program	High-protein, low-carb	Calories aren't counted, but proportions of foods at meals are controlled	High choles-terol, low blood sugar levels, poten-tial calcium and fiber deficiencies	No	2
Choose to Lose	Balanced, reduced-calorie	1,500 to 1,600 per day	No risks	Yes	5
Curves	Reduced-carb and reduced-calorie, higher protein	1,200 to 1,600 calo-ries, then 2,500 to 3,000	Could be low in several nutrients dur-ing Phase 1	Depends on your food choices	3
Eat, Drink, and Be Healthy	Mostly plant-based with little dairy	Sample menus pro-vide 2,000 calories a day	No risks	Yes. Could be low in calcium and vitamin D	4

Diet	Diet type	Calories	Risks	Nutritionally balanced?	Stick-to-it-ability rating
Eat More, Weigh Less	Very low-fat (10% of calories), plant-based diet	There are no calorie counts, food exchanges, or allowances	No risks	Yes. Could be low in some essential fatty acids	1
Jenny Craig	Prepackaged diet foods	Individualized at 1,000 to 2,300 a day	Relapsing when prepackaged food is gradually eliminated	Yes	3
The 90/10 Weight-Loss Plan	Low-calorie; allows a 250-calorie "splurge"	1,200-, 1,400-, and 1,600-calorie-a-day plans	Could be low in several nutrients on the 1,200-calorie plan	Yes, on the higher-calorie plan	4
Nutri/System	Prepackaged diet foods	Averages 1,200 calories a day for women and 1,500 for men	Relapsing when prepackaged food is gradually eliminated	Yes	3
Overeaters Anonymous	Support group for compulsive eaters	There are no calorie counts	Underlying problems not addressed and could get worse	n/a	2

Diet	Diet type	Calories	Risks	Nutritionally balanced?	Stick-to-it-ability rating
Richard Simmons	Balanced, reduced-calorie	Minimum of 1,200 calories a day	None	Yes	5
Schwarzbein Principle	High-protein, high-fat, low-carbohydrate	There are no calorie counts	Heart disease, possible calcium and vitamin D deficiencies	No. Falls short on calcium, vitamin D, folic acid, and fiber	2
Dr. Shapiro's Picture Perfect Weight Loss	Low calorie-concentration, high-volume	There are no calorie counts	Could result in low nutrient intakes	No	2
Slim-Fast	Liquid diet	1,200 or 1,500 calories a day	Constipation, also low in phytochemicals found in fruits and vegetables	No	2
South Beach	Modified low-carbohydrate, low-fat	There are no calorie counts	Could be low in several nutrients during Phase 1	Yes	4

Diet	Diet type	Calories	Risks	Nutritionally balanced?	Stick-to-it-ability rating
SugarBusters!	Low-sugar	There are no calorie counts	May not provide enough quick energy for people who exercise heavily	Yes	4
TOPS	There is no official diet	Offers plans of 1,200-, 1,500-, and 1,800-calories a day	None	Yes	3
Volumetrics	Reduced-calorie, large volume	There are no calorie counts	None	Yes	5
Weight Watchers	Reduced-calorie	Uses a point system rather than counting calories	None	Yes	5
Enter the Zone	High-protein, low-carb	800 to 1,200 calories a day	Low in B vitamins, magnesium, zinc, calcium, vitamin D; too low in calories	No	2

personalize your weight-loss plan

You've learned the fundamentals of weight loss—what it takes to lose weight and keep it off. And you've read reviews of popular weight-loss plans. Now it's time to get started on your weight-loss quest by learning strategies that will help you plot a course and stay on it. Whether you follow one of the reviewed weight-loss plans or create your own depends on your goals, tastes, lifestyle, and health. Once you choose your approach, use the practical techniques in this section to turn your goals into reality with a personalized eating and activity plan that will help you win at losing.

taking stock

Now that you've got the nutritional information you need under your belt, as well as a better understanding of the ready-made diet programs out there, it's time to get personal. You need to "weigh" your own situation—your overall health, your current weight versus your optimum weight, your fitness level, and your weight-loss goals. Evaluating where you are now and where you want to be is the first leg of your weight-loss journey.

ready or not?

The road to weight loss doesn't begin at the grocery store, the kitchen table, or the gym. There's only one place to find "Start," and that's in your head. Losing weight and keeping it off means making changes—in your thoughts, perceptions, lifestyle, eating habits, and activities. But you can only make the necessary changes if you're mentally ready.

How can you be sure? Ask yourself the following questions to evaluate your readiness to change (be honest in your answers!):

1. Have I recently experienced any major life upheavals, such as moving, changing jobs, having a baby, or getting divorced?
2. Am I losing weight primarily to make someone else happy?
3. Do I have my family's support?
4. Will I be satisfied losing weight gradually—about one or two pounds per week?
5. Am I willing to learn more about nutrition and take time to read nutrition labels?
6. Can I make time for physical activity at least three times per week?
7. Will I be too discouraged if my weight levels off for a while?
8. Do I understand that even after I reach my goal weight, I can't go back to my former eating habits?

If you answered "yes" to the first question, you may need to rethink your timing. It's not a good idea to try to lose weight during periods of major stress and change. Dieting is stressful by itself, and it's best for other areas of your life to be stable when you're making such significant lifestyle changes. Get through this trying period before you begin your weight-loss efforts. Likewise, if you answered "yes" to the second question, you need to reevaluate your motives before attempting to lose weight. You'll only be able to successfully lose weight and keep it off if you're doing it for yourself.

If you answered "yes" to questions three through eight, though, you have the right outlook for achieving weight loss. You know that changing your lifestyle takes commitment, and you don't expect immediate results. And you know what to do if your dieting efforts plateau: Stay the course!

SMART weight-loss goals

You want to get on the road to weight loss already, but before you set out, you need some kind of a road map. The more detailed the map, the better your chances of arriving at your destination without getting lost or detoured along the way. Your map will not only show you the way, but it will also help you stay focused on your goals.

Try the SMART method for mapping out your weight-loss plans.

Specific
Be specific about your goals and the results you want to achieve. You can break down your main goal into several smaller goals, especially if what

you want to achieve seems daunting at first. Once you meet an interim goal, set a new one that's closer to your ultimate goal.

Measurable
Set goals with results you can measure, and give yourself reasonable time frames, such as one month, three months, or six months. You can monitor the number on the scale or you can simply use the fit of your clothing or changes in your waist and hip circumference as your measurable results.

Attainable
Be sure your goal is attainable. Setting an unrealistic weight-loss goal only sets you up for failure. Oftentimes, losing just 5 to 10 percent of your current weight can lead to big changes in your overall health and appearance. But if you're not sure what a realistic goal would be, a health-care professional can help. A registered dietitian or your health-care provider can help you determine what a healthy weight is for you. Or, you can use the tools provided in this chapter. If you set sensible goals for yourself, chances are you'll be able to meet them. And you'll have a better chance of keeping the weight off.

Rewarding
It's good to reward yourself along the way. Positive reinforcement, whether it's from yourself or others, can be a

How fit are you?

Take this simple test to gauge how fit you are when it comes to aerobic ability, strength, and flexibility.

Aerobic:
After walking up more than one flight of stairs, I feel

1	**2**	**3**	**4**	**5**
no discomfort				short of breath

Strength:
After lifting and carrying heavy items, such as groceries or a small child, I feel

1	**2**	**3**	**4**	**5**
no discomfort				weak and tired

Flexibility:
When bending and stretching to make a bed or tie my shoes, I feel

1	**2**	**3**	**4**	**5**
no discomfort				uncomfortable

If your total score is 9 points or higher, your level of fitness could use some help. Use the guidelines in chapter 3 to help design a physical activity routine that fits into your lifestyle. If your total score was less than 9 points, you're on the right track to fitness. You can still benefit from increasing your daily physical activity.

strong motivator. When you pass a milestone on the way to your goal, give yourself a nonfood reward, such as a new pair of walking shoes or a healthy cookbook. Share your progress with family and friends; their praise may be all the reward you need to keep moving toward your ultimate goal.

Trackable
Keep track of what you eat, your physical activity, and your weight on a chart or in a daily journal. By checking this record, you can see what's working and what's not. The record can help you reassess and find another way to reach your ultimate goal. For example, if walking doesn't turn out to be an activity that you enjoy, you can try some other activities, such as biking or an exercise class. (For more on keeping a food journal, see Building Your Own Weight-Loss Diet, page 82.)

rate your weight

Today, the most widely accepted method for determining whether you need to lose weight is the body mass index, or BMI. The BMI has been found to be more accurate than the traditional height and weight tables at assessing whether your weight falls into a range that's optimal for health. This measurement also gives you an indication of how much extra fat you are carrying around. A BMI between 19 and 24.9 is considered to be in the healthy range, the one associated with the least risk of heart disease. A BMI of 25 to 29.9 indicates that you are overweight. If your BMI is more than 30, you are obese and have a much higher risk of serious illness such as high blood pressure, diabetes, and heart disease.

It's also important to take into consideration where you carry your extra weight and whether you have weight-related health problems. Guidelines from the National Institutes of Health advise measuring both your BMI and waist size, as well as taking into consideration your current health status to determine if you need to lose weight. Follow these three steps:

#1. Calculate your BMI.

- Weigh yourself first thing in the morning.
- Confirm your height, and convert this to inches.
- Using a calculator, multiply your weight (in pounds) by 700. Divide this result by your height in inches. Then divide this result again by your height in inches. This number is your BMI.
- Record this and move on to step 2.

#2. Measure your waistline.

- Place a tape measure around your waist, just below your rib cage and above your belly button.
- Record your waist circumference in inches, then move on to step 3.

#3. Consider whether your weight may be affecting your health.

- Record any current health problems you have that are related to your weight, such as high blood pressure, type 2 diabetes, high blood cholesterol, gallstones, sleep apnea, and arthritis.

You should think seriously about losing weight if any one of these descriptions fit you:

- Your BMI is 30 or greater
- Your BMI is 25 to 29.9 **and** you have two or more weight-related health problems

- Your waist circumference exceeds 40 inches (for men) or 35 inches (for women) **and** you have two or more weight-related health problems

If your BMI is in the upper 20s or your waist circumference is high but you don't have weight-related health problems, you can still benefit from losing some weight to prevent future health problems. At the very least, you should make an effort not to gain any more weight. Note: BMI doesn't apply to children, people over 74, or conditioned athletes who weigh more because they're muscular.

your healthy weight

Before you can set a goal weight, you need to know how much you should weigh. But how do you know your optimal weight? Experts say there is no one exact weight that's right for any individual. You should strive for the weight at which you feel your best, both mentally and physically, as long as it is within a healthy range.

If you have a goal weight in mind, you can easily find out if your desired weight is in a healthy range by refiguring your BMI using your goal weight instead of your current weight. If your desired weight falls within the 19 to 24.9 range, then it's a healthy one, and you can use this to determine your daily calorie needs (see below). If it falls below or above that range, adjust your weight-loss goal and repeat the formula to make sure it's in the healthy range.

There's another way to get a ballpark figure for your desired weight, one that's used by nutritionists for quick assessments. Although experts no longer recommend an "ideal" weight based on your height, you can get a general idea of a desirable weight based on your height using this technique:

- For women, allow 100 pounds for your first five feet of height. Add five pounds for every inch above that. (If you're under five feet, subtract four pounds for every inch under.) So, if you're five feet four inches tall, your desirable weight would be about 120 pounds.
- For men, allow 106 pounds for your first five feet of height. Add six pounds for every inch over that. So if you're five feet nine inches tall, your desirable weight would be about 160 pounds.

Keep in mind that the suggested weight you get from this method may or may not be realistic for you. That's because the amount of muscle you have and your frame size both impact your weight. Muscle weighs more than fat, so when you have more muscle, you will weigh more even if you look lean. This is primarily an issue for people who work out a lot, not for the average dieter. For most people, if the number on the scale is higher than it

should be, it's because they have more fat than they should, not more muscle. Frame size, though, is a consideration for everyone. If you have a large bone structure, your desirable weight will be higher—about 10 percent more than the desirable weight you just figured. And if you have a small frame, your desirable weight may be about 10 percent lower.

calorie control

Even if your weight-loss strategy doesn't require you to count calories, it is a good idea to figure your daily calorie needs. Knowing how many calories you need to maintain your current weight will help you select foods and physical activities that will help you lose weight. Remember that to shed a pound, you need to "lose" 3,500 calories, which you can accomplish by reducing calories from food, increasing your calorie-burning activities, or both. Of course, the last option is the healthiest and most effective approach for the long haul.

The following quick calculation will give you a ballpark estimate of your daily personal energy needs.

1. My current weight: _____ ×10 (for women) or ×11 (for men) = _____
2. I am:
- Inactive (mainly sitting, driving a car, standing, reading, typing, or other low-intensity activities): Add 300 to the result of #1.

- Moderately active (active throughout the day with very little sitting; may include heavy housework, gardening, brisk walking): Add 500 to the result of #1.
- Active (active, physical sports or in a labor-intensive job such as construction): Add 700 to the result of #1.

3. I want to lose:

- One pound per week: Subtract 500 from the result of #2.
- Two pounds per week: Subtract 1,000 from the result of #2.

4. My daily calorie needs to lose weight (result of #3): _____

Another way to use this formula is to determine the number of calories you need each day for your goal weight. You can then consume that number of calories, which will be fewer than the number you need to maintain your current weight. Say you weigh 150 pounds and your goal weight is 130. An inactive person of 150 pounds needs 1,800 calories a day, while an inactive person who weighs 130 pounds needs 1,600 calories a day. If you reduce your daily intake to 1,600 calories a day, you are consuming 200 calories less a day—or 1,400 calories less a week. With some calorie-burning activity added in, you'd lose about one-half pound a week.

calories in perspective

Although you may be anxious to lose weight as rapidly as possible, be careful not to reduce your daily calorie intake so much that you jeopardize your health. Women should not take in less than 1,200 calories a day, while men should get no less than 1,800 calories a day. It's hard to get all the vitamins and minerals you need each day when you reduce your intake below these amounts. In fact, it's still difficult even at these calorie levels, so consider taking a daily multivitamin and mineral supplement. If you boost your physical activity level at the same time that you reduce calories, you'll be able to take in a healthy and more satisfying number of calories while still losing weight.

If you've watched the number on the scale creep up but don't think you're eating more or exercising less, it may have to do with the aging process. As you get older, your calorie needs decrease very gradually. That's because you begin to lose lean tissue, notably muscle, which is typically replaced by fat. Since muscle demands more calories for its upkeep than fat, losing muscle tissue means you need fewer calories. That's why doing physical activities that help you maintain and build muscle is even more crucial as you age. It's never too late to build muscle and rev up your calorie-burning capacity. See Exercises to Move You, page 91, for help in creating your own physical activity and muscle-building plan.

building your own weight-loss diet

Choosing a weight-loss plan is a bit like shopping for a pair of pants: The fit has to be comfortable, and the style has to mesh with your personality and lifestyle. When you looked over the weight-loss plans reviewed earlier, did any of them seem to be the right fit? Have you "tried on" any of the diet plans to see if they suit you?

If none of the weight-loss plans reviewed earlier fit you perfectly, you may do better with a custom fit. In fact, dieters who personalize their weight-loss programs are more likely to lose weight and keep it off. But you'll need to tailor more than just the diet itself. Dieters who develop their own social support systems, personal coping strategies, and physical activity plans are most likely to win at losing.

put it in writing

The first thing you need to do is raise your awareness of what you actually eat. The best way to do that is to log the foods you eat every day in a food journal. A food journal will dispel any illusions you may have about your

eating habits, and it will make you more conscious of what you're eating when you're eating it. That consciousness may be enough to change some of your eating behaviors. You may be less likely to scarf down that doughnut on your way to work or snack while reading because you'll be recording those foods. Using a food journal is also a great way to monitor your portions and track your progress to see if you're moving toward your goals.

There's no question that emotions play a big role in when, where, and how much you eat. A food journal can also help you identify how emotions affect your eating habits, and that's the first step to taking control. Just write down how you're feeling when you eat and where you happen to be (in front of the television, standing at the kitchen counter) in the journal. And rate how hungry you are on a scale of one to five, with one being the least hungry. All these bits of information are part of your personal diet puzzle.

Buy a small notebook or a planner especially made for food journaling that you can carry with you at all times. Every time you eat something, record the following information in your journal:

- Time
- Food eaten and portion size (use the portion chart to estimate your portion size)
- Hunger rating before eating
- Your mood
- Who you're eating with
- Where you're eating

You may also want to keep track of the calories you consume each time you eat. When you tally the number of calories at the end of each day, you'll know how close you've come to the goal you set for your daily calorie intake. If you're not sure how many calories are in a particular food, look on the product's Nutrition Facts label or look the food up in the nutrient counter section on pages 100–127.

After keeping your food journal for a week or so, take some time to examine your records. Look for patterns in your eating behaviors. Do you see any problem areas? Can you identify certain situations or emotions that caused you to overeat or to make poor choices? Are you getting enough servings from all the food groups? Use this information to do some problem solving. Keep up the food journal, and review it periodically to assess how you're doing and how you can fine-tune your diet.

strategic eating

Think of your new eating plan as a long-term investment in your health—one with a pretty good rate of return if you make strategic choices along the way. So, how do you put together carbohydrate, fat, and protein along with vitamins and minerals to create a strategic eating plan that will help you

Fill up, not out

Use these tactics to help fill up on less food. Don't feel bad that some of these tips involve "tricking" your stomach—the rest of your body will thank you!

- Eat more slowly. It takes your stomach about 20 minutes to tell your brain that it's feeling full, so eating slower means you'll eat less by the time your brain announces you've had enough.
- Take three bites less of everything. Leaving a couple of bites on your plate at each meal can spare you significant calories.
- Choose foods with more fiber and water, such as vegetables, fruits, whole grains, and soups. These help fill you up because they take up more space in your stomach. Avoid eating lots of dry, low-fiber foods, such as pretzels or crackers, that are easy to overeat and don't leave you feeling satisfied.
- Go nutty. Even though nuts are a higher-fat food, they can help you eat fewer calories. The fat, fiber, and protein in nuts help to quell your appetite. When you eat a handful of nuts for a snack, you tend to feel satisfied for longer.
- Drink water or a low-calorie beverage, such as fat-free milk, with your meals to help fill in the spaces in your stomach.
- Don't let tastes go to your waist. A bite here, a taste there, and you can easily run up 100 calories or more in just a few swallows. Fight the urge to finish off the last bit of juice in the carton, the last few crackers in the box, and the last bites of food on your child's plate.
- If dessert is calling your name, have a small portion right after your meal. When you're already feeling full, you'll be less likely to overindulge. Just a few bites may be enough to satisfy your desire.
- Keep your mouth busy. If you tend to nibble mindlessly, chew sugar-free gum to keep your mouth occupied. Or brush and floss your teeth right after eating. You may be less willing to put food in your clean mouth.

lose weight and that you can stick with over the long term? Here's some help in figuring it out.

nutrient math

In the previous chapter, you determined how many calories you need each day. Based on that, you can also calculate the approximate amounts of carbohydrate, protein, and fat you should be eating each day. The recommended amounts (called dietary reference intakes, or DRIs) of these three energy-producing nutrients are based on percentages of your total calories. These ranges are established by the Food and Nutrition Board of the Institute of Medicine as the amounts of nutrients needed to meet daily nutritional needs while minimizing risk of disease.

- Carbohydrate: 45 to 65 percent of your total calories
- Fat: 20 to 35 percent of your total calories
- Protein: 10 to 35 percent of your total calories

Here's how you can figure the recommended ranges for each nutrient:

Carbohydrate

Your calorie total ____ ×0.45 = ____ calories from carbohydrates
Your calorie total ____ ×0.65 = ____ calories from carbohydrates

Next, divide your calories from carbohydrate by 4 calories/gram to figure a range of carbohydrate you should have each day:

____ to ____ grams of carbohydrates

Fat

Your calorie total ____ ×0.20 = ____ calories from fat
Your calorie total ____ ×0.35 = ____ calories from fat

Next, divide your calories from fat by 9 calories/gram to figure a range of fat grams you should have each day:

____ to ____ grams of fat

Protein

Your calorie total ____ ×0.10 = ____ calories from protein
Your calorie total ____ ×0.35 = ____ calories from protein

Next, divide your calories from protein by 4 calories/gram to figure a range of protein you should have each day:

____ to ____ grams of protein

variety is key

You're probably familiar with the USDA's Food Guide Pyramid, which often appears on food labels. This is just one of several pyramids, but not all are based on sound science. While the USDA Pyramid is undergoing some reconstruction, the overall philosophy still holds: The foundation of your diet should be composed of whole grains, vegetables, and fruits. Protein-rich foods, such as lean meats, legumes, nuts, eggs, and low-fat and fat-free milk, yogurt, and cheese are next in order of dietary importance. At the top of the pyramid, which means you should eat fewer of these, are taste-enhancing extras, such as occasional sweets, fats from mono- and polyunsaturated oils, herbs, spices, and garlic.

As you can see, if you follow the pyramid's approach you will eat a diet that includes considerable variety. And that's essential to healthful eating. If that sounds familiar, it may be because you've been hearing that since health class in grade school. But just in case your memory is a little foggy, here is a refresher on making smart choices for healthful eating:

fill up on fruits and vegetables. It works! If there is one thing that most people lack in their diets, it's foods from this group. When you eat more fruits and vegetables, these low-calorie, high-volume foods will usually take the place of some other more calorie-dense (and less nutritious!) food. Fresh produce is loaded with vitamins, minerals, and phytonutrients. Aim to get at least five servings every day—closer to nine is even better. Fruit juice can count as a fruit serving, but keep in mind that it lacks the fiber and the "chew factor" that come with the whole fruit.

go for the whole grain. Make a simple switch to whole-grain breads (whole wheat is the most common), cereals (whole oats, corn, or wheat), and other grains (brown rice, whole-wheat pasta, or barley). Look for products that list a whole grain, such as whole wheat, oats, brown rice, or corn, as the first ingredient. Besides providing fiber, which helps to fill you up, whole-grain foods supply a host of other health benefits, such as lowering blood cholesterol levels and reducing your risk for cancer. Aim for at least six servings of grains per day, and make at least half of them whole grain.

make low-fat and fat-free dairy products a habit. There are many lower-fat options for milk, yogurt, and cheese products. Especially when these are combined with other foods, you won't even notice the difference. But your body will notice that you're consuming fewer calories but still getting the many nutrients that dairy products provide. And there's an added weight-loss benefit from the calcium and protein in dairy foods. New evidence suggests that calcium aids the body in burning fat, while protein helps build and maintain muscle. Dropping dairy foods as a calorie- or carbohydrate-cutting tactic can actually make it harder to lose weight. Dairy foods that aren't included in this group are butter, cream, cream cheese, and sour cream because these are made from high-fat cream. Try to get at least three servings a day of fat-free or low-fat milk, yogurt, or cheese.

When to call in an expert

If you've diligently kept a food journal and made some positive changes in your eating and activity habits but don't see results, it may be time to call in an expert—a registered dietitian (RD). An RD can take an objective look at your food journal, analyze your choices, and recommend ways to get beyond obstacles to losing weight. Having the support and advice of a food and nutrition professional may give you the boost of confidence you need to continue on your path to weight loss.

lean on meat, poultry, fish, eggs, nuts, and legumes. These all are excellent sources of protein. Stick with lean cuts of meat, poultry, and fish—and keep them lean by using a low-fat cooking method such as grilling, broiling, roasting, or stir-frying. Legumes, tofu, and nuts offer fiber and other essential nutrients in addition to protein. Eggs and egg substitutes offer another option for getting high-quality protein without a lot of fat. You need about 5 to 7 ounces a day from this group. One-half cup legumes or tofu, 1 egg, 2 tablespoons peanut butter, or ⅓ cup nuts count as 1 ounce of meat.

add in some "extras." Be realistic. Don't swear off sweets or go cold turkey on added fats. Chances are you'll grow bored and give up on this tactic. Instead, include some extras for flavor and fun. Try to use lower-fat and lower-calorie versions of mayonnaise, salad dressing, sour cream, and spreads. Try low- or no-calorie sweeteners, spreads, toppings, and drinks for sweet flavor with fewer calories.

downsize your portions

Being aware of serving size is important to weight control. You'll find serving sizes listed on the Nutrition Facts panel on food labels. You can also find standard serving sizes accompanying various food guide pyramids, and many diet plans include their own suggested serving amounts.

What many people don't realize is that a serving is not necessarily the amount you usually eat. What you actually eat is a *portion* of food, which may be bigger or smaller than a recommended serving size. And a serving is not the amount that fills your plate, bowl, or cup either. Serving sizes are established so you can judge the overall amount of food recommended by a specific food guide. These are based on the total number of recommended servings per day. So if you eat a larger portion, this may count as more than one serving. (For example, a single serving of pasta is ½ cup according to the USDA Food Guide Pyramid. A typical dinner portion, though, might be 1 or 1½ cups, which would be equivalent to 3 servings of the 6 to 11 recommended daily servings.) What's important is the total number of servings that you eat in a day.

One of today's biggest challenges is controlling portion sizes. We have become conditioned to expect larger portions of food, especially when eating out. We've all but lost the ability to gauge the amount of food that's enough. Regaining your perspective and control over portion size is one of the most successful dieting strategies.

A straightforward yet more involved way to keep tabs on portions is to weigh and measure your food. Use liquid measuring cups for liquids and measuring cups and spoons for solids.

For foods measured in ounces or grams, such as meats, it's best to use a food scale. Once you've measured different types of foods several times, you'll be familiar enough with portion sizes to "eyeball" them instead of measuring.

Another eyeballing method is to compare food amounts to common household items. Here's a quick guide for sizing up portions from each food group:

Food	A serving is... *	About the size of a...
Grains, starchy vegetables, and legumes	1 slice bread, 1 pancake, or 1 waffle	stack of 3 computer diskettes
	½ cup cooked cereal, rice, pasta, or legumes	hockey puck
	¾ cup dry cereal	handful
	1 small baked potato	small computer mouse
Other vegetables	¾ cup vegetable juice	half of a soda can
	½ cup cooked vegetables	60-watt lightbulb
	1 cup raw vegetables or leafy greens	woman's fist
Fruits	1 small piece of fruit	tennis ball
	¾ cup juice	half of a soda can
	½ cup canned fruit	cupcake wrapper
	2 tablespoons raisins	Ping-Pong ball
Milk, yogurt, and cheese	1 cup fat-free or low-fat milk or yogurt	baseball
	1½ to 2 ounces cheese	4 dominos
Protein (meat, poultry, fish, eggs, cheese, nuts)	2 to 3 ounces cooked meat, fish, or chicken	deck of cards
	½ cup tofu	bar of soap
	⅓ cup nuts	small handful
Fats and oils	1 tablespoon regular salad dressing or light mayonnaise	2 casino chips
	1 teaspoon margarine	tip of a thumb
	2 tablespoons light salad dressing	Ping-Pong ball
Sugary foods	1 plain cake donut	hockey puck
	1/12 of angel food cake	2 cassette tapes
	1 tablespoon maple syrup	2 casino chips

*Most serving sizes listed are defined by the USDA Food Guide Pyramid.

manage your meals

Mealtime management is essential to your weight-loss plan. This includes the timing of your meals, the foods and nutrients that compose your meals, and the size of your meals. These factors all have one important thing in common—they help you manage your hunger so you can manage your weight. Better meal management, combined with some extra activity, may be all it takes to get rid of those extra pounds.

time it right. Did you know that you're more likely to overeat when you undereat? No kidding. Skipping meals, especially breakfast, can unleash your hunger and cause you to overeat at your next meal or give in to excessive between-meal snacking. In the end, you usually wind up eating more calories than you would have if you'd eaten the meal you skipped. Studies show that people who skip breakfast tend to be heavier than those who eat a morning meal. Your body is programmed to require food every three to four hours during your waking hours, so you're better off eating a regular progression of meals and snacks throughout the day. Eating more often—and including planned snacks—is a great way to prevent binges and keep your hunger at bay. And you're more likely to meet your daily needs for vitamins and minerals when you eat regular meals and snacks.

balance your meals. The foods (and nutrients) that compose your meals determine how satisfied you will feel after your meal and how much you eat. For example, a meal that's heavy on carbohydrates such as bread, pasta, and fruit may not supply enough long-lasting energy to get you through until your next meal. This also explains why your energy and alertness may take a nosedive shortly after eating a meal that's laden with carbohydrate. When you include protein and some fat with your carbohydrates, your meal or snack becomes much more satisfying and will hold you over longer. This could mean adding grilled chicken or tofu to your pasta, for instance, or spreading peanut butter on your toast, eating a slice of cheese with your crackers, or serving up some yogurt with your fruit.

be size wise. The size of your meals obviously has an effect on your caloric intake. Eating one or two small meals and then a large evening meal often results in a higher total calorie intake than does eating four to six smaller meals. Use the tips in "Fill up, not out," page 83, for ways to feel full on less food.

tools for losing

Any job is easier when you have the right tools. The same holds true for weight loss. Putting the following tools and tips to good use can help you achieve your weight-loss goals.

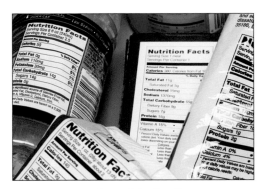

scrutinize food labels

Food labels give you the information you need to decide how a particular product fits into your calorie budget and your diet plan. Follow these five steps to scrutinize a food label. They will become second nature in no time.

1. Size up the serving. The nutrient information on food labels is for the serving size listed, so be sure to compare the serving size to how much YOU actually eat. (For instance, a can of soup that you consider one lunchtime serving may actually contain two servings if you consult the label.) If you eat more or less than the serving listed, you'll need to adjust the nutrition information up or down.

2. Look over the Daily Values. Daily Value information at the very bottom of the label is a handy reminder of the suggested daily amounts of key nutrients for two different calorie levels: 2,000 and 2,500 calories. Some Daily Values identify the maximum daily amounts, such as for fat, cholesterol, and sodium, while others—carbohydrate and fiber—are target amounts. Remember, if your calorie needs are less than 2,000 calories, these maximum daily amounts will be lower.

3. Rate your choices with the % Daily Values. The % Daily Values make it easy to judge the nutritional quality of a food. As a quick guide, 5% Daily Value or less is considered low, and 20% Daily Value or more is high. For nutrients you need to limit, such as fat and sodium, choose plenty of foods with 5% Daily Value or less. For nutrients you need more of, such as calcium and iron, look for foods with 10% to 20% Daily Value or more.

4. Rely on the adjectives. Descriptors on food labels, such as "low," "high," and "free," have legal definitions. This means that a food product must contain a defined amount of the specific nutrient before the label can boast about the food's nutritional merits. For example, a low-fat food can have no more than three grams of fat in the serving size noted on the label.

5. Browse the ingredient list. It displays the food's ingredients in order by weight and is useful for finding out the main ingredients.

manage your food cravings

We all have food cravings, and they may become more intense when the foods we crave are forbidden. Scientists can't really explain food cravings, but most seem to be related to emotions. Some research suggests that there may also be a biological basis to cravings. If you're unable to resist and then feel like a failure for giving in, you're likely to overindulge. Instead, control cravings with these tips:

- Get up and move. Your craving will temporarily subside while you're active and you'll feel better about taking such a proactive approach.
- Grab something to drink. Cravings for food may be thirst in disguise.
- Eat a food that contains protein, fat, or fiber. These nutrients keep blood sugar levels more even and help keep such cravings under control.
- Surrender to your craving. Give in and eat a reasonably small portion. In moderation, favorite higher-calorie foods can actually help you stay on your weight-loss track.

surviving the supermarket

Food shopping can be dangerous when you're trying to lose weight. It is easy to buy impulsively. Arm yourself with these top ten survival skills.

1. Plan ahead. Prepare a weekly menu, including regular meals and snacks to minimize impulse buying.
2. Make a list before you go shopping, and stick to it. Let your list be a compass that guides you on a safe course through the supermarket. And be sure to make up the list at home—after you've eaten!
3. Choose a nutrition-friendly grocery store. Look for a store with shelf-labeling, nutrition booklets, recipe cards, and a variety of healthy foods at reasonable prices.
4. Keep your shopping trips to a minimum—once a week, if possible. This saves time and limits temptation.
5. Get into the label-reading habit. Check the serving size, calories, and fat per serving so you know what you're getting.
6. Bypass the danger zones: aisles filled with your "problem" foods and tasting islands with free food samples.
7. Shop when you're well-rested and well-fed. You're more likely to purchase high-calorie junk food when you're hungry.
8. Do not overbuy or become coupon driven. Avoid the economy size of "problem" foods. If you have trouble controlling your portions, buy single-serve containers.
9. Take your groceries home unopened. Don't nibble on food in the store or on the way home.
10. Ask your local grocery-store manager to stock any items that you can't find. The wider variety of lower-calorie foods on your supermarket shelves is largely due to customer requests.

physical activities to move you

Physical activity is so essential to weight loss that many experts suggest focusing on it *first,* before you make any changes to your diet. Becoming more physically active will give you a jump-start by revving up your metabolism. Then, when you begin to make changes in your eating habits, your body will be more responsive to losing body fat. And as you start to see results from being more active, you may be more motivated to alter your diet to achieve your weight-loss goals. No matter what diet approach you choose—if you're

serious about losing weight and keeping it off, you'll make a commitment to fitting more physical activity into your daily life.

fitting in physical activity

Ideally, a well-rounded physical activity plan will include aerobic, strength training, and flexibility activities. But if you've been sedentary, your first goal should simply be to get your body moving. Any type of physical activity will help you burn extra calories. Once you've become more active, you can focus on increasing the time, intensity, and frequency of your activities.

What's the best activity to choose to help you lose weight? It's the one that you will enjoy and are willing and able

Stay on your activity course

It's a good idea to plan for barriers to exercise as well as strategies to overcome them. Sticking with an activity program requires different strategies than when you're just getting started. Keep these strategies in mind to help you stay on course—or to jumpstart your exercise program if you find yourself straying from your goals.

- Continually review your progress in your food and activity log
- Find an activity partner to hold you accountable
- Seek out environments where others are being active
- Try a new form of physical activity, such as kick-boxing, weight training, or Irish dancing
- Hire a personal trainer
- Set goals and give yourself rewards to provide motivation
- Make appointments with yourself for activity
- Look for everyday ways to put more activity in your day
- Be a role model to those around you, such as children or a spouse, to help them increase their activity

to do regularly over the long run—not just to lose weight. Physical activity is the key not just to taking off weight but to keeping it off for good. As long as the activity gets your heart pumping harder, your breath coming quicker, and your muscles moving, it can be part of your activity plan—especially if it keeps you committed. So choose a range of activities that you like and make sure that together they give you some variety and flexibility in terms of weather, level of difficulty, ease of access, companionship, interest, and cost. Having options means that you won't be prevented from pursuing your weight-loss goals.

Fortunately, there's more than one approach to improving your level of fitness. You can take a more formal approach or a less structured "lifestyle" approach—or a combination of the two. There are advantages and disadvantages to each.

structured approach

With a structured approach, you'll be doing the bulk of your physical activity at a set time. The time can change from day to day or week to week, but you'll be committing a block of time, say 20 to 30 minutes, to the activity of your choice. It doesn't matter where you are or what activity you do. Many people are very successful using a structured approach. They enjoy the discipline of it and the way it allows them to monitor their growing muscle and aerobic strength. And they know that when they're done with their allotted time for the day, they're done: Any other physical activity is gravy. If you're looking for the fast track to weight loss, aerobic conditioning, and increased muscle, you'll want to try the structured approach.

should you join a gym or take a class?

Let's face it, some of us need company to keep motivated. If you thrive on a regular routine but you're not sure whether joining a gym or taking an exercise class is right for you, ask yourself the following questions:

- Am I very self-disciplined? If you are, consider home exercise equipment, exercise videos, swimming, and outdoor activities you can do on your own.
- Do I need the inspiration of a group or an instructor? If so, consider taking classes or joining a gym or health club. You may be able to find special rates if you join with a friend or partner.
- How do I feel about the trendy music that is often blasted in fitness classes and clubs? For some, the music makes exercising more fun. For others, it's just painful noise. If loud music helps to get your body moving, then try taking a class. If it doesn't, you'll be happier on your own.

- How experienced am I? If you're an exercising novice, you may want some expert instruction, particularly in strength training and toning exercises, to get the most out of your workouts.
- Do I want to learn something new? Boredom can doom an exercise program. A gym will likely offer a variety of equipment as well as classes. Local community centers and park districts also offer exercise, sports, and recreation programs.
- How much time do I have? If you're pressed for time, exercising at home is likely to be ideal. There's no travel time, and you don't have to wait to use exercise machines.

lifestyle approach

Some people find it daunting to regularly set aside a block of time for exercise. For them the lifestyle approach works better. With the lifestyle approach, you augment your weight-loss efforts by adding short segments of physical activity to your everyday routine. Most lifestyle activities can be done anytime by just about anyone. Your goal still is to include at least 30 minutes of physical activity on most days of the week, but with the lifestyle approach you will accumulate that amount over the course of the day. With the lifestyle approach, you may not see results in terms of weight loss or fitness improvements as quickly, but if

you haven't been active in the past or if a structured approach just isn't right for you, this can be a good way to get started. And the lifestyle approach can still go a long way toward lowering your risk for disease, such as heart disease, stroke, diabetes, and cancer.

Here's an example of how easily the minutes can add up with a lifestyle approach. Times are just examples and will vary from person to person and activity to activity.

Activity:	Time:
Vacuum briskly	5 minutes
Walk the dog	10 minutes
Take the stairs instead of the elevator	3 minutes
Walk to get lunch instead of getting it delivered	7 minutes
Make extra trips carrying in groceries or bringing laundry up the stairs	5 minutes
Wash your car instead of going through a car wash	15 minutes
Rake leaves	15 minutes
Total time:	60 minutes

You can pump up the benefits of these everyday activities by putting some extra movement into them. For example, do some lunges as you vacuum or pump your arms when you walk the dog. Here are some ideas for

Taking your pulse

During physical activity, check your pulse to see if you're in your target heart-rate zone:

- Place the index and middle finger of one hand across the underside of the wrist of your other hand. You should be able to feel your pulse just below the heel of your hand. If you don't feel your pulse right away, slide your fingers around the wrist area until you can feel the beats.
- Count the beats for 15 seconds. Then multiply that number by four to get the beats per minute.
- Try to take your pulse while continuing to perform the activity if possible, or take it as quickly as you can so your heart rate doesn't have a chance to drop.
- If your pulse is below your target zone, you'll want to pick up the pace a bit. If your pulse is above your target zone, ease up on the intensity. After some practice, you may find that you can tell if you're working in your target zone based just on how hard you're breathing. Still, it doesn't hurt to check your pulse from time to time to be sure.

making your daily activities more physical:

- Go beyond talking. Do some strength-building activities (upper-arm curls, side-arm raises, leg lifts, or leg kicks) while talking on the phone. This is easiest to do when you have a portable phone and a headset.
- Get out and play. Instead of watching TV with your kids, do something active with them, such as shooting hoops or throwing a Frisbee.
- Use your feet every chance you get. Walk to the store, to the post office, or around the neighborhood or a mall. Whenever you can, skip the elevators and escalators and work your leg muscles with stair climbing.
- Make reading a physical activity. Walk on a treadmill, ride a stationary bike, or do leg lifts as you read.
- Stretch as you sit. When sitting at a computer, in the car in a traffic jam, or while watching TV, do some stretching exercises for your neck and shoulders. Watching TV also lends itself to leg lifts.

If you're unsure what kind of physical activity or what kind of activity plan is right for you, the lifestyle approach is a great place to start. Later, you may want to add some structured activities to intensify your weight-loss efforts.

physical activity tools for losing

For optimal health and the best weight-loss results, try to include a combination of aerobic, strength-training, and flexibility activities throughout the week. The rule of thumb used to be that you should exercise until you nearly dropped from exhaustion. Today, experts have a very different view of how much physical activity it takes to get fit, lose weight, and stay healthy. Here's what you need to know:

frequency: Three times a week is the minimum for aerobic activities. If you're really serious about losing body fat, however, shoot for five times a week or even every day. Build up to that frequency gradually, though, especially if you've been relatively inactive.

Two times a week is the minimum for strength-training activities. Don't strength train two days in a row, though, unless you're working different muscle groups. Your muscles need a day off to repair and build themselves.

Include stretching and flexibility movements as part of your regular routine. Try to do some warmup and cooldown stretching before and after your aerobic and strength-training activities.

intensity: If your aerobic activity feels light to somewhat hard, then it's probably about right. You should be able to carry on a conversation, but if you could easily belt out a tune, you need to pick up the pace a bit.

Monitoring your heart rate is a more exact way to measure intensity. You'll get the best results by working out in your "target heart-rate zone," which is 65 to 85 percent of your maximum heart rate per minute. If you're in good health, you can get a reasonably accurate idea of your maximum heart rate by subtracting your age from 220. Once you know your maximum heart rate, multiply it by 0.65 and 0.85 to find the lower and upper ends of your target zone, respectively. During physical activity, check your pulse occasionally (see "Taking your pulse" on page 94 for instructions) to be sure you are working in your target zone.

time: While a total of 20 minutes in your target zone is the minimum recommended, for weight-loss results it's best to aim for at least 30 minutes. There's no upper limit, so keep going if and when you can. If you can stretch your aerobic session to 40, 50, or even 60 minutes a day, you'll burn even more body fat and your heart will reap even more benefits. However, if you have been inactive, be sure to start with shorter workouts and increase the time gradually.

On days when your time is limited and you can't spare the whole 20 to 30 minutes, pick up the pace for one- to three-minute intervals during your workout. For example, try alternating five or ten minutes of moderate effort with three minutes of more intense effort throughout the activity session. Or divide your workout time into shorter but more intense sessions, working at the higher end of your target zone if you can. You may not get the same fat-burning effect as you would by exercising for a continuous 30 minutes, but you will still burn calories.

how many calories do you burn?

The amount of energy, or calories, you use to power your physical activity depends on several things—the type of activity, the intensity, and the length of time spent doing it. But it also depends on how much you weigh. The less you weigh, the more time is required to burn the same amount of calories as a person at a higher weight doing the same activity. That's because a lighter body requires fewer calories to move itself about. Working harder or faster for a given activity will increase the calories spent, but not as much as lengthening the time spent on your activity. Find out how many calories you burn doing various activities:

Approximate Calories Burned Per Hour

Sedentary activities

Activity	125-pound person	175-pound person
Lying down or sleeping	38	53
Sitting: reading or watching TV	68	95
Sitting: card playing or typing	76	106

Moderate activities

Activity	125-pound person	175-pound person
Aerobic dancing (low impact)	330	462
Bicycling (5 mph)	145	203
Bicycling (stationary, moderate)	420	588
Dancing (disco, ballroom, square)	330	462
Golf (carrying clubs)	330	462
Hiking (cross country)	360	504
In-line or ice skating (general)	420	588
Stair step machine (general)	360	504
Swimming (general)	360	504
Tennis (general)	420	588
Walking (slow pace, 2 mph)	240	336
Walking (brisk pace, 4½ mph)	300	420
Weight lifting (general)	180	252

Vigorous activities

Activity	125-pound person	175-pound person
Aerobic dancing (step, high impact)	600	840
Bicycling (stationary, vigorous)	630	882
Bicycling (15 mph)	600	840
Circuit weight training	480	672
Cross-country skiing	480	672
Jumping rope	600	840
Martial arts (karate, kickboxing)	600	840
Rowing (stationary, vigorous)	510	714
Running (8 min/mile)	750	1,050
Running (12 min/mile)	480	672
Swimming (laps, vigorous)	600	840

walk this way

Walking has stepped to the forefront of popularity for both seasoned and novice exercisers. For most people, a more convenient activity cannot be found. You can easily adjust walking to your fitness level by changing the speed, duration, or terrain. It's a weight-bearing activity, so it can help strengthen your bones. At the same time, walking strengthens and tones your abdomen, hips, buttocks, arms, shoulders, calves, thighs, ankles—even your feet.

And, best of all, because walking is aerobic and works the large muscle groups, it's a great calorie-burning activity. You can expect to burn 100 to 200 calories during a moderately paced 30-minute walk. If you walked this much every day, over the course of a year you'd burn off at least 36,500 calories—or the equivalent of about 10 pounds. If you pump your arms as you stride along, you'll burn even more calories.

To lose weight, it's more important to walk longer than harder. For instance, you are better off walking a longer distance for 25 minutes at a slower pace than trying to jog, getting tired, and quitting after only 10 minutes. In fact, you burn almost the same number of calories whether you walk or run a mile—it just takes longer to walk it.

To get the most from your walking workout, follow these pointers:

- Be sure to warm up and cool down. Walk slowly for 5 minutes to warm up, walk briskly for 20 minutes, then walk slowly for 5 minutes to cool down. Check your pulse during the 20-minute brisk walk to be sure you're in your target heart-rate zone. If you're not, pick up the pace.
- Stand tall. Hold your head high, and walk with your rib cage up and your shoulders back. Don't slouch or stare

Stretch and flex

To increase your flexibility and help prevent injury, spend a few minutes before and after your workout stretching your muscles. Try these stretches, holding each for 20 to 60 seconds.

Ankles: Rotate each ankle through a full range of motion by tracing large circles with your toes, first in a clockwise direction and then counterclockwise.

Shins: Sit down with your legs extended and your heels on the ground. Gently point your toes toward the ground.

Calves: Lean forward against a wall, with your palms on the wall and your fingers pointing up. Step back with one leg. Keep your back leg straight and gently press the heel into the floor. Switch leg positions and repeat.

Quadriceps (front of thigh): Stand with your right hand on a wall or chair for balance. Bend your left knee and, grasping the left ankle with your left hand, pull your left foot toward your buttocks. Repeat with the opposite leg.

Hamstrings (back of thigh): Lie face up on the floor with your right leg bent, your right foot flat on the floor, and your left leg extended. Grasping the back of your left knee, bend your left knee and pull your left leg toward your chest. Then gently straighten the left knee and push your left heel toward the ceiling. Release and repeat with the right leg.

Lower back: Lie on your back and pull both legs to your chest until your hips lift off the floor.

at the ground as you walk; this restricts your breathing.

- Bend your elbows at a 90-degree angle so that each arm forms an "L," and make a slight pumping action with your arms as you walk. You will walk faster and burn 5 to 10 percent more calories.

- Stride smoothly. Plant your heel so that your foot is at a 90-degree angle to your leg. The back of the heel should strike first, and your weight should roll forward so that you end each step by pushing off with your toes. Push off fully with your rear leg to work the entire leg and the buttocks.

- Wear a comfortable walking shoe that provides adequate support and cushioning. And never wear ankle weights, which can alter your gait.

give your body a lift

Building and toning your muscles, also referred to as strength training, weight training, weight lifting, and resistance training, should be an integral part of your fitness program. A weight-loss regimen that relies on a reduced-calorie diet and aerobic activity is missing the many benefits that come with having more muscle.

When your body has more muscle, it makes everyday tasks easier. Muscular strength can improve your posture and your overall ability in physical activities. You can see dramatic improvements in your appearance as you tone your muscles—making your body appear slimmer, toned, and younger. When you have more muscle, your metabolism speeds up, so you burn more calories at rest. And your bones also get stronger, making them less susceptible to injury.

When you think of strength training, you may have visions of struggling with heavy weights or weight machines. But you don't need a set of weights or a membership to an expensive gym to build strong muscles. Building and toning muscle occurs when your muscle contracts against resistance or a load. That resistance can simply be the weight of your own body, as in calisthenics such as sit-ups, push-ups, leg lifts, and squats. Of course, you can also use hand and ankle weights or weight machines to build strength. Once you learn the various options for strength training, you can pick the approach that works best for you.

lifting tips

To start building and toning your muscles, all you need is gravity, your body, and a wall, the floor, or a chair. For exercises that use weights, you can use anything from phone books and milk jugs filled with sand to store-bought weights. Here are some practical pointers before you get started. (See "Body building," page 99, for some starter strength-training exercises.)

learn the lingo. When you are strength training, the number of times you lift or do a movement is called a *repetition,* or a *rep.* A *set* is the amount of times you complete a group of repetitions. For example, if you are instructed to do three sets of push-ups at 12 reps each, you do 12 push-ups, rest, do 12 more, rest, do 12 more, and you're done.

think light and long. If you want to tone your muscles, use lighter weights and do more sets. When you do fewer repetitions with heavier weights, you are building more muscle. Don't worry about becoming bulky, though. To get that weight-lifter's look, you have to lift very heavy weights and do lengthy workouts.

breathe right. There's a proper way to breathe when you are strength training. Always exhale as you contract the muscle or lift the weight. Then inhale as you relax the muscle or lower the weight.

do uppers and lowers. Make sure you work both your upper body and your lower body. You can work your upper body one day and your lower body the next, or you can work both every time you work out and rest a day in between.

take a break. Strength training stresses your muscles. To rebuild that muscle and make it stronger, give it at least a day of rest. But there's no need to rest from your aerobic activity routine. An aerobic workout can help alleviate any soreness from your strength training.

consider a trainer. If you're interested in getting the most from strength training, you may want to consider investing in the services of a personal trainer. This strength-training expert can set you up on a training program that's personalized to your needs and teach you proper form. This is particularly important when you're using free weights. Exercise videos and books can also help to demonstrate proper form.

Body building

Your body can be the best, and cheapest, muscle-building equipment. Try the following exercises a few times a week: Basic sit-ups, squats, and leg lifts are also good muscle-building exercises.

Wall push-up (for upper body):
Stand two to three feet away from the wall, placing your feet shoulder-distance apart. Place your hands on the wall so that they are even with your shoulders. Slowly bend your arms at the elbow until your nose is a few inches away from the wall. Hold your abdominal muscles tight so your belly isn't falling toward the wall. Push yourself back to a standing position. Repeat 10 to 12 times.

Basic lunge (for lower body):
You'll need to hold onto a chair or wall with one hand for support. Place your right leg about three feet in front of your left. Keeping your back straight and placing your free hand on your hips, slowly lower your body, keeping your weight evenly distributed between your legs and making sure your right knee doesn't extend over your ankle. Push back up into a standing position. Repeat four times and switch legs.

the nutrient counter

When you're trying to lose weight, it's particularly important to choose foods carefully and knowledgably. As you may have discovered, that's easier said than done!

How do you assess whether that English muffin you're eyeing or the banana you want to slice on top of your cereal will make or break your calorie budget? How can you be certain that the foods you're eating provide the amounts of carbohydrate, protein, and fat that your body requires and that your diet plan allows? Getting enough fiber, as you've learned in this book, is essential to good health and an important component of any weight-loss program. But you can't tell how much fiber a food contains by looking at it.

That's where this nutrient counter comes in. The counter lists nutrient values for hundreds of foods so you can compare them side-by-side to decide which fit best in your weight-loss plan.

For each food item, the counter lists the calories and the number of grams of total carbohydrate, fiber, protein, total fat, and saturated fat in a portion. (While the total carbohydrate value for a food includes its fiber content, we've broken out the number of fiber grams where available so you can see how many of a food's carb grams come from beneficial, indigestible fiber.) Values have been rounded to the nearest whole number. If "Tr" (which stands for trace) appears in a column, it means there's less than half a gram of that nutrient in a single portion of that food. If "NA" appears, that means the value was not available to us. When comparing foods, remember to check the portion sizes listed to be sure you're looking at equal portions of each food.

The counter can also help you deal with reality. Despite your best intentions, there will be times when your food choices do not exactly comply with your diet. Instead of giving up on your diet because you couldn't pass up that piece of apple pie or you just didn't want to say no to a slice of your co-worker's birthday cake, you can account for it. Use the counter to get an idea of how many extra calories and grams of fat you took in, then look for lower-calorie, lower-fat foods for your next few meals to help balance them out and get back on track.

Thank you, uncle sam

This nutrient counter was adapted from: U.S. Department of Agriculture, Agricultural Research Service. 2004. USDA Nutrient Database for Standard Reference, Release 16-1. Nutrient Data Laboratory Home Page, http://www.nal.usda.gov/fnic/foodcomp

Food, portion	Calories	Total Fat (g)	Sat Fat (g)	Protein (g)	Total Carb (g)	Fiber (g)	Calcium (mg)	Sodium (mg)
Baked Products								
Bagel, cinnamon-raisin, 3½″ dia	195	1	Tr	7	39	2	13	229
Bagel, plain (includes onion, poppy, sesame), 3½″ dia	289	2	Tr	11	56	2	19	561
Biscuit, mixed-grain, refrigerated dough, 2½″ dia	116	2	1	3	21	NA	7	295
Biscuit, plain or buttermilk, commercially baked, 2½″ dia	127	6	1	2	17	Tr	17	368
Biscuit, plain or buttermilk, prepared from recipe, 2½″ dia	212	10	3	4	27	1	141	348
Bread, cornbread, dry mix, prepared, 1 piece	188	6	2	4	29	1	44	467
Bread, cracked-wheat, 1 slice	65	1	Tr	2	12	1	11	135
Bread crumbs, grated, seasoned, 1 oz	104	1	Tr	4	20	1	28	751
Bread, French or Vienna (includes sourdough), 4″×2½″×1¾″	175	2	Tr	6	33	2	48	390
Bread, Italian, 1 slice	54	1	Tr	2	10	1	16	117
Bread, mixed-grain (includes whole-grain, 7-grain), 1 slice	65	1	Tr	3	12	2	24	127
Bread, raisin, 1 slice	71	1	Tr	2	14	1	17	101
Bread, rye, 1 slice	83	1	Tr	3	15	2	23	211
Bread stick, plain, 7⅝″×⅝″	41	1	Tr	1	7	Tr	2	66
Bread stuffing, dry mix, 6 oz package	656	6	1	19	130	5	165	2703
Bread, wheat (includes wheat berry), 1 slice	65	1	Tr	2	12	1	26	133
Bread, wheat, reduced-calorie, 1 slice	46	1	Tr	2	10	3	18	118
Bread, white, 1 slice	67	1	Tr	2	13	1	38	170
Bread, whole-wheat, 1 slice	69	1	Tr	3	13	2	20	148
Cake, angelfood, commercially prepared, 1/12 of 12 oz cake	72	Tr	Tr	2	16	Tr	39	210

Food, portion	Calories	Total Fat (g)	Sat Fat (g)	Protein (g)	Total Carb (g)	Fiber (g)	Calcium (mg)	Sodium (mg)
Baked Products (cont.)								
Cake, chocolate, with chocolate frosting, ⅛ of 18 oz cake	235	10	3	3	35	2	28	214
Cake, pound, ⅒ of cake	116	6	3	2	15	Tr	11	119
Cake, shortcake, biscuit-type, prepared from recipe, 1 oz	98	4	1	2	14	NA	58	143
Cake, sponge, 1/12 of 16 oz cake	110	1	Tr	2	23	Tr	27	93
Cake, white, prepared from recipe, no frosting, 1/12 of 9" dia	264	9	2	4	42	1	96	242
Cheesecake, ⅙ of 17 oz cake	257	18	8	4	20	Tr	41	166
Coffee cake, fruit, ⅛ cake	156	5	1	3	26	1	23	193
Cookie, chocolate sandwich, with creme filling, 1 cookie	47	2	Tr	Tr	7	Tr	3	60
Cookies, butter, 1 cookie	23	1	1	Tr	3	Tr	1	18
Cookies, chocolate chip, soft-type, 1 cookie	69	4	1	1	9	Tr	2	49
Cookies, fig bars, 1 cookie	56	1	Tr	1	11	1	10	56
Cookies, fortune, 1 cookie	30	Tr	Tr	Tr	7	Tr	1	22
Cookies, oatmeal, commercially prepared, 1 oz	128	5	1	2	19	1	10	109
Cookies, peanut butter, 1 cookie	72	4	1	1	9	Tr	5	62
Cookies, raisin, soft-type, 1 cookie	60	2	1	1	10	Tr	7	51
Cookies, sugar (includes vanilla), 1 cookie	72	3	1	1	10	Tr	3	54
Crackers, cheese, 1 cracker, 1" sq	5	Tr	Tr	Tr	1	Tr	2	10
Crackers, cheese, sandwich-type, with peanut butter filling, 1 sandwich	32	2	Tr	1	4	Tr	3	46
Crackers, matzo, plain, 1 matzo	111	Tr	Tr	3	23	1	4	1
Crackers, melba toast, plain, 1 round	12	Tr	Tr	Tr	2	Tr	3	25
Crackers, rye, wafers, plain, 1 cracker	37	Tr	Tr	1	9	3	4	87

Food, portion	Calories	Total Fat (g)	Sat Fat (g)	Protein (g)	Total Carb (g)	Fiber (g)	Calcium (mg)	Sodium (mg)
Crackers, saltines (includes oyster, soda, soup), 1 cup	195	5	1	4	32	1	54	586
Crackers, sandwich-type, with peanut butter filling, 1 sandwich	32	2	Tr	1	4	Tr	5	47
Crackers, wheat, 1 cracker	9	Tr	Tr	Tr	1	Tr	1	16
Croissants, butter, 1 croissant	231	12	7	5	26	1	21	424
Croutons, seasoned, 1 cup	186	7	2	4	25	2	38	495
Cupcake, creme-filled, chocolate with frosting, 1 cupcake	188	7	1	2	30	Tr	37	213
Danish pastry, cheese, 1 pastry	266	16	5	6	26	1	25	320
Doughnuts, cake-type, plain, sugared, or glazed, 3" dia	192	10	3	2	23	1	27	181
Doughnuts, yeast-leavened, glazed (includes honey buns), 3" dia	242	14	3	4	27	1	26	205
English muffins, plain (includes sourdough), 1 muffin	134	1	Tr	4	26	2	99	264
English muffins, wheat, 1 muffin	127	1	Tr	5	26	3	101	218
French toast, prepared from recipe, with 2% milk, 1 slice	149	7	2	5	16	NA	65	311
Ice cream cones, cake or wafer-type, 1 cone	17	Tr	Tr	Tr	3	Tr	1	6
Muffins, blueberry, 1 medium	313	7	2	6	54	3	64	505
Muffins, corn, 1 medium	345	9	2	7	58	4	84	589
Muffins, plain, prepared from recipe, with 2% milk, 1 muffin	169	6	1	4	24	2	114	266
Pancakes, buttermilk, prepared from recipe, 1 pancake, 6" dia	175	7	1	5	22	NA	121	402
Pancakes, plain, dry mix, complete, prepared, 1 pancake, 6" dia	149	2	Tr	4	28	1	97	484
Pie, apple, ⅛ of 9" dia	411	19	5	4	58	NA	11	327
Pie, blueberry, ⅛ of 9" dia	290	13	2	2	44	1	10	406

Food, portion	Calories	Total Fat (g)	Sat Fat (g)	Protein (g)	Total Carb (g)	Fiber (g)	Calcium (mg)	Sodium (mg)
Baked Products (cont.)								
Pie, chocolate creme, commercially prepared, ¼ of 6" pie	301	19	5	3	33	2	36	135
Pie, pumpkin, ⅙ of 8" pie	229	10	2	4	30	3	65	307
Pita, white, 6½" dia	165	1	Tr	5	33	1	52	322
Rolls, dinner, French, 1 roll	105	2	Tr	3	19	1	35	231
Rolls, dinner, plain, 1 oz roll	84	2	Tr	2	14	1	33	146
Rolls, dinner, wheat, 1 oz roll	76	2	Tr	2	13	1	49	95
Rolls, dinner, whole-wheat, 1 submarine	250	4	1	8	48	7	100	449
Rolls, hamburger or hot dog, plain, 1 roll	120	2	Tr	4	21	1	59	206
Rolls, hard (includes kaiser), 3½" dia	167	2	Tr	6	30	1	54	310
SHAKE 'N' BAKE original recipe, 1 serving	106	1	0	2	22	NA	NA	795
Strudel, apple, 1 piece	195	8	1	2	29	2	11	191
Taco shells, baked, 5" dia	62	3	Tr	1	8	1	21	49
Toaster pastries, fruit (includes apple, blueberry, cherry, strawberry), 1 pastry	204	5	1	2	37	1	14	218
Tortillas, flour, 6" dia	104	2	1	3	18	1	12	153
Waffles, EGGO Golden Oat Waffles, 1 waffle	69	1	Tr	2	13	1	23	135
Waffles, EGGO Lowfat Homestyle Waffles, 1 waffle	83	1	Tr	2	15	Tr	20	155
Waffles, plain, ready-to-heat (includes buttermilk), 1 waffle	95	3	Tr	2	15	1	84	284
Beef Products								
Beef, ground, 95% lean meat, pan-browned, 3 oz	164	6	3	25	0	0	8	72
Beef, ground, patties, frozen, broiled, medium, 3 oz	240	17	7	21	0	0	9	65
Breakfast strips, cured, cooked, 3 slices	153	12	5	11	Tr	0	3	766

FOOD, PORTION	CALORIES	TOTAL FAT (G)	SAT FAT (G)	PROTEIN (G)	TOTAL CARB (G)	FIBER (G)	CALCIUM (MG)	SODIUM (MG)
Brisket, whole, braised, 3 oz	247	17	6	23	0	0	6	55
Chuck, top blade, broiled, 3 oz	173	9	3	22	0	0	6	58
Rib, eye, broiled, 3 oz	174	8	3	25	0	0	14	51
Rib, prime, broiled, 3 oz	250	18	8	21	0	0	7	60
Short loin, porterhouse steak, broiled, 3 oz	235	16	6	20	0	0	6	55
Short loin, T-bone steak, broiled, 3 oz	168	8	3	22	0	0	3	60
Tenderloin, broiled, 3 oz	175	8	0	25	0	0	14	50
BEVERAGES								
Beer, light, 12 fl oz	99	0	0	1	5	0	18	11
Beer, regular, 12 fl oz	117	Tr	0	1	6	Tr	18	14
Carbonated beverage, low-calorie, other than cola or pepper, no caffeine, 12 fl oz	0	0	0	Tr	0	0	14	21
Chocolate syrup, 2 tbsp	109	Tr	Tr	1	25	1	5	28
Clam and tomato juice, canned, 5.5 oz	80	Tr	Tr	1	18	Tr	20	601
Club soda, 12 fl oz	0	0	0	0	0	0	18	75
Cocoa mix, powder, 1 serving	111	1	1	2	24	1	39	141
Coffee, brewed from grounds, prepared with tap water, 8 fl oz	9	2	0	Tr	0	0	2	2
Cola, carbonated, contains caffeine, 12 fl oz	155	0	0	Tr	40	0	11	15
Cranberry juice cocktail, bottled, 8 fl oz	144	Tr	Tr	0	36	Tr	8	5
Cream soda, carbonated, 12 fl oz	189	0	0	0	49	0	19	45
Fruit punch juice drink, frozen concentrate, prepared with water, 8 fl oz	124	Tr	Tr	Tr	30	Tr	17	12
Ginger ale, carbonated, 12 fl oz	124	0	0	0	32	0	11	26
Grape juice drink, canned, 8 fl oz	125	0	0	Tr	32	0	8	3
KOOL-AID Tropical Punch, sweetened, powder, 1 serving	64	0	0	0	16	0	28	2

Food, portion	Calories	Total Fat (g)	Sat Fat (g)	Protein (g)	Total Carb (g)	Fiber (g)	Calcium (mg)	Sodium (mg)
Beverages (cont.)								
Lemonade, COUNTRY TIME, pink, sugar-free mix, 1 portion	5	Tr	0	Tr	2	NA	NA	Tr
Lemonade, frozen concentrate, white, prepared with water, 8 fl oz	131	Tr	Tr	Tr	34	Tr	10	7
NESTEA Iced Tea, Lemon Flavor, ready-to-drink, 8 fl oz	89	1	Tr	0	20	0	NA	0
Orange juice drink, 8 fl oz	132	0	0	Tr	33	0	5	5
Pepper-type cola, carbonated, 12 fl oz	151	Tr	Tr	0	38	0	11	37
Pineapple and grapefruit juice drink, canned, 8 fl oz	118	Tr	Tr	1	29	Tr	18	35
RICE DREAM, canned, 8 fl oz	120	2	Tr	Tr	25	0	20	86
Root beer, 12 fl oz	152	0	0	0	39	0	19	48
Shake, chocolate, 8 fl oz	211	6	4	6	34	3	188	161
Shake, vanilla, 8 fl oz	184	5	3	6	30	Tr	203	136
Tea, brewed, prepared with tap water, 8 fl oz	2	0	Tr	0	1	0	0	7
Wine, table, red, 1 glass, 3.5 fl oz	74	0	0	Tr	2	0	8	5
Wine, table, white, 1 glass, 3.5 fl oz	70	0	0	Tr	1	0	9	5
Breakfast Cereals								
APPLE CINNAMON CHEERIOS, ¾ cup	118	2	Tr	2	25	1	100	120
BANANA NUT CRUNCH Cereal, 1 cup	249	6	1	5	44	4	21	253
BASIC 4, 1 cup	202	3	Tr	4	42	3	196	316
Bran flakes with raisins, 1 cup	187	1	Tr	5	46	8	27	360
CHEERIOS, 1 cup	111	2	Tr	3	22	3	100	273
CORN CHEX, 1 cup	112	Tr	Tr	2	26	1	100	288
CORN FLAKES, 1 cup	101	Tr	Tr	2	24	1	2	203
CORN POPS, 1 cup	118	Tr	Tr	1	28	Tr	5	120

Food, portion	Calories	Total Fat (g)	Sat Fat (g)	Protein (g)	Total Carb (g)	Fiber (g)	Calcium (mg)	Sodium (mg)
CREAM OF WHEAT, instant, prepared with water, 1 cup	149	1	Tr	4	32	1	154	10
CRISPIX, 1 cup	109	Tr	Tr	2	25	Tr	6	210
FIBER ONE, ½ cup	59	1	Tr	2	24	14	100	129
FROSTED FLAKES, ¾ cup	114	Tr	Tr	1	28	1	2	148
FROSTED WHEATIES, ¾ cup	112	Tr	Tr	2	27	1	100	204
GOLDEN GRAHAMS, ¾ cup	112	1	Tr	2	25	1	350	269
HONEY BUNCHES OF OATS Honey Roasted Cereal, ¾ cup	118	2	Tr	2	25	1	6	193
HONEY NUT CHEERIOS, 1 cup	112	1	Tr	3	24	2	100	269
Multi-Bran CHEX, 1 cup	166	1	Tr	3	41	6	89	322
POST 100% BRAN Cereal, ⅓ cup	83	1	Tr	4	23	8	22	121
POST GRAPE-NUTS Cereal, ½ cup	208	1	Tr	6	47	5	20	354
PRODUCT 19, 1 cup	100	Tr	Tr	2	25	1	5	207
QUAKER Instant Oatmeal, apples and cinnamon, 1 packet, prepared	130	1	Tr	3	26	3	110	165
QUAKER OAT LIFE, plain, ¾ cup	120	1	Tr	3	25	2	112	164
RAISIN BRAN, 1 cup	195	2	Tr	5	47	7	29	362
RICE KRISPIES, 1¼ cups	119	Tr	Tr	2	29	Tr	5	319
SPECIAL K, 1 cup	117	Tr	Tr	7	22	1	9	224
TOTAL Corn Flakes, 1⅓ cups	112	Tr	Tr	2	26	1	1000	209
TRIX, 1 cup	117	1	Tr	1	27	1	100	194
WHEATIES, 1 cup	107	1	Tr	3	24	3	0	218
Whole Grain TOTAL, ¾ cup	97	1	Tr	2	23	2	1000	192
Cereal Grains and Pasta								
Barley, 1 cup	651	4	1	23	135	32	61	22
Corn, yellow, 1 cup	606	8	1	16	123	12	12	58
Cornmeal, whole-grain, yellow, 1 cup	442	4	1	10	94	9	7	43

Food, portion	Calories	Total Fat (g)	Sat Fat (g)	Protein (g)	Total Carb (g)	Fiber (g)	Calcium (mg)	Sodium (mg)
Cereal Grains and Pasta (cont.)								
Couscous, cooked, 1 cup	176	Tr	Tr	6	36	2	13	8
Macaroni, cooked, enriched, 1 cup small shells	162	1	Tr	5	33	1	8	1
Noodles, Chinese, chow mein, 1 cup	237	14	2	4	26	2	9	198
Noodles, egg, cooked, enriched, 1 cup	213	2	Tr	8	40	2	19	11
Noodles, somen, cooked, 1 cup	231	Tr	Tr	7	48	NA	14	283
Oat bran, cooked, 1 cup	88	2	Tr	7	25	6	22	2
Pasta, fresh-refrigerated, plain, cooked, 2 oz	75	1	Tr	3	14	NA	3	3
Rice, brown, long-grain, cooked, 1 cup	216	2	Tr	5	45	4	20	10
Rice flour, white, 1 cup	578	2	1	9	127	4	16	0
Rice noodles, cooked, 1 cup	192	Tr	Tr	2	44	2	7	33
Rice, white, cooked, 1 cup	169	Tr	Tr	4	37	2	3	9
Rice, white, long-grain, cooked, 1 cup	205	Tr	Tr	4	45	1	16	2
Rye, 1 cup	566	4	Tr	25	118	25	56	10
Spaghetti, cooked, enriched, 1 cup	197	1	Tr	7	40	2	10	1
Wheat flour, white, enriched, 1 cup	455	1	Tr	13	95	3	19	3
Wheat flour, whole-grain, 1 cup	407	2	Tr	16	87	15	41	6
Wheat, sprouted, 1 cup	214	1	Tr	8	46	1	30	17
Wild rice, cooked, 1 cup	166	1	Tr	7	35	3	5	5
Dairy and Egg Products								
Butter, salted, 1 tbsp	102	12	6	Tr	Tr	0	3	82
Cheese, American, 1 oz	94	7	4	6	2	0	141	274
Cheese, blue, 1 cup, crumbled	477	39	25	29	3	0	713	1883
Cheese, brick, 1 oz	105	8	5	7	1	0	191	159
Cheese, cheddar, 1 slice	113	9	6	7	Tr	0	202	174
Cheese, cream, 1 tbsp	51	5	3	1	Tr	0	12	43

Food, portion	Calories	Total Fat (g)	Sat Fat (g)	Protein (g)	Total Carb (g)	Fiber (g)	Calcium (mg)	Sodium (mg)
Cheese, feta, 1 cup, crumbled	396	32	22	21	6	0	740	1674
Cheese, Gouda, 1 oz	101	8	5	7	1	0	198	232
Cheese, Mexican, queso anejo, 1 oz	106	8	5	6	1	0	193	321
Cheese, mozzarella, part skim milk, 1 oz	72	5	3	7	1	0	222	175
Cheese, Parmesan, grated, 1 cup	431	29	17	38	4	0	1109	1529
Cheese, provolone, 1 slice	98	7	5	7	1	0	212	245
Cheese, Swiss, 1 slice	106	8	5	8	2	0	221	54
CHEEZ WHIZ cheese sauce, 2 tbsp	91	7	4	4	3	Tr	118	541
Cottage cheese, lowfat, 2% milkfat, 1 cup	203	4	3	31	8	0	156	918
Cream, half-and-half, 1 fl oz	39	3	2	1	1	0	32	12
Cream, sour, cultured, 1 tbsp	26	3	2	Tr	1	0	14	6
Dessert topping, pressurized, 1 tbsp	11	1	1	Tr	1	0	Tr	2
Egg substitute, liquid, 1 cup	211	8	2	30	2	0	133	444
Egg, white, raw, fresh, 1 large	17	Tr	0	4	Tr	0	2	55
Egg, whole, cooked, hard-boiled, 1 large	78	5	2	6	1	0	25	62
Egg, whole, cooked, scrambled, 1 large	101	7	2	7	1	0	43	171
Egg, yolk, raw, fresh, 1 large	55	5	2	3	1	0	22	8
Eggnog, 1 cup	343	19	11	10	34	0	330	137
KRAFT FREE Singles, American, nonfat, 1 slice	31	Tr	Tr	5	2	Tr	150	273
Milk, fluid, 2% milkfat, 1 cup	122	5	2	8	11	0	271	115
Milk, fluid, whole, 1 cup	146	8	5	8	11	0	246	105
Milk, imitation, nonsoy, 1 cup	112	5	1	4	13	0	200	134
Milk, nonfat, 1 cup	83	Tr	Tr	8	12	0	223	108
Yogurt, fruit variety, nonfat, 8 oz	213	Tr	Tr	10	43	0	345	132
Yogurt, plain, low-fat, 8 oz	143	4	2	12	16	0	415	159
Yogurt, vanilla, low-fat, 8 oz	193	3	2	11	31	0	388	150

Food, portion	Calories	Total Fat (g)	Sat Fat (g)	Protein (g)	Total Carb (g)	Fiber (g)	Calcium (mg)	Sodium (mg)
Fast Foods								
Biscuit, with egg and ham, 1 biscuit	442	27	6	20	30	1	221	1382
Biscuit, with egg and sausage, 1 biscuit	581	39	15	19	41	1	155	1141
Biscuit, with sausage, 1 biscuit	485	32	14	12	40	1	128	1071
Burrito, with beans and cheese, 2 pieces	378	12	7	15	55	NA	214	1166
Burrito, with beans, cheese, and beef, 2 pieces	331	13	7	15	40	NA	130	991
Cheeseburger, large, double patty, with condiments and vegetables, 1 sandwich	704	44	18	38	40	NA	240	1148
Cheeseburger, large, single patty, with condiments and vegetables, 1 sandwich	563	33	15	28	38	NA	206	1108
Chicken, breaded and fried, boneless pieces, 6 pieces	319	21	5	18	15	0	14	513
Chicken, breaded and fried, boneless pieces, with BBQ sauce, 6 pieces	330	18	6	17	25	NA	21	829
Chicken, breaded and fried, light meat (breast or wing), 2 pieces	494	30	8	36	20	NA	60	975
Chicken fillet sandwich, plain, 1 sandwich	515	29	9	24	39	NA	60	957
Chili con carne, 1 cup	256	8	3	25	22	NA	68	1007
Coleslaw, ¾ cup	147	11	2	1	13	NA	34	267
Corn-on-the-cob with butter, 1 ear	155	3	2	4	32	NA	4	29
Croissant, with egg, cheese, and sausage, 1 croissant	523	38	18	20	25	NA	144	1115
Egg and cheese sandwich, 1 sandwich	340	19	7	16	26	NA	225	804
Enchilada, with cheese and beef, 1 enchilada	323	18	9	12	30	NA	228	1319
English muffin, with egg, cheese, and sausage, 1 muffin	487	31	12	22	31	NA	196	1135
Fish fillet, battered or breaded, and fried, 1 fillet	211	11	3	13	15	Tr	16	484

Food, portion	Calories	Total Fat (g)	Sat Fat (g)	Protein (g)	Total Carb (g)	Fiber (g)	Calcium (mg)	Sodium (mg)
Fish sandwich, with tartar sauce, 1 sandwich	431	23	5	17	41	NA	84	615
French toast with butter, 2 slices	356	19	8	10	36	NA	73	513
Ham and cheese sandwich, 1 sandwich	352	15	6	21	33	NA	130	771
Hamburger, large, double patty, with condiments and vegetables, 1 sandwich	540	27	11	34	40	NA	102	791
Hamburger, large, single patty, with condiments, 1 sandwich	427	21	8	23	37	2	134	731
Hot dog, plain, 1 sandwich	242	15	5	10	18	NA	24	670
Nachos, with cheese, 6–8 nachos	346	19	8	9	36	NA	272	816
Pizza with cheese, meat, and vegetables, 1 slice	184	5	2	13	21	NA	101	382
Pizza with pepperoni, 1 slice	181	7	2	10	20	NA	65	267
Potato, baked and topped with cheese sauce and broccoli, 1 piece	403	21	9	14	47	NA	336	485
Potato, french fried in vegetable oil, 1 medium	458	25	5	6	53	5	19	265
Potato salad, 1/3 cup	108	6	1	1	13	NA	13	312
Roast beef sandwich, plain, 1 sandwich	346	14	4	22	33	NA	54	792
Salad, vegetable, tossed, without dressing, with chicken, 1½ cups	105	2	1	17	4	NA	37	209
Salad, vegetable, tossed, without dressing, with pasta and seafood, 1½ cups	379	21	3	16	32	NA	71	1572
Shrimp, breaded and fried, 6–8 shrimp	454	25	5	19	40	NA	84	1446
Steak sandwich, 1 sandwich	459	14	4	30	52	NA	92	798
Submarine sandwich, with cold cuts, 1 submarine	456	19	7	22	51	NA	189	1651
Sundae, hot fudge, 1 sundae	284	9	5	6	48	0	207	182
Taco, 1 large	568	32	17	32	41	NA	339	1233
Taco salad, 1½ cups	279	15	7	13	24	NA	192	762

Food, portion	Calories	Total Fat (g)	Sat Fat (g)	Protein (g)	Total Carb (g)	Fiber (g)	Calcium (mg)	Sodium (mg)
Fats and Oils								
Lard, 1 tbsp	115	13	5	0	0	0	0	0
Margarine, 80% fat, stick, 1 tbsp	99	11	2	Tr	Tr	0	Tr	92
Margarine spread, fat-free, tub, 1 tbsp	6	Tr	Tr	Tr	1	0	1	85
Margarine, spread, soybean, 1 tbsp	87	10	2	Tr	Tr	NA	1	98
Margarine-butter blend, 60% corn oil margarine and 40% butter, 1 tbsp	102	11	4	Tr	Tr	0	4	127
Mayonnaise dressing, no cholesterol, 1 tbsp	103	12	2	0	Tr	0	1	73
MIRACLE WHIP FREE, nonfat, 1 tbsp	13	Tr	Tr	Tr	2	Tr	1	126
Oil, canola, 1 tbsp	124	14	1	0	0	0	0	0
Oil, corn, 1 tbsp	120	14	2	0	0	0	0	0
Oil, olive, 1 tbsp	119	14	2	0	0	0	Tr	Tr
Oil, palm, 1 tbsp	120	14	7	0	0	0	0	0
Oil, soybean, 1 tbsp	120	14	2	0	0	0	0	0
Salad dressing, Caesar, 1 tbsp	78	8	1	Tr	Tr	Tr	4	158
Salad dressing, French, 1 tbsp	73	7	1	Tr	2	0	4	134
Salad dressing, Italian, 1 tbsp	43	4	1	Tr	2	0	1	243
Salad dressing, peppercorn, 1 tbsp	76	8	1	Tr	Tr	0	3	143
Salad dressing, thousand island, 1 tbsp	59	6	1	Tr	2	Tr	3	138
Salad dressing, vinegar and oil, 1 tbsp	72	8	1	0	Tr	0	0	Tr
Finfish and Shellfish Products								
Anchovy, European, canned in oil, drained, 1 anchovy	8	Tr	Tr	1	0	0	9	147
Catfish, breaded and fried, 3 oz	195	11	3	15	7	1	37	238
Clam, breaded and fried, 20 small	380	21	5	27	19	NA	118	684
Clam, canned, drained, 3 oz	126	2	Tr	22	4	0	78	95
Cod, Atlantic, cooked, dry heat, 3 oz	89	1	Tr	19	0	0	12	66

Food, portion	Calories	Total Fat (g)	Sat Fat (g)	Protein (g)	Total Carb (g)	Fiber (g)	Calcium (mg)	Sodium (mg)
Crab, Alaska king, cooked, moist heat, 1 leg	130	2	Tr	26	0	0	79	1436
Fish sticks, frozen, preheated, 1 stick	76	3	1	4	7	Tr	6	163
Flatfish (flounder and sole), cooked, dry heat, 3 oz	99	1	Tr	21	0	0	15	89
Halibut, Atlantic and Pacific, cooked, dry heat, 3 oz	119	2	Tr	23	0	0	51	59
Herring, Pacific, cooked, dry heat, 3 oz	213	15	4	18	0	0	90	81
Lobster, northern, cooked, 3 oz	83	1	Tr	17	1	0	52	323
Mackerel, king, cooked, 3 oz	114	2	Tr	22	0	0	34	173
Ocean perch, cooked, dry heat, 3 oz	103	2	Tr	20	0	0	116	82
Oyster, wild, cooked, moist heat, 3 oz	116	4	1	12	7	0	77	359
Pike, northern, cooked, dry heat, 3 oz	96	1	Tr	21	0	0	62	42
Roughy, orange, cooked, dry heat, 3 oz	76	1	Tr	16	0	0	32	69
Salmon, Atlantic, farmed, cooked, 3 oz	175	10	2	19	0	0	13	52
Sardine, Atlantic, canned in oil, drained solids with bone, 2 sardines	50	3	Tr	6	0	0	92	121
Scallop, breaded and fried, 2 large	67	3	1	6	3	NA	13	144
Shrimp, mixed, breaded and fried, 3 oz	206	10	2	18	10	Tr	57	292
Shrimp, mixed, cooked, moist heat, 3 oz	84	1	Tr	18	0	0	33	190
Snapper, mixed, cooked, dry heat, 3 oz	109	1	Tr	22	0	0	34	48
Surimi, 3 oz	84	1	Tr	13	6	0	8	122
Swordfish, cooked, dry heat, 3 oz	132	4	1	22	0	0	5	98
Trout, rainbow, wild, cooked, dry heat, 3 oz	128	5	1	19	0	0	73	48
Tuna, light, canned in water, drained, 1 can	191	1	Tr	42	0	0	18	558
Tuna salad, 3 oz	159	8	1	14	8	0	14	342

Food, portion	Calories	Total Fat (g)	Sat Fat (g)	Protein (g)	Total Carb (g)	Fiber (g)	Calcium (mg)	Sodium (mg)
Fruits and Fruit Juices								
Apple juice, canned or bottled, unsweetened, 1 cup	117	Tr	Tr	Tr	29	Tr	17	7
Apples, canned, sweetened, sliced, 1 cup	137	1	Tr	Tr	34	3	8	6
Apples, raw, with skin, 2¾" dia	72	Tr	Tr	Tr	19	3	8	1
Applesauce, canned, sweetened, 1 cup	194	Tr	Tr	Tr	51	3	10	8
Bananas, 7" to 7⅞" long	105	Tr	Tr	1	27	3	6	1
Blackberries, 1 cup	62	1	Tr	2	14	8	42	1
Blueberries, 1 cup	83	Tr	Tr	1	21	3	9	1
Cantaloupe, 1 wedge, ⅛ of melon	35	Tr	Tr	1	8	1	9	16
Casaba, 1 cup, cubes	48	Tr	Tr	2	11	2	19	15
Cherries, sweet, 1 cup, with pits	74	Tr	Tr	1	19	2	15	0
Cranberries, 1 cup, whole	44	Tr	Tr	Tr	12	4	8	2
Cranberry juice, unsweetened, 1 cup	116	Tr	Tr	1	31	Tr	20	5
Cranberry sauce, canned, sweetened, 1 cup	418	Tr	Tr	1	108	3	11	80
Dates, deglet noor, 1 date	23	Tr	Tr	Tr	6	1	3	Tr
Figs, raw, 1 medium	37	Tr	Tr	Tr	10	1	18	1
Fruit cocktail (peach, pineapple, pear, grape, cherry), juice pack, solids and liquids, 1 cup	109	Tr	Tr	1	28	2	19	9
Fruit salad, (peach, pear, apricot, pineapple, cherry), juice pack, solids and liquids, 1 cup	125	Tr	Tr	1	32	2	27	12
Grapefruit juice, white, canned, sweetened, 1 cup	115	Tr	Tr	1	28	Tr	20	5
Grapefruit, raw, pink and red, ½ fruit, 3¾" dia	37	Tr	Tr	1	9	1	18	0
Grapes, red or green, 1 grape, seedless	3	Tr	Tr	Tr	1	Tr	1	Tr

FOOD, PORTION	CALORIES	TOTAL FAT (G)	SAT FAT (G)	PROTEIN (G)	TOTAL CARB (G)	FIBER (G)	CALCIUM (MG)	SODIUM (MG)
Honeydew, ⅛ of a melon	45	Tr	Tr	1	11	1	8	23
Kiwi fruit, fresh, 1 fruit without skin	56	Tr	Tr	1	13	3	31	3
Kumquats, 1 fruit	13	Tr	Tr	Tr	3	1	12	2
Mangos, 1 fruit	135	1	Tr	1	35	4	21	4
Nectarines, 1 fruit	60	Tr	Tr	1	14	2	8	0
Olives, ripe, canned, 1 large	5	Tr	Tr	Tr	Tr	Tr	4	38
Orange juice, 1 cup	112	Tr	Tr	2	26	Tr	27	2
Orange juice, canned, unsweetened, 1 cup	105	Tr	Tr	1	25	Tr	20	5
Orange-grapefruit juice, canned, unsweetened, 1 cup	106	Tr	Tr	1	25	Tr	20	7
Oranges, 1 fruit	62	Tr	Tr	1	15	3	52	0
Papayas, 5⅛" long×3" dia	119	Tr	Tr	2	30	5	73	9
Peaches, canned, juice pack, 1 cup, halves or slices	109	Tr	Tr	2	29	3	15	10
Peaches, 1 fruit	38	Tr	Tr	1	9	1	6	0
Pears, raw, 1 fruit	96	Tr	Tr	1	26	5	15	2
Pineapple, canned, juice pack, drained, 1 cup, chunks	109	Tr	Tr	1	28	2	29	2
Pineapple juice, canned, unsweetened, 1 cup	140	Tr	Tr	1	34	1	43	3
Pineapple, 1 slice	27	Tr	Tr	Tr	7	1	7	1
Plums, 1 fruit	30	Tr	Tr	Tr	8	1	4	0
Prune juice, canned, 1 cup	182	Tr	Tr	2	45	3	31	10
Prunes, uncooked, 1 cup, pitted	408	1	Tr	4	109	12	73	3
Raisins, seedless, 1 miniature box, ½ oz	42	Tr	Tr	Tr	11	1	7	2
Raspberries, 1 cup	64	1	Tr	1	15	8	31	1
Rhubarb, 1 cup, diced	26	Tr	Tr	1	6	2	105	5
Strawberries, 1 cup, whole	46	Tr	Tr	1	11	3	23	1

Food, portion	Calories	Total Fat (g)	Sat Fat (g)	Protein (g)	Total Carb (g)	Fiber (g)	Calcium (mg)	Sodium (mg)
Fruits and Fruit Juices (cont.)								
Tangerines (mandarin oranges), 1 medium	37	Tr	Tr	1	9	2	12	1
Watermelon, ¹⁄₁₆ of melon	86	Tr	Tr	2	22	1	20	3
Lamb and Veal Products								
Lamb, ground, cooked, broiled, 3 oz	241	17	7	21	0	0	19	69
Lamb, leg, (shank and sirloin), roasted, 3 oz	162	7	3	23	0	0	8	61
Veal, ground, cooked, broiled, 3 oz	146	6	3	21	0	0	14	71
Veal, loin, cooked, roasted, 3 oz	184	10	4	21	0	0	16	79
Veal, rib, cooked, braised, 3 oz	185	7	2	29	0	0	20	84
Veal, sirloin, cooked, braised, 3 oz	214	11	4	27	0	0	14	67
Legumes and Legume Products								
Bacon bits, meatless, 1 tbsp	33	2	Tr	2	2	1	7	124
Bacon, meatless, 1 strip	16	1	Tr	1	Tr	Tr	1	73
Beans, baked, canned, 1 cup	236	1	Tr	12	52	13	127	1008
Beans, baked, canned, with franks, 1 cup	368	17	6	17	40	18	124	1114
Beans, black, boiled, 1 cup	227	1	Tr	15	41	15	46	2
Beans, kidney, boiled, 1 cup	225	1	Tr	15	40	11	62	2
Beans, navy, boiled, 1 cup	258	1	Tr	16	48	12	127	2
Chili with beans, canned, 1 cup	287	14	6	15	30	11	120	1336
Cowpeas (blackeyes, crowder, southern), cooked, boiled, 1 cup	200	1	Tr	13	36	11	41	7
Falafel, home-prepared, 1 patty, 2¼" dia	57	3	Tr	2	5	NA	9	50
GREEN GIANT, HARVEST BURGER, 1 patty	138	4	1	18	7	6	102	411
Hummus, commercial, 1 cup	415	24	4	20	36	15	95	948
Lentils, boiled, 1 cup	230	1	Tr	18	40	16	38	4
Lima beans, boiled, 1 cup	216	1	Tr	15	39	13	32	4

FOOD, PORTION	CALORIES	TOTAL FAT (G)	SAT FAT (G)	PROTEIN (G)	TOTAL CARB (G)	FIBER (G)	CALCIUM (MG)	SODIUM (MG)
MORI-NU, Tofu, silken, soft, 1 slice	46	2	Tr	4	2	Tr	26	4
Peanut butter, chunk style, with salt, 2 tbsp	188	16	3	8	7	2	17	150
Peanut butter, smooth style, with salt, 2 tbsp	192	17	3	8	6	2	15	160
Peanuts, dry-roasted, without salt, 1 cup	854	73	10	35	31	12	79	9
Peanuts, raw, 1 cup	828	72	10	38	24	12	134	26
Peas, split, boiled, 1 cup	231	1	Tr	16	41	16	27	4
Refried beans, canned, 1 cup	237	3	1	14	39	13	88	753
Soy milk, fluid, 1 cup	120	5	1	9	11	3	10	29
Soy sauce, soy and wheat (shoyu), 1 tbsp	8	Tr	Tr	1	1	Tr	3	914
Soy sauce, soy (tamari), 1 tbsp	11	Tr	Tr	2	1	Tr	4	1005
Soyburger, 1 patty	125	4	1	13	9	3	20	385
Tofu, fried, 1 piece	35	3	Tr	2	1	1	48	2
Tofu yogurt, 1 cup	246	5	1	9	42	1	309	92
Vegetarian fillets, 1 fillet	247	15	2	20	8	5	81	417

MEALS, ENTRÉES, AND SIDEDISHES

FOOD, PORTION	CALORIES	TOTAL FAT (G)	SAT FAT (G)	PROTEIN (G)	TOTAL CARB (G)	FIBER (G)	CALCIUM (MG)	SODIUM (MG)
BANQUET Chicken Pot Pie, frozen, 1 serving	382	22	9	10	36	1	28	948
BANQUET Turkey & Gravy with Dressing Meal, frozen meal, 1 serving	280	10	3	14	34	3	47	1061
Beef stew, canned, 1 serving	218	12	5	11	16	3	28	947
CHEF BOYARDEE Spaghetti & Meatballs in Tomato Sauce, 1 serving	250	9	4	9	34	2	17	941
CHUN KING Sweet & Sour Vegetables & Sauce with Chicken, canned, 1 serving	165	2	0	6	32	NA	NA	564
Cinnamon Swirl French Toast with Sausage, 1 serving	415	23	7	13	38	2	NA	502
GREEN GIANT, Broccoli in Cheese Flavored Sauce, frozen, 1 serving	75	3	1	3	10	NA	NA	538
HAMBURGER HELPER, Cheeseburger Macaroni, dry mix, 1 serving	178	5	1	5	29	NA	NA	914

Food, portion	Calories	Total Fat (g)	Sat Fat (g)	Protein (g)	Total Carb (g)	Fiber (g)	Calcium (mg)	Sodium (mg)
Meals, Entrées, and Sidedishes (cont.)								
HEALTHY CHOICE Chicken Teriyaki with Rice Medley, frozen, 1 serving	268	6	3	17	37	3	37	602
HORMEL Chili with Beans, 1 cup	240	4	2	17	34	8	69	1163
HOT POCKETS Ham 'N Cheese, frozen, 1 serving	340	14	6	15	38	NA	251	666
KRAFT Macaroni and Cheese Dinner Original Flavor, unprepared, 1 serving	259	3	1	11	48	1	92	561
LEAN CUISINE Rice and Chicken Stir-Fry with Vegetables, frozen, 1 serving	270	7	1	12	40	6	NA	632
LIPTON, Alfredo Egg Noodles in a Creamy Sauce, dry mix, 1 serving	259	7	3	10	39	NA	79	1097
MARIE CALLENDER'S Escalloped Noodles & Chicken, frozen entrée, 1 cup	397	21	7	13	38	NA	104	1007
STOUFFER'S, Creamed Spinach, frozen, 1 serving	169	13	4	4	9	2	141	335
THE BUDGET GOURMET Italian Sausage Lasagna, frozen, 1 serving	456	24	8	21	40	3	316	903
Tortellini, pasta with cheese filling, ¾ cup	249	6	3	11	38	2	123	279
TYSON Beef Stir Fry Kit, frozen, 1 serving	433	5	0	26	71	NA	NA	1584
TYSON Chicken Fajita Kit, frozen, 1 serving	129	3	1	8	17	NA	NA	350
Nut and Seed Products								
Almonds, 1 cup, whole	827	72	6	30	28	17	355	1
Chestnuts, European, roasted, 1 cup	350	3	1	5	76	7	41	3
Coconut meat, dried, sweetened, flaked, 1 cup	351	24	21	2	35	3	10	189
Hazelnuts or filberts, 1 cup, whole	848	82	6	20	23	13	154	0
Macadamia nuts, dry roasted, 1 cup, whole or halves	962	102	16	10	18	11	94	5

Food, portion	Calories	Total Fat (g)	Sat Fat (g)	Protein (g)	Total Carb (g)	Fiber (g)	Calcium (mg)	Sodium (mg)
Mixed nuts, peanuts, dry roasted, salt added, 1 cup	814	70	9	24	35	12	96	917
Pecans, 1 cup, halves	684	71	6	9	14	10	69	0
Pistachio nuts, dry roasted, salt added, 1 cup	699	57	7	26	33	13	135	498
Sunflower seed kernels, dried, 1 cup	821	71	7	33	27	15	167	4
Pork Products								
Bacon, cured, pan-fried, 1 slice cooked	42	3	1	3	Tr	0	1	192
Canadian-style bacon, cured, grilled, 2 slices	87	4	1	11	1	0	5	727
Ham, boneless, 11% fat, roasted, 3 oz	151	8	3	19	0	0	7	1275
Ham, cured, boneless, extra lean, roasted, 3 oz	140	7	2	19	Tr	0	7	1177
Ham, leg, shank half, roasted, 3 oz	246	17	6	22	0	0	13	50
Pork, fresh, ground, cooked, 3 oz	252	18	7	22	0	0	19	62
Pork, sirloin (chops), boneless, braised, 3 oz	149	6	2	23	0	0	11	39
Pork, tenderloin, roasted, 3 oz	147	5	2	24	0	0	5	47
Poultry Products								
Chicken, breast, meat and skin, fried, batter, ½ breast, bone removed	364	18	5	35	13	Tr	28	385
Chicken, dark meat and skin, roasted, ½ chicken, bone removed	423	26	7	43	0	0	25	145
Chicken, drumstick, meat and skin, fried, batter, 1 drumstick, bone removed	193	11	3	16	6	Tr	12	194
Chicken, leg, meat and skin, roasted, 1 leg, bone removed	264	15	4	30	0	0	14	99
Chicken, light meat and skin, fried, batter, ½ chicken, bone removed	521	29	8	44	18	NA	38	540
Chicken, thigh, meat and skin, roasted, 1 thigh, bone removed	153	10	3	16	0	0	7	52

Food, portion	Calories	Total Fat (g)	Sat Fat (g)	Protein (g)	Total Carb (g)	Fiber (g)	Calcium (mg)	Sodium (mg)
Poultry Products (cont.)								
Chicken wing, meat and skin, fried, batter, 1 wing, bone removed	159	11	3	10	5	Tr	10	157
Cornish game hens, meat and skin, roasted, 1 bird	668	47	13	57	0	0	33	164
Ground turkey, cooked, 4 oz patty	193	11	3	22	0	0	21	88
Turkey, breast, meat and skin, roasted, ½ breast, bone removed	1633	64	18	248	0	0	181	544
Turkey, leg, meat and skin, roasted, 1 leg	148	7	2	20	0	0	23	55
Turkey, wing, meat and skin, roasted, 1 wing, bone removed	426	23	6	51	0	0	45	113
Sausages and Luncheon Meats								
Beef, cured, pastrami, 1 oz	98	8	3	5	1	0	3	344
Beef, sausage, smoked, 1 sausage	134	12	5	6	1	0	3	486
Bologna, beef, 1 serving	87	8	3	3	1	0	9	302
Bologna, turkey, 1 serving	59	4	1	3	1	Tr	34	351
Chicken breast, oven-roasted, fat-free, sliced, 1 serving	33	Tr	Tr	7	1	0	3	457
Frankfurter, beef, 1 frankfurter	149	13	5	5	2	0	6	513
Ham, sliced, 11% fat, 1 slice	46	2	1	5	1	Tr	7	365
Pastrami, beef, 98% fat-free, 1 serving	54	1	0	11	1	0	5	576
Pepperoni, pork, beef, 1 oz	130	11	5	6	1	Tr	6	501
Salami, cooked, beef, 1 slice	67	6	3	3	Tr	0	2	296
Sausage, Italian, pork, cooked, 1 link	268	21	8	17	1	0	20	765
Sausage, Polish, pork and beef, smoked, 1 serving	229	20	7	9	2	0	5	644
SPAM, pork with ham, minced, 1 serving	174	15	6	7	2	0	8	767
Turkey sausage, reduced fat, brown and serve, 1 cup	256	13	4	22	14	Tr	40	790

Food, portion	Calories	Total Fat (g)	Sat Fat (g)	Protein (g)	Total Carb (g)	Fiber (g)	Calcium (mg)	Sodium (mg)
SNACKS								
Banana chips, 3 oz	441	29	25	2	50	7	15	5
Beef jerky, chopped and formed, 1 piece	82	5	2	7	2	Tr	4	443
Cheese puffs and twists, low fat, 1 oz	122	3	1	2	21	3	101	364
CHEX mix, 1 oz	120	5	2	3	18	2	10	288
Granola bars, soft, uncoated, chocolate chip, 1 bar	118	5	3	2	19	1	26	76
Popcorn, air-popped, 1 cup	31	Tr	Tr	1	6	1	1	Tr
Popcorn, caramel-coated, with peanuts, 1 oz	113	2	Tr	2	23	1	19	84
Potato chips, made from dried potatoes, plain, 1 can, 7 oz	1105	76	19	12	101	7	48	1299
Potato chips, plain, salted, 1 bag, 8 oz	1217	79	25	16	120	10	54	1348
Pretzels, hard, plain, unsalted, 10 twists	229	2	Tr	5	48	2	22	173
Pretzels, soft, 1 medium	389	4	1	9	80	2	26	1615
Puffs or twists, corn-based, extruded, cheese-flavor, 1 bag, 8 oz	1258	78	15	17	122	2	132	2384
Rice cake, cracker, 1 cubic inch	16	Tr	Tr	Tr	3	Tr	Tr	3
Sesame sticks, wheat-based, salted, 1 oz	153	10	2	3	13	1	48	422
Tortilla chips, plain, 1 oz	142	7	1	2	18	2	44	150
Trail mix, with chocolate chips, salted nuts and seeds, 1 cup	707	47	9	21	66	NA	159	177
SOUPS, SAUCES, AND GRAVIES								
Barbecue sauce, 1 cup (8 fl oz)	188	5	1	5	32	3	48	2038
CHEF-MATE Basic Cheddar Cheese Sauce, 1 serving	82	5	2	2	8	0	46	471
Gravy, beef, canned, 1 cup	123	5	3	9	11	1	14	1305
Gravy, turkey, canned, 1 cup	121	5	1	6	12	1	10	1373
LJ MINOR Sweet N' Sour Sauce, 1 serving	40	1	Tr	Tr	8	Tr	6	116

Food, portion	Calories	Total Fat (g)	Sat Fat (g)	Protein (g)	Total Carb (g)	Fiber (g)	Calcium (mg)	Sodium (mg)
Soups, Sauces, and Gravies (cont.)								
LJ MINOR Teriyaki Sauce, 1 serving	21	1	Tr	Tr	4	0	1	159
Sauce, pasta, spaghetti/marinara, ready-to-serve, 1 cup	143	5	1	4	21	4	55	1030
Soup, beef stroganoff, canned, chunky style, 1 cup	235	11	6	12	22	1	48	1044
Soup, black bean, canned, prepared with equal volume water, 1 cup	116	2	Tr	6	20	4	44	1198
Soup, chicken noodle, canned, prepared with equal volume water, 1 cup	75	2	1	4	9	1	17	1106
Soup, chicken vegetable, canned, prepared with equal volume water, 1 cup	75	3	1	4	9	1	17	945
Soup, cream of chicken, prepared with equal volume milk, 1 cup	191	11	5	7	15	Tr	181	1047
Soup, cream of potato, canned, prepared with equal volume milk, 1 cup	149	6	4	6	17	Tr	166	1061
Soup, lentil with ham, canned, 1 cup	139	3	1	9	20	NA	42	1319
Soup, onion, canned, condensed, 1 cup	113	3	1	8	16	2	54	2116
Soup, pea, green, canned, prepared with equal volume milk, 1 cup	239	7	4	13	32	3	173	970
Soup, tomato, canned, prepared with equal volume water, 1 cup	85	2	Tr	2	17	Tr	12	695
Soup, vegetarian vegetable, canned, prepared with equal volume water, 1 cup	72	2	Tr	2	12	Tr	22	822
Sweets								
3 MUSKETEERS Bar, 1 bar, 1.81 oz	212	7	3	2	39	1	43	99
ALMOND JOY Candy Bar, 1 package, 1.76 oz	235	13	9	2	29	2	31	70
BABY RUTH Bar, 1 bar, 0.75 oz	97	5	3	1	13	1	9	45
BUTTERFINGER Bar, 1 bar, fun size	100	4	2	1	15	Tr	7	45

Food, portion	Calories	Total Fat (g)	Sat Fat (g)	Protein (g)	Total Carb (g)	Fiber (g)	Calcium (mg)	Sodium (mg)
Caramels, 1 piece	39	1	1	Tr	8	Tr	14	25
Frostings, chocolate, creamy, ready-to-eat, 2 tbsp	163	7	2	Tr	26	Tr	3	75
Frozen yogurts, chocolate, 1 cup	221	6	4	5	38	4	174	110
Fruit and juice bars, 1 bar, 2.5 fl oz	63	Tr	0	1	16	1	4	3
Gumdrops, starch jelly, 10 gummy bears	87	0	0	0	22	Tr	1	10
Hard candies, 1 piece	24	Tr	0	0	6	0	Tr	2
Honey, 1 tbsp	64	0	0	Tr	17	Tr	1	1
Ice creams, chocolate, ½ cup	143	7	4	3	19	1	72	50
Ice creams, vanilla, ½ cup	145	8	5	3	17	1	92	58
Jams and preserves, 1 tbsp	56	Tr	Tr	Tr	14	Tr	4	6
Jellybeans, 10 1-oz pieces	105	Tr	0	0	26	Tr	1	14
KIT KAT BIG KAT Bar, 1 bar, 1.94 oz	286	15	10	3	35	1	76	35
KRACKEL Chocolate Bar, 1 bar, 1.45 oz	210	11	7	3	26	1	65	80
"M&M's" Milk Chocolate Candies, 1 package, 1.69 oz	236	10	6	2	34	1	50	29
"M&M's" Peanut Chocolate Candies, 1 package, 1.67 oz	243	12	5	4	28	2	47	23
Marshmallows, 1 regular	23	Tr	Tr	Tr	6	Tr	Tr	6
Milk chocolate, 10 kisses	246	14	7	4	27	2	87	36
MILKY WAY Bar, 1 bar, 1.9 oz	228	9	4	2	39	1	70	130
Molasses, 1 tbsp	58	Tr	Tr	0	15	0	41	7
MR. GOODBAR Chocolate Bar, 1 bar, 1.75 oz	264	16	7	5	27	2	54	20
Pie fillings, canned, cherry, 1 can	684	Tr	Tr	2	167	4	65	107
Puddings, chocolate, ready-to-eat, 5 oz	197	6	1	4	33	1	128	183
Puddings, rice, ready-to-eat, 5 oz	231	11	2	3	31	Tr	74	121
Puddings, tapioca, ready-to-eat, 5 oz	169	5	1	3	28	Tr	119	226

Food, portion	Calories	Total Fat (g)	Sat Fat (g)	Protein (g)	Total Carb (g)	Fiber (g)	Calcium (mg)	Sodium (mg)
Sweets (cont.)								
RAISINETS Chocolate-Covered Raisins, 1 package	185	7	3	2	32	2	49	16
REESE'S Peanut Butter Cups, 1 package, 1.6 oz	232	14	5	5	25	2	35	141
REESE'S PIECES Candy, 1 package, 1.63 oz	229	11	8	6	28	1	32	89
Sherbet, orange, 1 bar, 2.75 fl oz	95	1	1	1	20	2	36	30
SKITTLES Bite Size Candies, 1 package, 2 oz	231	2	Tr	Tr	52	0	0	9
SNICKERS Bar, 1 bar, 2 oz	273	14	5	5	34	1	54	152
SPECIAL DARK Chocolate Bar, 1 bar, 1.45 oz	218	13	0	2	24	3	12	2
Sugars, granulated, 1 tsp	16	0	0	0	4	0	Tr	0
Syrups, chocolate, fudge-type, 2 tbsp	133	3	2	2	24	1	38	131
Syrups, table blends, pancake, 1 tbsp	47	0	0	0	12	Tr	1	16
Toppings, strawberry, 2 tbsp	107	Tr	Tr	Tr	28	Tr	3	9
TWIZZLERS Strawberry Twists Candy, 4 pieces	133	1	0	1	30	0	0	109
YORK Peppermint Pattie, 1 patty, 1.5 oz	165	3	2	1	35	1	5	12
Vegetables and Vegetable Products								
Artichoke, cooked, boiled, with salt, 1 artichoke	60	Tr	Tr	4	13	6	54	397
Asparagus, frozen, boiled, with salt, 1 cup	32	1	Tr	5	3	3	32	432
Bamboo shoots, boiled, drained, 1 cup	14	Tr	Tr	2	2	1	14	5
Beans, lima, canned, solids and liquids, ½ cup	88	Tr	Tr	5	17	4	35	312
Beans, snap, green, boiled, drained, 1 cup	44	Tr	Tr	2	10	4	55	1
Beets, sliced, boiled, drained, ½ cup	37	Tr	Tr	1	8	2	14	65

Food, portion	Calories	Total Fat (g)	Sat Fat (g)	Protein (g)	Total Carb (g)	Fiber (g)	Calcium (mg)	Sodium (mg)
Broccoli, chopped, boiled, drained, ½ cup	27	Tr	Tr	2	6	3	31	32
Brussels sprouts, boiled, drained, 1 sprout	8	Tr	Tr	1	1	1	8	4
Cabbage (pak-choi), boiled, drained, 1 cup	20	Tr	Tr	3	3	2	158	58
Carrot juice, canned, 1 cup	94	Tr	Tr	2	22	2	57	68
Carrots, baby, 1 medium	4	Tr	Tr	Tr	1	Tr	3	8
Carrots, 1 medium	25	Tr	Tr	1	6	2	20	42
Catsup, 1 tbsp	14	Tr	Tr	Tr	4	Tr	3	167
Cauliflower, boiled, drained, ½ cup	14	Tr	Tr	1	3	2	10	9
Celery, diced, 1 cup	17	Tr	Tr	1	4	2	48	96
Coleslaw, home-prepared, ½ cup	41	2	Tr	1	7	1	27	14
Collards, chopped, boiled, drained, 1 cup	49	1	Tr	4	9	5	266	30
Corn, sweet, yellow, canned, cream style, 1 cup	184	1	Tr	4	46	3	8	8
Corn, sweet, yellow, raw, 1 ear	123	2	Tr	5	27	4	3	21
Cucumber, sliced, peeled, 1 cup	14	Tr	Tr	1	3	1	17	2
Eggplant, boiled, drained, 1 cup	35	Tr	Tr	1	9	2	6	1
Grape leaves, canned, 1 leaf	3	Tr	Tr	Tr	Tr	NA	12	114
Kale, boiled, drained, 1 cup	36	1	Tr	2	7	3	94	30
Leeks (bulb and lower leaf-portion), 1 leek	54	Tr	Tr	1	13	2	53	18
Lettuce, cos or romaine, 1 inner leaf	2	Tr	Tr	Tr	Tr	Tr	3	1
Lettuce, iceberg, 1 leaf	2	Tr	Tr	Tr	Tr	Tr	3	1
Mountain yam, steamed, 1 cup, cubed	119	Tr	Tr	3	29	NA	12	17
Mung beans, sprouted, stir-fried, 1 cup	62	Tr	Tr	5	13	2	16	11
Mushrooms, canned, drained solids, 1 medium	3	Tr	Tr	Tr	1	Tr	1	51
Mushrooms, shiitake, dried, 1 mushroom	11	Tr	Tr	Tr	3	Tr	Tr	Tr
Mustard greens, boiled, drained, 1 cup	21	Tr	Tr	3	3	3	104	22

Food, portion	Calories	Total Fat (g)	Sat Fat (g)	Protein (g)	Total Carb (g)	Fiber (g)	Calcium (mg)	Sodium (mg)
Vegetables and Vegetable Products (cont.)								
Okra, sliced, boiled, drained, ½ cup	18	Tr	Tr	1	4	2	62	5
Onion rings, breaded, frozen, heated in oven, 10 rings, 2–3" dia	244	16	5	3	23	1	19	225
Onions, 2½" dia	46	Tr	Tr	1	11	2	24	3
Onions, 1 slice, thin	4	Tr	Tr	Tr	1	Tr	2	Tr
Peas and carrots, frozen, boiled, drained, ½ cup	38	Tr	Tr	2	8	2	18	54
Peas, green, boiled, drained, 1 cup	134	Tr	Tr	9	25	9	43	5
Peppers, jalapeño, 1 pepper	4	Tr	Tr	Tr	1	Tr	1	Tr
Peppers, sweet, green, 1 pepper	24	Tr	Tr	1	6	2	12	4
Peppers, sweet, red, 1 pepper	31	Tr	Tr	1	7	2	8	2
Pickle, sweet, 1 slice	8	Tr	Tr	Tr	2	Tr	Tr	66
Pickle relish, sweet, 1 tbsp	20	Tr	Tr	Tr	5	Tr	Tr	122
Pickles, dill, 1 slice	1	Tr	Tr	Tr	Tr	Tr	1	90
Potato, baked, flesh and skin, 1 medium	161	Tr	Tr	4	37	4	26	17
Potato salad, home-prepared, 1 cup	358	21	4	7	28	3	48	1323
Potatoes, au gratin, home-prepared from recipe using butter, 1 cup	323	19	12	12	28	4	292	1061
Potatoes, boiled, cooked without skin, flesh, with salt, 1 medium	144	Tr	Tr	3	33	3	13	402
Potatoes, french fried, frozen, heated in oven, with salt, 10 strips	100	4	1	2	16	2	4	133
Potatoes, hashed brown, home-prepared, 1 cup	413	20	2	5	55	5	22	534
Potatoes, mashed, prepared from flakes, whole milk and butter, 1 cup	204	11	6	4	23	2	61	344
Potatoes, white, flesh and skin, baked, 1 medium	163	Tr	Tr	4	36	4	17	12

FOOD, PORTION	CALORIES	TOTAL FAT (G)	SAT FAT (G)	PROTEIN (G)	TOTAL CARB (G)	FIBER (G)	CALCIUM (MG)	SODIUM (MG)
Spinach, canned, solids and liquids, 1 cup	44	1	Tr	5	7	5	194	176
Spinach, frozen, chopped or leaf, boiled, drained, ½ cup	30	Tr	Tr	4	5	4	145	92
Squash, summer, sliced, boiled, drained, 1 cup	36	1	Tr	2	8	3	49	2
Sweet potato, cooked, baked in skin, 1 medium	103	Tr	Tr	2	24	4	43	41
Sweet potato, cooked, candied, home-prepared, 1 piece	144	3	1	1	29	3	27	74
Tomato juice, canned, 1 fl oz	5	Tr	Tr	Tr	1	Tr	3	3
Tomato products, canned, paste, with salt added, 6 oz can	139	1	Tr	7	32	8	61	1343
Tomato products, canned, sauce, with mushrooms, 1 cup	86	Tr	Tr	4	21	4	32	1107
Tomatoes, red, canned, stewed, 1 cup	66	Tr	Tr	2	16	3	87	564
Tomatoes, red, canned, whole, 1 medium	21	Tr	Tr	1	5	1	33	11
Tomatoes, red, cooked, 1 cup	43	Tr	Tr	2	10	2	26	26
Tomatoes, red, raw, 1 cup	38	1	Tr	2	8	2	9	16
Tomatoes, red, 1 cherry	4	Tr	Tr	Tr	1	Tr	1	2
Tomatoes, sun-dried, 1 cup	139	2	Tr	8	30	7	59	1131
Vegetable juice cocktail, canned, 1 cup	46	Tr	Tr	2	11	2	27	653
Vegetables, mixed, canned, drained solids, 1 cup	80	Tr	Tr	4	15	5	44	243
Waterchestnuts (matai), sliced, ½ cup	60	Tr	Tr	1	15	2	7	9
Yam, cubed, boiled, drained, or baked, 1 cup	158	Tr	Tr	2	38	5	19	11
Zucchini, baby, raw, 1 medium	2	Tr	Tr	Tr	Tr	Tr	2	Tr
Zucchini, includes skin, frozen boiled, drained, 1 cup	38	Tr	Tr	3	8	3	38	4

winning weight-loss recipes

You'll be amazed at how delicious losing weight can be with the recipes in this section. Packed with flavor, they won't pack on the pounds. Whether you're looking to break the boring breakfast routine or satisfy your sweet tooth, you'll find a recipe here that works with your weight-loss plans. The nutrient information that accompanies each recipe is your key to losing weight healthfully.

balanced breakfasts

stuffed french toast with fresh berry topping

nutrients per serving:

1 sandwich (without powdered sugar or syrup)

Calories: 339
Carbohydrate: 54 g
Calories From Fat: 14%
Total Fat: 7 g
Saturated Fat: 2 g
Cholesterol: 112 mg
Sodium: 420 mg
Dietary Fiber: 3 g
Protein: 14 g

- 2 cups mixed fresh berries (strawberries, raspberries, blueberries and/or blackberries)
- 2 tablespoons granulated sugar
- ⅔ cup lowfat ricotta cheese
- ¼ cup strawberry preserves
- 3 large eggs
- ⅔ cup NESTLÉ® CARNATION® Evaporated Fat Free Milk
- 2 tablespoons packed brown sugar
- 2 teaspoons vanilla extract
- 12 slices (about ¾-inch-thick) French bread
- 1 tablespoon vegetable oil, butter or margarine
  Powdered sugar (optional)
  Maple syrup, heated (optional)

COMBINE berries and granulated sugar in small bowl. Combine ricotta cheese and strawberry preserves in another small bowl; mix well. Combine eggs, evaporated milk, brown sugar and vanilla extract in pie plate or shallow bowl; mix well.

SPREAD ricotta-preserve mixture evenly over *6 slices* of bread. Top with *remaining* slices of bread to form sandwiches.

HEAT small amount of vegetable oil in large, nonstick skillet or griddle over medium heat. Dip sandwiches in egg mixture, coating both sides. Cook on each side for about 2 minutes or until golden brown.

SPRINKLE with powdered sugar. Serve with berries and maple syrup.

Makes 6 servings

stuffed french toast with fresh berry topping

zucchini-tomato frittata

Nonstick olive oil-flavored cooking spray
1 cup sliced zucchini
1 cup broccoli florets
1 cup diced red or yellow bell pepper
3 whole eggs, lightly beaten*
5 egg whites, lightly beaten*
½ cup 1% low-fat cottage cheese
½ cup rehydrated sun-dried tomatoes (1 ounce dry),
  coarsely chopped
¼ cup chopped green onions with tops
¼ cup chopped fresh basil
⅛ teaspoon ground red pepper
2 tablespoons Parmesan cheese
  Paprika (optional)

Or, substitute with cholesterol free egg substitute to equal 6 large eggs.

1. Preheat broiler. Spray 10-inch ovenproof nonstick skillet with cooking spray. Place zucchini, broccoli and bell pepper in skillet; cook and stir over high heat 3 to 4 minutes or until crisp-tender.

2. Combine whole eggs, egg whites, cottage cheese, tomatoes, onions, basil and ground red pepper in medium bowl; mix well. Pour egg mixture over vegetables in skillet. Cook, uncovered, gently lifting sides of frittata so uncooked egg flows underneath. Cook 7 to 8 minutes or until frittata is almost firm and golden brown on bottom. Remove from heat. Sprinkle with Parmesan.

3. Broil about 5 inches from heat 3 to 5 minutes or until golden brown on surface. Garnish with paprika, if desired. Cut into wedges. Serve immediately.

Makes 4 servings

zucchini-tomato frittata

tooty fruitys

nutrients per serving:

1 biscuit (without powdered sugar)

Calories: 93
Carbohydrate: 16 g
Calories From Fat: 24%
Total Fat: 3 g
Saturated Fat: <1 g
Cholesterol: 0 mg
Sodium: 230 mg
Dietary Fiber: 1 g
Protein: 2 g

1 package (10 ounces) extra-light flaky biscuits
10 (1½-inch) fruit pieces, such as plum, apple, peach or pear
1 egg white
1 teaspoon water
   Powdered sugar (optional)

1. Preheat oven to 425°F. Spray baking sheets with nonstick cooking spray; set aside.

2. Separate biscuits. Place on lightly floured surface. Roll each biscuit with lightly floured rolling pin or flatten dough with fingers to form 3½-inch circles. Place 1 fruit piece in center of each circle. Bring 3 edges of dough up over fruit; pinch edges together to seal. Place on prepared baking sheets.

3. Beat egg white with water in small bowl; brush over dough.

4. Bake until golden brown, 10 to 15 minutes. Remove to wire rack to cool. Serve warm or at room temperature. Sprinkle with powdered sugar, if desired, just before serving.

Makes 10 servings

Sweet Tooty Fruitys: Prepare dough circles as directed. Gently press both sides of dough circles into granulated or cinnamon-sugar to coat completely. Top with fruit and continue as directed, except do not brush with egg white mixture or sprinkle with powdered sugar.

Cheesy Tooty Fruitys: Prepare dough circles as directed. Top each circle with ½ teaspoon softened reduced-fat cream cheese in addition to the fruit. Continue as directed.

tooty fruitys

spinach feta frittata

1½ cups cholesterol-free egg substitute
⅓ cup evaporated skimmed milk
1 package (10-ounces) frozen chopped spinach, thawed and squeezed dry
½ cup finely chopped green onions
1½ teaspoons dried oregano or basil leaves
¼ teaspoon salt
⅛ teaspoon black pepper
2 cups cooked spaghetti noodles (4 ounces uncooked)
4 ounces crumbled sun-dried tomato and basil or plain feta cheese
Nonstick cooking spray
Diced red bell pepper (optional)

1. Preheat broiler.

2. Combine egg substitute and milk in medium bowl; whisk together until well blended. Stir in spinach, green onions, oregano, salt and black pepper. Stir in noodles and feta.

3. Spray 10-inch cast iron or ovenproof skillet with cooking spray. Heat over medium heat. Add egg mixture and cook 5 minutes or until nearly cooked through, stirring occasionally.

4. Place skillet under broiler 3 to 5 minutes or until just beginning to lightly brown and set. Remove from broiler. Cut into 4 wedges. Top each wedge with diced bell pepper, if desired.

Makes 4 servings

spinach feta frittata

nutrients per serving:

½ of total recipe

Calories: 458
Carbohydrate: 92 g
Calories From Fat: 11%
Total Fat: 6 g
Saturated Fat: 1 g
Cholesterol: 0 mg
Sodium: 141 mg
Dietary Fiber: 13 g
Protein: 14 g

harvest apple oatmeal

1 cup apple juice
1 cup water
1 medium apple, cored and chopped
1 cup uncooked old-fashioned oats
¼ cup raisins
⅛ teaspoon salt
⅛ teaspoon ground cinnamon

Microwave Directions

1. Combine juice, water and apple in 2-quart microwavable bowl. Microwave at HIGH (100%) 3 minutes, stirring halfway through cooking time.

2. Add oats, raisins, salt and cinnamon; stir until well blended.

3. Microwave at MEDIUM (50% power) 4 to 5 minutes or until thick; stir before serving. *Makes 2 servings*

Conventional Directions: To prepare conventionally, bring apple juice, water and apple to a boil in medium saucepan over medium-high heat. Stir in oats, raisins, cinnamon and salt until well blended. Cook, uncovered, over medium heat 5 to 6 minutes or until thick, stirring occasionally.

tip

Oats are one of the most nutritious of grains. Quick-cooking rolled oats and old-fashioned rolled oats are essentially the same; the quick-cooking oats simply cook faster because they have been rolled into thinner flakes.

harvest apple oatmeal

creamy fruit blend

nutrients per serving:

⅓ of total recipe (without fresh fruit)

Calories: 221
Carbohydrate: 51 g
Calories From Fat: 3%
Total Fat: 1 g
Saturated Fat: <1 g
Cholesterol: 2 mg
Sodium: 71 mg
Dietary Fiber: 3 g
Protein: 6 g

   1 cup fat-free (skim) milk
   ½ cup white grape juice
   ½ cup fresh or frozen unsweetened strawberries
   1 small ripe peach, peeled, pitted and quartered
   1 ripe banana, peeled and quartered
   2 tablespoons brown sugar
   1 tablespoon lemon juice
   ½ teaspoon almond extract
      Fresh fruit for garnish (optional)

Process all ingredients in blender or food processor until smooth. Serve immediately. Garnish with fresh fruit, if desired.   *Makes 2 to 3 servings*

english muffin breakfast sandwiches

nutrients per serving:

1 Muffin half

Calories: 233
Carbohydrate: 17 g
Calories From Fat: 35%
Total Fat: 9 g
Saturated Fat: 3 g
Cholesterol: 233 mg
Sodium: 836 mg
Dietary Fiber: 1 g
Protein: 18 g

   2 English muffins, split into halves and toasted
   2 tablespoons plain nonfat yogurt
   1 tablespoon spicy brown or Dijon mustard
   ½ teaspoon dried tarragon or basil leaves
   4 slices Canadian bacon
   4 large tomato slices (about ¼-inch thick)
   2 (1 ounce each) slices reduced-fat Swiss cheese, cut crosswise
      into halves
   4 poached eggs, kept warm
      Paprika (optional)

1. Preheat broiler.

2. Place muffin halves on baking sheet or broiler pan.

3. Combine yogurt, mustard and tarragon in small bowl; stir until well blended. Spread ¼ of yogurt mixture evenly over each muffin half. Top each muffin half with Canadian bacon and tomato slice.

4. Top each tomato slice with cheese slice half. Place muffin halves on broiler pan; broil 4 inches from heat source 1 minute or until cheese begins to brown slightly. Top with poached eggs. Sprinkle with paprika, if desired.   *Makes 4 servings*

creamy fruit blend

cheddar cheese strata

1 pound French bread, cut into ½- to ¾-inch slices with crusts removed, divided
2 cups (8 ounces) shredded reduced-fat Cheddar cheese, divided
2 whole eggs
3 egg whites
4 cups fat-free (skim) milk
1 teaspoon dry mustard
1 teaspoon grated fresh onion
½ teaspoon salt
Paprika to taste

1. Spray 13×9-inch glass baking dish with nonstick cooking spray. Place half the bread slices in bottom of prepared dish, overlapping slightly if necessary. Sprinkle with 1¼ cups cheese. Place remaining bread slices on top of cheese.

2. Whisk whole eggs and egg whites in large bowl. Add milk, mustard, onion and salt; whisk until well blended. Pour evenly over bread and cheese. Cover with remaining ¾ cup cheese and sprinkle with paprika. Cover and refrigerate 1 hour or overnight.

3. Preheat oven to 350°F. Bake about 45 minutes or until cheese is melted and bread is golden brown. Let stand 5 minutes before serving. Garnish with red bell pepper stars and fresh Italian parsley, if desired. *Makes 8 servings*

nutrients per serving:

⅛ of total recipe (without red pepper stars and parsley)

Calories: 297
Carbohydrate: 38 g
Calories From Fat: 23%
Total Fat: 7 g
Saturated Fat: 3 g
Cholesterol: 70 mg
Sodium: 962 mg
Dietary Fiber: <1 g
Protein: 18 g

banana yogurt shake

1½ cups 2% low-fat milk
2 ripe bananas, peeled
1 cup low-fat plain yogurt
¼ cup honey
1 teaspoon vanilla
½ teaspoon ground cinnamon
Dash ground nutmeg
5 ice cubes

Combine all ingredients except ice cubes in blender or food processor; process until thick and creamy. With motor running, add ice cubes; process until smooth. Pour into tall glasses to serve. *Makes 4 cups*

Favorite recipe from **National Honey Board**

nutrients per serving:

1 cup Shake

Calories: 206
Carbohydrate: 40 g
Calories From Fat: 12%
Total Fat: 3 g
Saturated Fat: 2 g
Cholesterol: 11 mg
Sodium: 90 mg
Dietary Fiber: 2 g
Protein: 7 g

cheddar cheese strata

apple cinnamon quesadillas

Spiced Yogurt Dipping Sauce (recipe follows)
1 medium McIntosh apple, cored and chopped
¾ cup no-sugar-added applesauce
⅛ teaspoon ground cinnamon
4 (6-inch) flour tortillas
¼ cup (1 ounce) shredded reduced-fat Cheddar cheese
Nonstick cooking spray

1. Prepare Spiced Yogurt Dipping Sauce; set aside.

2. Combine apple, applesauce and cinnamon in small bowl; mix well.

3. Spoon half of apple mixture onto tortilla; sprinkle with half of cheese. Top with another tortilla. Repeat with remaining tortillas, apple mixture and cheese.

4. Spray large nonstick skillet with cooking spray; heat over medium heat until hot. Cook quesadillas, one at a time, about 2 minutes on each side or until golden brown. Cut each quesadilla into four wedges. Serve with Spiced Yogurt Dipping Sauce.

Makes 4 servings

spiced yogurt dipping sauce

½ cup vanilla low-fat yogurt
2 tablespoons no-sugar-added applesauce
Dash ground cinnamon

Combine yogurt, applesauce and cinnamon in small bowl; mix well. Refrigerate until ready to use.

apple cinnamon quesadillas

sunrise french toast

nutrients per serving:

2 sandwiches (without powdered sugar or syrup)

Calories: 431
Carbohydrate: 82 g
Calories From Fat: 7%
Total Fat: 4 g
Saturated Fat: 1 g
Cholesterol: 1 mg
Sodium: 687 mg
Dietary Fiber: <1 g
Protein: 16 g

2 cups cholesterol-free egg substitute
½ cup evaporated skimmed milk
1 teaspoon grated orange peel
1 teaspoon vanilla
¼ teaspoon ground cinnamon
1 loaf (1 pound) Italian bread, cut into ½-inch-thick slices (about 20 slices)
1 jar (10 ounces) no-sugar-added orange marmalade
Nonstick cooking spray
Powdered sugar (optional)
Maple-flavored syrup (optional)

1. Preheat oven to 400°F. Combine egg substitute, milk, orange peel, vanilla and cinnamon in medium bowl. Set aside.

2. Spread 1 bread slice with 1 tablespoon marmalade to within ½ inch of edge. Top with another bread slice. Repeat with remaining bread and marmalade.

3. Spray griddle or large skillet with cooking spray; heat over medium heat until hot. Dip sandwiches in egg substitute mixture. Do not soak. Cook sandwiches in batches 2 to 3 minutes on each side or until golden brown.

4. Transfer toasted sandwiches to 15×10-inch jelly-roll pan. Bake 10 to 12 minutes or until sides are sealed. Dust with powdered sugar and serve with syrup, if desired.

Makes 5 servings

sunrise french toast

cinnamon flats

1¾ cups all-purpose flour
½ cup sugar
1½ teaspoons ground cinnamon
¼ teaspoon ground nutmeg
¼ teaspoon salt
½ cup (1 stick) cold margarine
3 egg whites, divided
1 teaspoon vanilla
1 teaspoon water
Sugar Glaze (recipe follows)

1. Preheat oven to 350°F. Combine flour, sugar, cinnamon, nutmeg and salt in medium bowl. Cut in margarine with pastry blender or two knives until mixture forms coarse crumbs. Beat in 2 egg whites and vanilla, forming crumbly mixture; mix with hands to form soft dough.

2. Divide dough into 6 equal pieces and place, evenly spaced, on greased 15×10-inch jelly-roll pan. Spread dough evenly to edges of pan using hands; smooth top of dough with metal spatula or palms of hands. Mix remaining egg white and water in small cup; brush over top of dough. Lightly score dough into 2×1½-inch squares.

3. Bake 20 to 25 minutes or until lightly browned and firm when lightly touched with fingertip. While still warm, cut into squares; drizzle or spread Sugar Glaze over squares. Let stand 15 minutes or until glaze is firm before removing from pan.

Makes 50 cookies

sugar glaze

1½ cups powdered sugar
2 to 3 tablespoons fat-free (skim) milk
1 teaspoon vanilla

Combine powdered sugar, 2 tablespoons milk and vanilla in small bowl. If glaze is too thick, add remaining 1 tablespoon milk.

Makes about ¾ cup

cinnamon flats

breakfast burritos with baked citrus fruit

    4 green onions, thinly sliced and divided
1 ¼ cups frozen cholesterol-free egg substitute, thawed
    2 tablespoons diced mild green chilies
    **½ cup (2 ounces) shredded reduced-fat Monterey Jack
       or Cheddar cheese**
    ¼ cup lightly packed fresh cilantro
    4 (7-inch) flour tortillas
    ¼ cup salsa
    ¼ cup reduced-fat sour cream
      Baked Citrus Fruit (recipe follows)

Spray large nonstick skillet with cooking spray. Heat over medium heat. Set aside ¼ cup green onions. Add remaining onions, egg substitute and chilies. Cook, stirring occasionally, about 4 minutes or until eggs are softly set. Stir in cheese and cilantro. Continue cooking, folding eggs over until eggs are cooked to desired doneness, about 1 minute.

Stack tortillas and wrap in paper towels. Microwave at HIGH about 1 minute or until hot. Place one-quarter of eggs in center of each tortilla. Fold sides over filling to enclose. Place burritos seam side down on plates. Top each with salsa, 1 tablespoon sour cream and reserved green onions. Serve with Baked Citrus Fruit. *Makes 4 servings*

Health Note: Check labels on egg substitutes to know what you are buying. Some contain no fat or cholesterol and others simply reduce the levels found in fresh eggs.

baked citrus fruit

    2 oranges, peeled and sliced
    1 grapefruit, peeled and sliced
1 ½ tablespoons lightly packed brown sugar
    ½ teaspoon ground cinnamon

Preheat oven to 400°F. Divide fruit slices into 4 portions. Arrange each portion on baking sheet, overlapping slices. Combine brown sugar and cinnamon in small bowl. Sprinkle 1 teaspoon brown sugar mixture over each serving of fruit. Bake 5 minutes or until fruit is hot. *Makes 4 servings*

breakfast burritos with baked citrus fruit

vegetable omelet

Ratatouille (page 154)
Nonstick cooking spray
5 whole eggs
6 egg whites *or* ¾ cup cholesterol-free egg substitute
¼ cup fat-free (skim) milk
½ teaspoon salt
⅛ teaspoon black pepper
4 to 6 slices Italian bread
2 cloves garlic, halved

1. Prepare Ratatouille; keep warm.

2. Spray 12-inch skillet with cooking spray; heat over medium heat. Beat whole eggs, egg whites, milk, salt and pepper in large bowl until foamy. Pour egg mixture into skillet; cook over medium-high heat 2 to 3 minutes or until bottom of omelet is set. Reduce heat to medium-low. Cover; cook 8 minutes or until top of omelet is set. Remove from heat.

3. Spoon half of Ratatouille down center of omelet. Carefully fold omelet in half; slide onto serving plate. Spoon remaining Ratatouille over top.

4. Toast bread slices; rub both sides of warm toast with cut garlic cloves. Serve omelet with toast and fresh fruit, if desired. *Makes 4 servings*

tip

Eggs are one of the world's most versatile foods. They can be prepared in many ways, from simple scrambled eggs to an elegant omelet. They provide an inexpensive and easy-to-prepare source of protein.

vegetable omelet

ratatouille

nutrients per serving:

½ cup Ratatouille

Calories: 31
Carbohydrate: 7 g
Calories From Fat: 7%
Total Fat: <1 g
Saturated Fat: <1 g
Cholesterol: 0 mg
Sodium: 5 mg
Dietary Fiber: 2 g
Protein: 1 g

Nonstick cooking spray
1 cup chopped onion
½ cup chopped green bell pepper
2 cloves garlic, minced
4 cups cubed unpeeled eggplant
1 medium yellow summer squash, sliced
1 cup chopped fresh tomatoes
¼ cup finely chopped fresh basil *or* 1 teaspoon dried basil leaves
1 tablespoon finely chopped fresh oregano *or* 1 teaspoon dried oregano leaves
2 teaspoons finely chopped fresh thyme *or* ½ teaspoon dried thyme leaves

Spray large skillet with cooking spray; heat over medium heat. Add onion, bell pepper and garlic; cook and stir 5 minutes. Add eggplant, summer squash, tomatoes, basil, oregano and thyme. Cover; cook over medium heat 8 to 10 minutes or until vegetables are tender. Uncover; cook 3 minutes or until liquid is absorbed. *Makes about 4 cups*

power breakfast

nutrients per serving:

1 bowl Power Breakfast (⅙ of total recipe) without granola and yogurt

Calories: 213
Carbohydrate: 44 g
Calories From Fat: 7%
Total Fat: 2 g
Saturated Fat: 1 g
Cholesterol: 4 mg
Sodium: 62 mg
Dietary Fiber: 2 g
Protein: 6 g

3 cups cooked brown rice
2 cups skim milk
¼ cup brown sugar
½ teaspoon cinnamon
½ cup whole milk
⅓ cup raisins
½ teaspoon vanilla extract
Sliced fresh fruit
¾ cup low-fat granola cereal (optional)
1 (6-ounce) container low-fat vanilla yogurt (optional)

Combine rice, skim milk, brown sugar and cinnamon in 2½- to 3-quart saucepan; heat over medium heat, stirring frequently, 10 to 12 minutes or until mixture thickens. Stir in whole milk, raisins and vanilla. Cook 5 minutes, stirring until mixture thickens slightly. Place rice mixture into serving bowls. Sprinkle with fruit. Top each serving with 2 tablespoons granola and yogurt, if desired. *Makes 6 servings*

Favorite recipe from **USA Rice Federation**

upside-down apricot pecan danish

2 tablespoons packed dark brown sugar
¼ cup pecan pieces
2 teaspoons ground cinnamon
1 package (11 ounces) refrigerated French bread dough
5 tablespoons plus 1 teaspoon diet margarine, divided
4 packets sucralose-based sugar substitute*
¼ cup finely chopped dried apricots

*Sold as the brand name Splenda®

1. Preheat oven to 350°F. Coat 9-inch round baking pan with nonstick cooking spray. Sprinkle brown sugar, pecans and cinnamon evenly over bottom; set aside.

2. On work surface, unroll the dough. Spread 3 tablespoons margarine evenly over dough. Sprinkle evenly with sugar substitute. Top with apricots. Gently roll dough to form log.

3. Using serrated knife, cut log into 12 slices. Place slices, cut side down, in prepared pan; bake 30 minutes or until golden brown. Immediately invert onto dinner plate. Add remaining margarine to hot pan; stir until melted. Drizzle over danish.

Makes 12 rolls

nutrients per serving:
1 roll

Calories: 275
Carbohydrate: 43 g
Calories From Fat: 24%
Total Fat: 7 g
Saturated Fat: <1 g
Cholesterol: 0 mg
Sodium: 498 mg
Dietary Fiber: 4 g
Protein: 8 g

cinnamon fruit crunch

1 cup low-fat granola cereal
¼ cup toasted sliced almonds
1 tablespoon margarine
2 tablespoons plus 1 teaspoon packed brown sugar, divided
2¼ teaspoons ground cinnamon, divided
½ cup low-fat vanilla yogurt
⅛ teaspoon ground nutmeg
2 cans (16 ounces each) mixed fruit chunks in juice, drained

Combine granola and almonds in small bowl. Melt margarine in small saucepan. Blend in 2 tablespoons brown sugar and 2 teaspoons cinnamon; simmer until sugar dissolves, about 2 minutes. Toss with granola and almonds; cool. Combine yogurt, 1 teaspoon brown sugar, ¼ teaspoon cinnamon and nutmeg in small bowl. To serve, spoon approximately ½ cup chunky mixed fruit onto each serving plate. Top with yogurt mixture and sprinkle with granola mixture. *Makes 6 servings*

nutrients per serving:
⅙ of total recipe

Calories: 259
Carbohydrate: 48 g
Calories From Fat: 21%
Total Fat: 6 g
Saturated Fat: 1 g
Cholesterol: 1 mg
Sodium: 109 mg
Dietary Fiber: 6 g
Protein: 4 g

satisfying soups & salads

spinach salad with orange-chili glazed shrimp

nutrients per serving:

¼ of total recipe

Calories: 177
Carbohydrate: 19 g
Calories From Fat: 29%
Total Fat: 6 g
Saturated Fat: 3 g
Cholesterol: 100 mg
Sodium: 311 mg
Dietary Fiber: 3 g
Protein: 14 g

  2 teaspoons sesame seeds
  ¼ cup orange juice
  1 tablespoon cider vinegar
  1 clove garlic, minced
  1 teaspoon grated orange peel
  1 teaspoon olive oil
  ½ teaspoon honey
  ⅛ teaspoon red pepper flakes
  1 ripe large mango or ripe medium papaya
  12 cups washed and torn fresh spinach leaves
  ½ cup crumbled feta cheese
     Orange-Chili Glazed Shrimp (recipe follows)

Heat small nonstick skillet over medium heat. Add sesame seeds and cook, stirring often, about 4 minutes or until golden. Remove from pan; place in small bowl. Add orange juice, vinegar, garlic, orange peel, oil, honey and red pepper; stir to combine. Set aside.

Peel mango. Cut fruit away from pit; cut into cubes or slices. Discard tough stems from spinach leaves. Place leaves in large bowl and toss with dressing. Top with mango, cheese and shrimp.   *Makes 4 servings*

orange-chili glazed shrimp

  ½ cup orange juice
  4 cloves garlic, minced
  1 teaspoon chili powder
  8 ounces large shrimp, peeled, deveined

Combine orange juice, garlic and chili powder in large nonstick skillet. Bring to a boil over high heat. Boil 3 minutes or until mixture just coats bottom of pan. Reduce heat to medium. Add shrimp; cook and stir 2 minutes or until shrimp are opaque and juice mixture coats shrimp. (Add additional orange juice or water to keep shrimp moist, if necessary.)   *Makes 4 servings*

spinach salad with orange-chili glazed shrimp

5-minute heat and go soup

nutrients per serving:

1 bowl of Soup
(¼ of total recipe)

Calories: 198
Carbohydrate: 34 g
Calories From Fat: 14%
Total Fat: 3 g
Saturated Fat: <1 g
Cholesterol: 0 mg
Sodium: 252 mg
Dietary Fiber: 9 g
Protein: 11 g

    1 can (16 ounces) low-sodium navy beans, rinsed and drained
    1 can (14½ ounces) diced tomatoes with green peppers and onions
    1 cup water
1½ teaspoons dried basil leaves
  ½ teaspoon sugar
  ½ teaspoon low-sodium chicken bouillon granules
    2 teaspoons olive oil

1. Place all ingredients, except oil, in medium saucepan. Bring to a boil over high heat. Reduce heat and simmer 5 minutes, uncovered. Remove from heat, stir in oil; serve.

2. To transport, if desired, place hot soup in vacuum flask or allow to cool and place in a plastic container. Reheat in microwave when needed.

Makes 3½ cups (4 servings)

chicken pasta salad supreme

nutrients per serving:

⅙ of total recipe

Calories: 310
Carbohydrate: 42 g
Calories From Fat: 9%
Total Fat: 3 g
Saturated Fat: 1 g
Cholesterol: 54 mg
Sodium: 511 mg
Dietary Fiber: 3 g
Protein: 27 g

    3 cups diced cooked chicken
    1 package (8 ounces) small shell pasta, cooked according to
        package directions, drained
    1 medium red pepper, cut in 1½×¼-inch strips
    1 package (8 ounces) frozen snow peas, thawed, drained
  ¼ cup sliced green onion
  ¾ cup bottled, reduced calorie oil and vinegar dressing
    1 cup cherry tomatoes, halved
    Lettuce leaves

In a large bowl, place chicken, pasta, red pepper, snow peas and green onion; toss to mix. Pour dressing over chicken mixture; toss to mix. Cover and chill until ready to serve. Add tomatoes; toss gently. Serve on lettuce-lined plates.   *Makes 6 servings*

*Favorite recipe from **Delmarva Poultry Industry, Inc.***

5-minute heat and go soup

crab spinach salad with tarragon dressing

nutrients per serving:

1 cup Salad with 1½ tablespoons Dressing and 2 cups Spinach

Calories: 170
Carbohydrate: 14 g
Calories From Fat: 18%
Total Fat: 4 g
Saturated Fat: <1 g
Cholesterol: 91 mg
Sodium: 481 mg
Dietary Fiber: 4 g
Protein: 22 g

12 ounces coarsely flaked cooked crabmeat *or* 2 packages (6 ounces each) frozen crabmeat, thawed and drained
1 cup chopped tomatoes
1 cup sliced cucumber
⅓ cup sliced red onion
¼ cup fat-free salad dressing or mayonnaise
¼ cup reduced-fat sour cream
¼ cup chopped fresh parsley
2 tablespoons fat-free (skim) milk
2 teaspoons chopped fresh tarragon *or* ½ teaspoon dried tarragon
1 clove garlic, minced
¼ teaspoon hot pepper sauce
8 cups torn washed stemmed spinach

1. Combine crabmeat, tomatoes, cucumber and onion in medium bowl. Combine salad dressing, sour cream, parsley, milk, tarragon, garlic and hot pepper sauce in small bowl.

2. Line four salad plates with spinach. Place crabmeat mixture on spinach; drizzle with dressing. *Makes 4 servings*

seafood salad

nutrients per serving:

¼ of total recipe

Calories: 273
Carbohydrate: 44 g
Calories From Fat: 10%
Total Fat: 3 g
Saturated Fat: 1 g
Cholesterol: 35 mg
Sodium: 798 mg
Dietary Fiber: 3 g
Protein: 18 g

1 bag SUCCESS® Rice
½ pound crabmeat, cooked
1 can (6 ounces) sliced water chestnuts, drained
½ cup sliced celery
¼ cup sliced green onions
¼ cup plain nonfat yogurt
¼ cup reduced-calorie sour cream
1 tablespoon lemon juice
¼ teaspoon salt

Prepare rice according to package directions. Cool.

Place rice in medium bowl. Add crabmeat, water chestnuts, celery and green onions; mix lightly.

Combine remaining ingredients in small bowl. Add to rice mixture; toss gently to coat. *Makes 4 servings*

crab spinach salad with tarragon dressing

nutrients per serving:

1 bowl Soup
(⅙ of total recipe)

Calories: 243
Carbohydrate: 32 g
Calories From Fat: 19%
Total Fat: 5 g
Saturated Fat: 1 g
Cholesterol: 32 mg
Sodium: 408 mg
Dietary Fiber: 7 g
Protein: 19 g

southwest corn and turkey soup

3 dried ancho chilies (each about 4 inches long) *or* **6 dried New Mexico chilies (each about 6 inches long)***
2 small zucchini
1 medium onion, thinly sliced
3 cloves garlic, minced
1 teaspoon ground cumin
3 cans (about 14 ounces each) fat-free reduced-sodium chicken broth
1½ to 2 cups (8 to 12 ounces) shredded cooked dark turkey meat
1 can (15 ounces) chick-peas (garbanzo beans) or black beans, rinsed and drained
1 package (10 ounces) frozen corn
¼ cup cornmeal
1 teaspoon dried oregano leaves
⅓ cup chopped fresh cilantro

*Chili peppers can sting and irritate the skin; wear rubber gloves when handling and do not touch eyes. Wash hands after handling.

1. Cut stems from chilies; shake out seeds. Place chilies in medium bowl; cover with boiling water. Let stand 20 to 40 minutes or until chilies are soft; drain. Cut open lengthwise and lay flat on work surface. With edge of small knife, scrape chili pulp from skin (thicker-skinned ancho chilies will yield more flesh than thinner-skinned New Mexico chilies). Finely mince pulp; set aside.

2. Cut zucchini in half lengthwise; slice crosswise into ½-inch-wide pieces. Set aside.

3. Spray large saucepan with cooking spray; heat over medium heat. Add onion; cook, covered, 3 to 4 minutes or until light golden brown, stirring several times. Add garlic and cumin; cook and stir about 30 seconds or until fragrant. Add chicken broth, reserved chili pulp, zucchini, turkey, chick-peas, corn, cornmeal and oregano; bring to a boil over high heat. Reduce heat to low; simmer 15 minutes or until zucchini is tender. Stir in cilantro; ladle into bowls and serve.   *Makes 6 servings*

southwest corn and turkey soup

salmon and green bean salad with pasta

nutrients per serving:

⅙ of total recipe

Calories: 210

Carbohydrate: 29 g

Calories From Fat: 15%

Total Fat: 3 g

Saturated Fat: 1 g

Cholesterol: 15 mg

Sodium: 223 mg

Dietary Fiber: 2 g

Protein: 16 g

1 can (6 ounces) red salmon
8 ounces small whole wheat or regular pasta shells
¾ cup fresh green beans, cut into 2-inch pieces
⅔ cup finely chopped carrots
½ cup fat-free cottage cheese
3 tablespoons plain nonfat yogurt
1½ tablespoons lemon juice
1 tablespoon chopped fresh dill
2 teaspoons grated onion
1 teaspoon Dijon mustard

1. Drain salmon and separate into chunks; set aside.

2. Cook pasta according to package directions, including ¼ teaspoon salt; add green beans during last 3 minutes of cooking. Drain; rinse under cold running water until pasta and green beans are cool. Drain.

3. Combine pasta, green beans, carrots and salmon in medium bowl.

4. Place cottage cheese, yogurt, lemon juice, dill, onion and mustard in food processor or blender; process until smooth. Pour over pasta mixture; toss to coat evenly.

Makes 6 servings

salmon and green bean salad with pasta

eggplant & orzo soup with roasted red pepper salsa

2 medium eggplants (1 pound each)
1½ cups finely chopped onions
2 cloves garlic, minced
2 cans (14.5 ounces each) low sodium chicken broth, defatted
1 jar (16 ounces) GUILTLESS GOURMET® Roasted Red Pepper Salsa
1 teaspoon coarsely ground black pepper
¾ cup uncooked orzo, cooked according to package directions
6 sprigs fresh thyme (optional)

Preheat oven to 425°F. Coat baking sheet with nonstick cooking spray. Halve eggplants lengthwise and place cut sides down on baking sheet. Bake about 15 to 20 minutes or until skins are wrinkled and slightly charred. Allow eggplants to cool until safe enough to handle. Peel eggplants; carefully remove and discard seeds. Finely chop eggplants; set aside.

Combine onions and garlic in 2-quart microwave-safe casserole. Cover with vented plastic wrap or lid; microwave on HIGH (100% power) 5 to 6 minutes or until onions are tender. Add eggplants, broth, salsa and pepper; cover. Microwave on HIGH 6 to 8 minutes more or until soup bubbles. To serve, place ⅓ cup orzo into each of 6 individual soup bowls. Ladle 1 cup soup over orzo in each bowl. Garnish with thyme, if desired.   *Makes 6 servings*

Stove Top Directions: Prepare eggplants as directed. Bring ¼ cup broth to a boil in 2-quart saucepan over medium-high heat. Add onions and garlic; cook and stir until onions are tender. Add eggplants, remaining broth, salsa and pepper. Return to a boil. Serve as directed.

green chili vegetable salad

4 cups torn washed romaine lettuce leaves
1 large green bell pepper, cut into strips
1 cup halved cherry tomatoes
3 tablespoons shredded reduced-fat colby or Cheddar cheese
¼ cup fat-free mayonnaise or salad dressing
2 tablespoons plain low-fat yogurt
1 can (4 ounces) diced green chilies, drained
¼ teaspoon ground cumin

1. Combine lettuce, bell pepper, tomatoes and cheese in large bowl. Combine mayonnaise, yogurt, green chilies and cumin in small bowl.

2. Add dressing to salad; toss to combine. *Makes 4 servings*

nutrients per serving:
about 1¾ cups Salad

Calories: 81
Carbohydrate: 14 g
Calories From Fat: 18%
Total Fat: 2 g
Saturated Fat: 1 g
Cholesterol: 4 mg
Sodium: 168 mg
Dietary Fiber: 4 g
Protein: 4 g

apricot chicken salad

12 ounces poached or baked skinless chicken
1 cup sliced celery
½ cup dried apricots, cut with scissors into strips
¼ cup slivered almonds
½ cup fat-free mayonnaise
¼ teaspoon black or white pepper
⅛ teaspoon ground ginger
8 to 10 cups romaine or leaf lettuce, torn into bite-size pieces
4 Roma tomatoes, sliced

1. Mix together chicken, celery, apricots, almonds, mayonnaise, pepper and ginger in large bowl. Refrigerate 1 hour or overnight to allow flavors to blend.

2. Line serving plates with lettuce and tomatoes. Top with chicken salad.
Makes 4 servings

Serving Suggestion: This chicken mixture also makes a great filling for pita bread.

nutrients per serving:
¼ of total recipe

Calories: 302
Carbohydrate: 28 g
Calories From Fat: 23%
Total Fat: 8 g
Saturated Fat: 1 g
Cholesterol: 72 mg
Sodium: 351 mg
Dietary Fiber: 2 g
Protein: 32 g

red bean & corn salad with lime-cumin dressing

nutrients per serving:

total recipe

Calories: 198
Carbohydrate: 33 g
Calories From Fat: 18%
Total Fat: 4 g
Saturated Fat: <1 g
Cholesterol: 0 mg
Sodium: 908 mg
Dietary Fiber: 9 g
Protein: 8 g

2 tablespoons fresh lime juice
1½ teaspoons canola oil
½ teaspoon ground cumin
½ teaspoon water
⅛ teaspoon salt
¾ cup canned red beans, rinsed and drained
½ cup frozen corn with bell pepper and onion, thawed
¼ cup chopped tomato
2 tablespoons chopped green onion, divided
2 large romaine lettuce leaves

1. Whisk together lime juice, oil, cumin, water and salt in medium bowl.

2. Add beans, corn, tomato and 1 tablespoon green onion; toss to coat. Serve on lettuce leaves. Top with remaining green onion.   *Makes 1 serving*

spinach-melon salad

nutrients per serving:

⅙ of total recipe

Calories: 99
Carbohydrate: 20 g
Calories From Fat: 18%
Total Fat: 2 g
Saturated Fat: <1 g
Cholesterol: 0 mg
Sodium: 54 mg
Dietary Fiber: 3 g
Protein: 3 g

6 cups torn stemmed washed spinach
4 cups mixed melon balls, such as cantaloupe, honeydew and/or watermelon
1 cup sliced zucchini
½ cup sliced red bell pepper
¼ cup thinly sliced red onion
¼ cup red wine vinegar
2 tablespoons honey
2 teaspoons olive oil
2 teaspoons lime juice
1 teaspoon poppy seeds
1 teaspoon dried mint leaves, crushed

Combine spinach, melon balls, zucchini, bell pepper and onion in large bowl.

For dressing, combine vinegar, honey, oil, lime juice, poppy seeds and mint in small jar with tight-fitting lid; shake well. Pour over salad; toss gently to coat.

Makes 6 servings

red bean & corn salad with lime-cumin dressing

nutrients per serving:

1 bowl Soup
(⅙ of total recipe)
with 2 Ravioli

Calories: 130
Carbohydrate: 21 g
Calories From Fat: 14%
Total Fat: 2 g
Saturated Fat: <1 g
Cholesterol: 26 mg
Sodium: 205 mg
Dietary Fiber: 2 g
Protein: 7 g

chicken ravioli soup

Chicken Ravioli (recipe follows)
8 cups fat-free reduced-sodium chicken broth
2 cups sliced fresh spinach leaves
1 cup sliced carrots
¼ teaspoon salt
⅛ teaspoon black pepper

1. Prepare Chicken Ravioli.

2. In large saucepan, heat chicken broth, spinach, carrots, salt and pepper to a boil. Reduce heat to low and simmer, covered, 10 minutes.

3. Return soup to a boil; add Chicken Ravioli. Reduce heat to low and simmer, uncovered, 2 to 3 minutes or until ravioli are tender and rise to surface of soup.

Makes 6 appetizer servings

chicken ravioli

⅓ cup ground chicken
1 tablespoon minced shallot or onion
1 clove garlic, minced
⅛ teaspoon salt
⅛ teaspoon ground nutmeg
⅛ teaspoon black pepper
24 wonton wrappers
Water

Combine chicken, shallot, garlic, salt, nutmeg and pepper in small bowl. Place rounded teaspoonful of chicken mixture in center of each of 12 wonton wrappers. Moisten edges of wonton wrappers with water. Top with remaining wonton wrappers; press to seal edges. Refrigerate, covered, until ready to cook. *Makes 12 ravioli*

chicken ravioli soup

light chicken vegetable salad

1¼ pounds skinless chicken breasts, cooked and cut into ¾-inch pieces
⅓ cup chopped zucchini
⅓ cup chopped carrot
2 tablespoons chopped onion
2 tablespoons chopped fresh parsley
⅓ cup fat-free mayonnaise
¼ cup fat-free sour cream
¼ teaspoon salt
⅛ teaspoon pepper
   Kale or lettuce leaves (optional)
3 tomatoes, cut into wedges
¼ cup sliced, toasted almonds

1. Combine chicken, zucchini, carrot, onion and parsley in large bowl.

2. Combine mayonnaise, sour cream, salt and pepper in small bowl. Add to chicken mixture; mix well. Cover and refrigerate at least 2 hours.

3. Line plates with kale leaves, if desired. Divide salad evenly among plates. Surround with tomato wedges; sprinkle with almonds. Garnish, if desired.

Makes 6 servings

turkey and black bean soup

1 can (14.5 ounces) HUNT'S® Diced Tomatoes with Roasted Garlic
2 cans (14.5 ounces) low fat and low sodium chicken broth
1 can (15 ounces) black beans, rinsed and drained
1 cup frozen whole kernel corn
1 teaspoon oregano leaves, crushed
¼ teaspoon ground cumin
6 ounces fully cooked reduced fat smoked turkey sausage,
   halved lengthwise and thinly sliced

1. In medium saucepan combine Hunt's® Tomatoes and *remaining* ingredients *except* sausage.

2. Bring to a boil. Reduce heat; simmer, uncovered, for 3 minutes.

3. Stir in sausage; heat through.

Makes 6 servings

light chicken vegetable salad

curried creamy sweet potato soup

nutrients per serving:

¾ cup Soup

Calories: 201
Carbohydrate: 35 g
Calories From Fat: 20%
Total Fat: 5 g
Saturated Fat: 3 g
Cholesterol: 13 mg
Sodium: 261 mg
Dietary Fiber: 4 g
Protein: 7 g

4 cups water
1 pound sweet potatoes, peeled and cut into 1-inch cubes
1 tablespoon plus 1 teaspoon butter or margarine, divided
2 cups finely chopped yellow onions
2 cups fat-free (skim) milk, divided
¾ teaspoon curry powder
½ teaspoon salt
Dash ground red pepper (optional)

Bring water to a boil in large saucepan over high heat. Add potatoes; return to a boil. Reduce heat to medium-low and simmer, uncovered, 15 minutes or until potatoes are tender.

Meanwhile, heat medium nonstick skillet over medium-high heat until hot. Coat with nonstick cooking spray; add 1 teaspoon butter and tilt skillet to coat bottom. Add onions; cook 8 minutes or until tender and golden.

Drain potatoes; place in blender with onions, 1 cup milk, curry powder, salt and ground red pepper. Blend until completely smooth. Return potato mixture to saucepan and stir in remaining 1 cup milk. Cook 5 minutes over medium-high heat or until heated through. Remove from heat and stir in remaining 1 tablespoon butter.

Makes 4 servings

fruit and green salad

nutrients per serving:

½ of total recipe

Calories: 102
Carbohydrate: 22 g
Calories From Fat: 11%
Total Fat: 1 g
Saturated Fat: <1 g
Cholesterol: 1 mg
Sodium: 14 mg
Dietary Fiber: 4 g
Protein: 2 g

2 tablespoons plain low-fat yogurt
1 teaspoon lemon juice
1 teaspoon sugar
1½ cups torn lettuce
1 orange, cubed
1 apple, cubed
1 teaspoon walnuts

In small bowl combine yogurt, lemon juice and sugar. In salad bowl toss lettuce, orange and apple. Pour dressing over salad and top with nuts. *Makes 2 servings*

*Favorite recipe from **The Sugar Association, Inc.***

curried creamy sweet potato soup

nutrients per serving:

1¼ cups Soup with 2 tablespoons crushed croutons

Calories: 284
Carbohydrate: 30 g
Calories From Fat: 16%
Total Fat: 5 g
Saturated Fat: 1 g
Cholesterol: 52 mg
Sodium: 721 mg
Dietary Fiber: 8 g
Protein: 28 g

skillet chicken soup

**¾ pound boneless skinless chicken breasts or thighs,
  cut into ¾-inch pieces**
1 teaspoon paprika
½ teaspoon salt
¼ teaspoon black pepper
2 teaspoons vegetable oil
1 large onion, chopped
1 red bell pepper, cut into ½-inch pieces
3 cloves garlic, minced
1 cup fat-free reduced-sodium chicken broth
**1 can (19 ounces) cannellini beans or small white beans,
  rinsed and drained**
3 cups sliced savoy or napa cabbage
½ cup fat-free herb-flavored croutons, slightly crushed

1. Toss chicken with paprika, salt and black pepper in medium bowl until coated.

2. Heat oil in large, deep nonstick skillet over medium-high heat until hot. Add chicken, onion, bell pepper and garlic. Cook until chicken is no longer pink, stirring frequently.

3. Add broth and beans; bring to simmer. Cover and simmer 5 minutes or until chicken is cooked through. Stir in cabbage; cover and simmer 3 additional minutes or until cabbage is wilted. Ladle into 4 shallow bowls; top evenly with crushed croutons.

Makes 4 servings

tip

Cannellini beans are cultivated white beans commonly used in Italian cooking. They are large white beans with a delicate flavor, which are used in soups, stews and salads. Great Northern beans may be substituted.

skillet chicken soup

green pea and potato soup

1 can (14½ ounces) fat-free reduced-sodium chicken broth
1 cup diced peeled potato
1 cup fresh or frozen green peas
½ cup sliced green onion tops
2 leaves green lettuce, chopped
1 teaspoon dried dill weed
⅛ teaspoon white pepper
1½ cups low-fat buttermilk
   Dash paprika

1. Combine chicken broth, potato, peas, green onions, lettuce, dill and pepper in medium saucepan. Bring to a boil over high heat. Reduce heat to medium. Cook, covered, 10 minutes or until potatoes are just tender. Let cool, uncovered, to room temperature.

2. Place vegetables and cooking liquid in food processor. Process 45 seconds or until almost smooth. Return mixture to saucepan; stir in buttermilk. Cook and stir over low heat 5 minutes or until heated through. Sprinkle with paprika.   *Makes 6 servings*

Note: Soup may be served cold. Chill at least 8 hours before serving.

italian fish soup

4 ounces fresh halibut or haddock steak, 1 inch thick
1 cup meatless spaghetti sauce
¾ cup fat-free, reduced-sodium chicken broth
¾ cup water
1 teaspoon dried Italian seasoning
¾ cup uncooked small pasta shells
1½ cups frozen vegetable blend, such as broccoli, carrots and water chestnuts or broccoli, carrots and cauliflower

1. Remove skin from fish. Cut fish into 1-inch pieces. Cover and refrigerate until needed.

2. Combine spaghetti sauce, broth, water and Italian seasoning in medium saucepan. Bring to a boil. Stir in pasta. Return to a boil. Reduce heat and simmer, covered, 5 minutes.

3. Stir in fish and frozen vegetables. Return to a boil. Reduce heat and simmer, covered, 4 to 5 minutes or until fish flakes easily when tested with fork and pasta is tender.

Makes 2 servings

nutrients per serving:
½ of total recipe

Calories: 331
Carbohydrate: 44 g
Calories From Fat: 21%
Total Fat: 8 g
Saturated Fat: 1 g
Cholesterol: 1 mg
Sodium: 734 mg
Dietary Fiber: 7 g
Protein: 21 g

mixed greens with honey raspberry vinaigrette

¼ cup raspberry vinegar or balsamic vinegar
¼ cup honey
1 tablespoon olive oil
½ teaspoon chopped fresh oregano, basil or thyme
8 cups mixed lettuce greens

Combine vinegar and honey in small bowl; mix well. To serve, drizzle 2 to 3 tablespoons vinegar-honey mixture, oil and oregano over lettuce greens. Toss to coat. Garnish with fruit, if desired.

Makes 4 servings

Variation: Use 2 to 3 tablespoons chopped fresh mint for mixed fruit salads in place of oregano, basil or thyme.

Note: Vinegar-honey mixture may be stored in covered jar for future use.

*Favorite recipe from **National Honey Board***

nutrients per serving:
¼ of total recipe

Calories: 111
Carbohydrate: 21 g
Calories From Fat: 27%
Total Fat: 4 g
Saturated Fat: <1 g
Cholesterol: 0 mg
Sodium: 10 mg
Dietary Fiber: 2 g
Protein: 2 g

shrimp and rice salad

nutrients per serving:

¼ of total recipe

Calories: 334
Carbohydrate: 47 g
Calories From Fat: 24%
Total Fat: 9 g
Saturated Fat: 1 g
Cholesterol: 97 mg
Sodium: 165 mg
Dietary Fiber: 3 g
Protein: 15 g

1 (2-cup) bag UNCLE BEN'S® Boil-in-Bag Rice
1¼ cups snow peas
½ pound cooked peeled, deveined shrimp
1 cup sliced celery
½ cup reduced-fat mayonnaise
½ cup thinly sliced carrot
½ cup diced red bell pepper
1 tablespoon fresh lemon juice

1. Cook rice according to package directions. Rinse under cold running water to cool; drain.

2. Meanwhile, slice snow peas into 1-inch lengths. In a medium bowl, combine snow peas and remaining ingredients.

3. Add drained rice; mix well. Serve immediately or chill until ready to serve.

Makes 4 servings

fiesta soup

nutrients per serving:

1 bowl Soup
(¼ of total recipe)

Calories: 281
Carbohydrate: 37 g
Calories From Fat: 13%
Total Fat: 4 g
Saturated Fat: 2 g
Cholesterol: 31 mg
Sodium: 1184 mg
Dietary Fiber: 8 g
Protein: 25 g

6 boneless, skinless chicken tenderloins, cut into 1-inch pieces
2 cans (14½ ounces) low-sodium chicken broth
1 can (15 ounces) kidney beans, undrained
1 cup salsa
1 cup frozen corn
½ cup UNCLE BEN'S® Instant Rice
⅓ cup shredded Monterey Jack cheese

1. In large saucepan, combine chicken, broth, kidney beans, salsa and corn.

2. Bring to a boil. Reduce heat and simmer uncovered 5 to 10 minutes or until chicken is no longer pink. Stir in rice. Cover; remove from heat and let stand covered 5 minutes. Top each serving with cheese. *Makes 4 servings*

Cook's Tip: Garnish with tortilla chips, sliced avocado or toasted tortilla strips.

shrimp and rice salad

nutrients per serving:

1½ cups Soup

Calories: 196
Carbohydrate: 35 g
Calories From Fat: 7%
Total Fat: 2 g
Saturated Fat: 0 g
Cholesterol: 0 mg
Sodium: 33 mg
Dietary Fiber: 5 g
Protein: 12 g

white bean and escarole soup

1½ cups dried baby lima beans
1 teaspoon olive oil
½ cup chopped celery
⅓ cup coarsely chopped onion
2 cloves garlic, minced
2 cans (10 ounces each) no-salt-added whole tomatoes, undrained, chopped
½ cup chopped fresh parsley
2 tablespoons fresh rosemary
¼ teaspoon black pepper
3 cups shredded fresh escarole

1. Place dried lima beans in large glass bowl; cover completely with water. Soak 6 to 8 hours or overnight. Drain beans; place in large saucepan or Dutch oven. Cover beans with about 3 cups water; bring to a boil over high heat. Reduce heat to low. Cover and simmer about 1 hour or until soft. Drain; set aside.

2. Heat oil in small skillet over medium heat. Add celery, onion and garlic; cook until onion is tender. Remove from heat.

3. Add celery mixture and tomatoes with juice to beans. Stir in parsley, rosemary and black pepper. Cover and simmer over low heat 15 minutes. Add escarole; simmer 5 minutes. *Makes 6 servings*

white bean and escarole soup

japanese petal salad

1 pound medium shrimp, cooked *or* 2 cups chicken, cooked and shredded
Romaine lettuce leaves
2 fresh California Nectarines, halved, pitted and thinly sliced
2 cups sliced cucumber
2 celery stalks, cut into 3-inch-matchstick pieces
⅓ cup shredded red radishes
Sesame Dressing (recipe follows) or low calorie dressing
2 teaspoons sesame seeds (optional)

Center shrimp on 4 lettuce-lined salad plates. Fan nectarines to right side of shrimp; overlap cucumber slices to left side. Place celery at top of plate; mound radishes at bottom of plate. Prepare dressing; pour 3 tablespoons over each salad. Sprinkle with sesame seeds, if desired.   *Makes 4 servings*

Sesame Dressing: In small bowl, combine ½ cup rice wine vinegar (not seasoned type), 2 tablespoons reduced-sodium soy sauce, 2 teaspoons sugar and 2 teaspoons dark sesame oil. Stir to dissolve sugar.

*Favorite recipe from **California Tree Fruit Agreement***

tip

Shrimp are found in most of the waters surrounding the United States. Shrimp are grouped for retail purposes by their size. The most common sizes are jumbo (11 to 15 per pound), large (21 to 30), medium (31 to 35) and small (36 to 45).

japanese petal salad

chicken & orzo soup

nutrients per serving:

1 bowl Soup
(½ of total recipe)
without additional
green onions

Calories: 176
Carbohydrate: 21 g
Calories From Fat: 8%
Total Fat: 2 g
Saturated Fat: <1 g
Cholesterol: 26 mg
Sodium: 182 mg
Dietary Fiber: 2 g
Protein: 18 g

Nonstick olive oil cooking spray
3 ounces boneless skinless chicken breast, cut into bite-size pieces
1 can (14½ ounces) fat-free reduced-sodium chicken broth
1 cup water
⅔ cup shredded carrot
⅓ cup sliced green onion
¼ cup uncooked orzo pasta
1 teaspoon grated fresh ginger
⅛ teaspoon ground turmeric
2 teaspoons lemon juice
Dash black pepper
Sliced green onions (optional)

1. Spray medium saucepan with cooking spray. Heat over medium-high heat. Add chicken. Cook and stir 2 to 3 minutes or until no longer pink. Remove from saucepan and set aside.

2. In same saucepan, combine broth, water, carrot, green onion, orzo, ginger and turmeric. Bring to a boil. Reduce heat and simmer, covered, 8 to 10 minutes or until orzo is tender. Stir in chicken and lemon juice; cook until hot. Season to taste with pepper.

3. Ladle into serving bowls. Sprinkle with additional green onions, if desired.

Makes 2 servings

chicken & orzo soup

caribbean callaloo soup

¼ cup plus 2 tablespoons shredded sweetened coconut
1½ pounds butternut squash
12 ounces boneless skinless chicken breasts
1 teaspoon olive oil
1 large onion, chopped
4 cloves garlic, minced
3 cans (about 14 ounces each) fat-free reduced-sodium
  chicken broth
2 jalapeño peppers,* stemmed, seeded and minced
2 teaspoons dried thyme leaves
½ package (10 ounces) spinach leaves, washed and torn

*Jalapeño peppers can sting and irritate the skin; wear rubber gloves when handling peppers and do not touch eyes. Wash hands after handling.

1. Preheat oven to 350°F. Place coconut in baking pan; bake 6 minutes, stirring every 2 minutes, until golden. Set aside. Peel squash; cut in half lengthwise and discard seeds. Cut into ½-inch cubes. Slice chicken crosswise into very thin strips.

2. Heat oil in large nonstick skillet over medium-low heat. Add onion and garlic; cook, covered, stirring often, 5 minutes or until onion is tender. Add squash, chicken broth, jalapeño peppers and thyme; bring to a boil over high heat. Reduce heat to low; simmer, covered, 15 to 20 minutes, until squash is very tender. Add chicken; cover and cook 2 minutes or until chicken is no longer pink in center. Remove skillet from heat; stir in spinach until wilted. Ladle into bowls and sprinkle with toasted coconut.

Makes 6 servings

meatball soup

¾ **pound ground turkey**
1 **egg white**
¼ **cup Italian-seasoned dry bread crumbs**
3 **cloves garlic, minced, divided**
3 **teaspoons dried Italian seasoning, divided**
¾ **teaspoon fennel seeds, crushed**
½ **teaspoon salt**
⅛ **teaspoon black pepper**
  Nonstick olive oil cooking spray
¾ **cup chopped onion**
8 **ounces hubbard or other winter yellow squash, peeled,
    seeded and cut into ¾-inch pieces**
3 **cans (14½ ounces each) fat-free reduced-sodium chicken broth**
1 **can (15½ ounces) great Northern beans, rinsed and drained**
2 **cups chopped tomatoes**
1 **cup frozen peas**
4 **ounces uncooked ditalini pasta**
  Salt and black pepper
  Minced fresh parsley

1. Preheat oven to 375°F.

2. Combine turkey, egg white, bread crumbs, 1 clove garlic, 1 teaspoon Italian seasoning, fennel seeds, ½ teaspoon salt and ⅛ teaspoon pepper in medium bowl. Shape turkey mixture into 18 meatballs.

3. Place meatballs in lightly greased baking pan and bake 15 to 20 minutes or until browned and no longer pink in center. Drain on paper towels.

4. Spray large saucepan with cooking spray; heat over medium heat until hot. Cook and stir onion, squash and remaining 2 cloves garlic about 5 minutes or until onion is tender. Add remaining 2 teaspoons Italian seasoning and cook 1 minute.

5. Add chicken broth, beans, tomatoes and peas; bring to a boil. Reduce heat and simmer, covered, 5 minutes. Add pasta and simmer, uncovered, about 10 minutes or until pasta is tender. Add meatballs during last 5 minutes of cooking time. Season to taste with salt and pepper. Ladle soup into bowls; sprinkle with parsley.

Makes 6 main-dish servings

nutrients per serving:

1 bowl Soup (about 2 cups)

Calories: 349
Carbohydrate: 46 g
Calories From Fat: 19%
Total Fat: 7 g
Saturated Fat: 2 g
Cholesterol: 28 mg
Sodium: 453 mg
Dietary Fiber: 3 g
Protein: 26 g

chicken caesar salad

4 small boneless skinless chicken breast halves
6 ounces uncooked gnocchi or other dried pasta
1 package (9 ounces) frozen artichoke hearts, thawed
1½ cups cherry tomatoes, quartered
¼ cup plus 2 tablespoons plain nonfat yogurt
2 tablespoons reduced-fat mayonnaise
2 tablespoons grated Romano cheese
1 tablespoon sherry or red wine vinegar
1 clove garlic, minced
½ teaspoon anchovy paste
½ teaspoon Dijon mustard
½ teaspoon white pepper
1 small head romaine lettuce, torn into bite-size pieces
1 cup toasted bread cubes

1. Grill or broil chicken breasts until no longer pink in center; set aside.

2. Cook pasta according to package directions, omitting salt. Drain and rinse well under cold water until pasta is cool; drain well. Combine pasta, artichoke hearts and tomatoes in large bowl; set aside.

3. Combine yogurt, mayonnaise, Romano cheese, sherry, garlic, anchovy paste, mustard and pepper in small bowl; whisk until smooth. Add to pasta mixture; toss to coat evenly.

4. Arrange lettuce on platter or individual plates. Spoon pasta mixture over lettuce. Thinly slice chicken breasts and place on top of pasta. Sprinkle with bread cubes.

Makes 4 main-dish servings

chicken caesar salad

hot gazpacho bean soup

1 tablespoon olive oil
1 cup chopped onion
1 cup chopped green bell pepper
1 clove garlic, minced
2 cans (11½ ounces each) no-salt-added vegetable juice
1 can (15 ounces) red kidney beans, rinsed and drained
1 can (15 ounces) garbanzo beans, rinsed and drained
2 beef bouillon cubes
2 tablespoons fresh lemon juice
¼ teaspoon red pepper flakes
3 cups chopped tomatoes, divided
1 cup chopped cucumber
½ cup chopped green onions
½ cup plain salad croutons

1. Heat olive oil in medium saucepan over medium-high heat until hot. Add onion, green pepper and garlic. Cook 3 minutes or until vegetables are crisp-tender.

2. Add vegetable juice, beans, bouillon cubes, lemon juice, red pepper flakes and 1½ cups tomatoes. Bring to a boil. Reduce heat to low. Cover and simmer 5 minutes.

3. Divide bean mixture among serving bowls. Top with remaining tomatoes, cucumber, green onions and croutons.   *Makes 6 servings*

Prep and Cook Time: 28 minutes

hot gazpacho bean soup

shantung twin mushroom soup

1 package (1 ounce) dried black Chinese mushrooms
2 teaspoons vegetable oil
1 large onion, coarsely chopped
2 cloves garlic, minced
2 cups sliced fresh button mushrooms
2 cans (about 14 ounces each) fat-free reduced-sodium chicken broth
2 ounces cooked ham, cut into thin slivers
½ cup thinly sliced green onions
1 tablespoon reduced-sodium soy sauce
1 tablespoon dry sherry
1 tablespoon cornstarch
6 whole wheat dinner rolls

1. Place dried mushrooms in small bowl; cover with warm water. Soak 20 minutes to soften. Drain; squeeze out excess water. Discard stems; slice caps.

2. Heat oil in large saucepan over medium heat until hot. Add chopped onion and garlic; cook 1 minute. Add both types of mushrooms; cook 4 minutes, stirring occasionally.

3. Add chicken broth; bring to a boil over high heat. Reduce heat to medium; simmer, covered, 15 minutes.

4. Stir in ham and green onions; heat through. Blend soy sauce and sherry into cornstarch in small bowl until smooth; stir into soup. Cook 2 minutes or until soup is thickened, stirring occasionally. Serve with whole wheat dinner rolls.

Makes 6 servings

shantung twin mushroom soup

savory sides

nutrients per serving:

¼ of total recipe (without added salt seasoning)

Calories: 58
Carbohydrate: 10 g
Calories From Fat: 19%
Total Fat: 1 g
Saturated Fat: <1 g
Cholesterol: <1 mg
Sodium: 37 mg
Dietary Fiber: 2 g
Protein: 3 g

citrus asparagus

Orange Sauce
   2 teaspoons reduced-fat margarine
   1 clove garlic, minced
   Juice of 1 large orange (about ⅓ cup)
1¼ teaspoons balsamic vinegar
   ¼ teaspoon Dijon mustard
   ½ teaspoon grated orange peel
   Salt (optional)

Asparagus
   Nonstick olive oil cooking spray
   1 small onion, diced
   1 pound fresh asparagus, lower half of stalks peeled*
   ⅔ cup diced red bell pepper
   ½ cup water

*If using pencil-thin asparagus, do not peel. Reduce cooking time to 4 to 5 minutes.

1. For Orange Sauce, heat margarine in small saucepan over medium heat. Add garlic; cook and stir 2 minutes or until soft. Stir in orange juice; bring to a boil. Add vinegar and mustard; reduce heat and simmer 2 minutes. Remove from heat and add orange peel. Season to taste with salt, if desired; reserve and keep warm.

2. For asparagus, spray medium saucepan with cooking spray; heat over medium-high heat. Add onion; cook and stir 2 minutes. Add asparagus, bell pepper and water. Reduce heat to medium-low. Cover and simmer 7 minutes or until asparagus is crisp-tender. Remove vegetables with slotted spoon to serving dish; serve with reserved Orange Sauce.

Makes 4 servings

citrus asparagus

ginger noodles with sesame egg strips

nutrients per serving:

¼ of total recipe

Calories: 111
Carbohydrate: 16 g
Calories From Fat: 19%
Total Fat: 2 g
Saturated Fat: 1 g
Cholesterol: 0 mg
Sodium: 226 mg
Dietary Fiber: <1 g
Protein: 7 g

5 egg whites
6 teaspoons teriyaki sauce, divided
3 teaspoons toasted sesame seeds,* divided
1 teaspoon dark sesame oil
½ cup fat-free reduced-sodium chicken broth
1 tablespoon minced fresh ginger
6 ounces uncooked Chinese rice noodles or vermicelli,
  cooked and well drained
⅓ cup sliced green onions

To toast sesame seeds, spread seeds in small skillet. Shake skillet over medium heat 2 minutes or until seeds begin to pop and turn golden.

1. Beat together egg whites, 2 teaspoons teriyaki sauce and 1 teaspoon sesame seeds.

2. Heat large nonstick skillet over medium heat. Add oil; heat until hot. Pour egg mixture into skillet; cook 1½ to 2 minutes or until bottom of omelet is set. Turn omelet over; cook 30 seconds to 1 minute. Slide out onto plate; cool and cut into ½-inch strips.

3. Add broth, ginger and remaining 4 teaspoons teriyaki sauce to skillet. Bring to a boil over high heat; reduce heat to medium. Add noodles; heat through. Add omelet strips and onions; heat through. Sprinkle with remaining 2 teaspoons sesame seeds.

Makes 4 side-dish servings

ginger noodles with sesame egg strips

festive polenta triangles

nutrients per serving:

6 triangles

Calories: 62
Carbohydrate: 9 g
Calories From Fat: 26%
Total Fat: 2 g
Saturated Fat: 1 g
Cholesterol: 6 mg
Sodium: 142 mg
Dietary Fiber: <1 g
Protein: 3 g

½ cup corn grits
1½ cups chicken broth, divided
2 cloves garlic, minced
½ cup (2 ounces) crumbled feta cheese
1 red bell pepper, roasted,* peeled and finely chopped
Nonstick cooking spray

Place pepper on foil-lined broiler pan; broil 15 minutes or until blackened on all sides, turning every 5 minutes. Place pepper in paper bag; close bag and let stand 15 minutes before peeling.

1. Combine grits and ½ cup broth; mix well and set aside. Pour remaining 1 cup broth into heavy large saucepan; bring to a boil. Add garlic and moistened grits; mix well and return to a boil. Reduce heat to low; cover and cook 20 minutes. Remove from heat; add feta cheese. Stir until cheese is completely melted. Add bell pepper; mix well.

2. Spray 8-inch square pan with cooking spray. Spoon grits mixture into prepared pan. Press grits evenly into pan with wet fingertips. Refrigerate until cold.

3. Preheat broiler. Turn polenta out onto cutting board and cut into 2-inch squares. Cut each square diagonally into 2 triangles. Spray baking sheet with cooking spray. Place polenta triangles on prepared baking sheet and spray tops lightly with cooking spray. Place under broiler until lightly browned. Turn triangles over and broil until browned and crisp. Serve warm or at room temperature. Garnish with fresh oregano and chives, if desired.

Makes 8 servings

festive polenta triangles

broccoli boutonnieres and buttons

1 large bunch fresh broccoli (about 1½ pounds)
2 teaspoons lemon juice
1 tablespoon cornstarch
1 cup water
1 teaspoon instant chicken bouillon granules
   White pepper
   Lemon wedges and mizuna greens for garnish

1. Trim leaves from broccoli stalks. Cut broccoli into florets. Peel stems, then cut crosswise into ¼-inch pieces to make "buttons."

2. Place steamer basket in large saucepan; add 1 inch of water. (Water should not touch bottom of basket.) Place buttons in steamer; top with florets. Cover; bring to a boil over high heat. Steam 4 to 6 minutes until bright green and crisp-tender, adding water if necessary.

3. Meanwhile, combine lemon juice and cornstarch in small saucepan. Stir in water and bouillon. Cook over medium heat until mixture thickens and begins to boil, stirring constantly.

4. Arrange buttons around edge of warm serving plate. Place florets in center. Drizzle with sauce; season with pepper to taste. Garnish, if desired.   *Makes 6 servings*

tip

To divide the broccoli head into florets, cut off the large stalk. Cut the broccoli head into individual florets to include a little stem with each floret. The stalks can be peeled and cut into crosswise slices. If the slices are more than ¼ inch thick, they may take longer to cook than the florets, so give them a 2- or 3-minute head start.

broccoli boutonnieres and buttons

red cabbage with apples

nutrients per serving:

⅛ of total recipe

Calories: 68
Carbohydrate: 17 g
Calories From Fat: 3%
Total Fat: <1g
Saturated Fat: <1 g
Cholesterol: 0 mg
Sodium: 13 mg
Dietary Fiber: 2 g
Protein: 1 g

1 small head red cabbage, shredded
2 large apples, peeled and thinly sliced
½ cup sliced onion
½ cup unsweetened apple juice
¼ cup lemon juice
2 tablespoons raisins
2 tablespoons brown sugar
Salt and pepper to taste (optional)

Combine cabbage, apples, onion, apple juice, lemon juice, raisins and brown sugar in large nonstick saucepan. Simmer, covered, 30 minutes. Season with salt and pepper.

Makes 8 servings

wild rice-cranberry-apple stuffing

nutrients per serving:

½ cup

Calories: 102
Carbohydrate: 20 g
Calories From Fat: 17%
Total Fat: 2 g
Saturated Fat: <1 g
Cholesterol: 0 mg
Sodium: 10 mg
Dietary Fiber: 1 g
Protein: 2 g

1 tablespoon olive oil or butter
2 stalks diced celery (about ⅔ cup)
1 medium apple, diced (about 1 cup)
1 clove garlic, minced (optional)
Pinch of dried or fresh thyme (optional)
Pinch of dried sage (optional)
1 cup hot, cooked wild rice
1 cup hot, cooked white or brown rice
½ cup orange juice
¼ to ½ cup dried cranberries
¼ cup sliced green onions (green tops only)
Salt and black pepper to taste (optional)

1. In large saucepan, heat olive oil over medium-high heat. Add celery, apple and garlic, if desired, and sauté until softened, about 5 minutes.

2. Reduce heat to medium-low and stir in thyme and sage, if desired. Cook a few seconds and stir in hot rices, orange juice and cranberries; cook until heated through, about 1 minute. Just before serving, stir in green onions and season with salt and pepper.

Makes 8 servings

red cabbage with apples

oven french fries

nutrients per serving:

⅙ of total recipe

Calories: 98
Carbohydrate: 18 g
Calories From Fat: 22%
Total Fat: 2 g
Saturated Fat: <1 g
Cholesterol: 0 mg
Sodium: 175 mg
Dietary Fiber: 2 g
Protein: 2 g

**4 medium potatoes
1 tablespoon CRISCO® Oil***
**½ teaspoon celery salt
⅛ teaspoon garlic powder
⅛ teaspoon pepper
⅛ teaspoon paprika**

*Use your favorite Crisco Oil product.

1. Heat oven to 425°F. Place cooling rack on countertop.

2. Peel potatoes. Cut into long ½-inch strips. Dry with paper towels. Place in large bowl. Add oil. Toss to coat. Place potatoes in single layer on unprepared baking sheet.

3. Combine celery salt, garlic powder, pepper and paprika in small bowl. Sprinkle potatoes with half of seasoning mixture. Turn potatoes over. Sprinkle with remaining seasoning mixture.

4. Bake at 425°F for 25 to 30 minutes or until potatoes are tender and evenly browned, turning occasionally. *Do not overbake.* Remove baking sheet to cooling rack. Serve warm. *Makes 6 servings*

orange sesame couscous

nutrients per serving:

1 cup

Calories: 236
Carbohydrate: 48 g
Calories From Fat: 8%
Total Fat: 2 g
Saturated Fat: <1 g
Cholesterol: 0 mg
Sodium: 103 mg
Dietary Fiber: 4 g
Protein: 7 g

1 cup fresh orange juice (3 SUNKIST® oranges)
½ cup chopped red or green bell pepper
1 teaspoon sesame oil
⅛ teaspoon salt
⅔ cup uncooked couscous
1 SUNKIST® orange, peeled and cut into bite-size pieces
3 tablespoons chopped green onions

In medium saucepan, combine orange juice, bell pepper, sesame oil and salt. Bring just to a boil; stir in couscous. Cover and remove from heat. Let stand 5 minutes. Stir with fork to fluff up mixture. Stir in orange pieces and green onions.

Makes 3 servings

boston baked beans

nutrients per serving:
⅛ of total recipe

Calories: 179
Carbohydrate: 31 g
Calories From Fat: 10%
Total Fat: 2 g
Saturated Fat: 1 g
Cholesterol: 5 mg
Sodium: 728 mg
Dietary Fiber: <1 g
Protein: 10 g

**2 cans (about 15 ounces each) navy or Great Northern beans,
   rinsed and drained**
½ cup beer (not dark beer)
⅓ cup minced red or yellow onion
⅓ cup ketchup
3 tablespoons light molasses
2 teaspoons Worcestershire sauce
1 teaspoon dry mustard
½ teaspoon ground ginger
4 slices turkey bacon

1. Preheat oven to 350°F. Place beans in 11×7-inch glass baking dish. Combine beer, onion, ketchup, molasses, Worcestershire sauce, mustard and ginger in medium bowl. Pour over beans; toss to coat.

2. Cut bacon into 1-inch pieces; arrange in single layer over beans. Bake, uncovered, 40 to 45 minutes or until most of liquid is absorbed and bacon is browned.

Makes 8 servings

rigatoni with broccoli

nutrients per serving:
¼ of total recipe

Calories: 278
Carbohydrate: 47 g
Calories From Fat: 17%
Total Fat: 5 g
Saturated Fat: 1 g
Cholesterol: 2 mg
Sodium: 72 mg
Dietary Fiber: 4 g
Protein: 11 g

8 ounces uncooked rigatoni pasta
**1 bunch fresh broccoli, trimmed and separated into florets with
   1-inch stems**
1 tablespoon FILIPPO BERIO® Extra Virgin Olive Oil
1 clove garlic, minced
Crushed red pepper
Grated Parmesan cheese

Cook pasta according to package directions until al dente (tender but still firm). Add broccoli during last 5 minutes of cooking time; cook until broccoli is tender-crisp. Drain pasta and broccoli; transfer to large bowl. Meanwhile, in small skillet, heat olive oil over medium heat until hot. Add garlic; cook and stir 1 to 2 minutes or until golden. Pour oil mixture over hot pasta mixture; toss until lightly coated. Season to taste with red pepper. Top with cheese.

Makes 4 servings

nutrients per serving:

1 cup Squash plus
1 cup sauce

Calories: 179
Carbohydrate: 35 g
Calories From Fat: 14%
Total Fat: 3 g
Saturated Fat: 1 g
Cholesterol: 4 mg
Sodium: 240 mg
Dietary Fiber: 6 g
Protein: 8 g

spaghetti squash primavera

1 medium spaghetti squash (about 3 pounds)
1 can (28 ounces) low-sodium diced tomatoes
2 cups sliced mushrooms
1 cup grated carrot
¼ cup diced red bell pepper
½ cup frozen green peas
1 teaspoon Italian seasoning or oregano
1 teaspoon prepared crushed garlic
1 tablespoon balsamic vinegar
¼ cup shredded Parmesan cheese

1. Pierce spaghetti squash to center in several places. Place on microwavable plate; microwave at HIGH (100% power) 20 minutes. (If microwave lacks turntable, turn squash three times during cooking.) Remove from microwave; cut in half lengthwise. When cool enough to handle, scrape out seeds. Set aside.

2. Place tomatoes in 2½-quart heavy saucepan. Bring to a boil over medium-high heat. Add mushrooms, carrots, bell pepper, peas, oregano, garlic and vinegar. Reduce heat; cover and simmer 15 minutes until sauce is thick.

3. To serve, shred spaghetti squash with fork into four pasta bowls, about 1 cup per bowl. Top with 1 cup sauce. Garnish each serving with cheese.   *Makes 4 servings*

Serving Suggestion: Serve with a large green salad and your favorite bottled low-fat dressing.

spaghetti squash primavera

nutrients per serving:

⅙ of total recipe

Calories: 123
Carbohydrate: 19 g
Calories From Fat: 24%
Total Fat: 3 g
Saturated Fat: 1 g
Cholesterol: 1 mg
Sodium: 200 mg
Dietary Fiber: 1 g
Protein: 5 g

green bean casserole

> **Ranch-Style White Sauce (recipe follows)**
> **1 cup chopped onion**
> **2 cloves garlic, minced**
> **1½ cups sliced fresh mushrooms**
> **1¼ pounds fresh green beans, cooked until crisp-tender**
> **1 cup fresh bread crumbs**
> **2 tablespoons minced fresh parsley**

1. Preheat oven to 350°F. Prepare Ranch-Style White Sauce; set aside. Spray medium skillet with nonstick cooking spray; heat over medium-high heat. Add onion and garlic; cook 2 to 3 minutes or until tender. Remove half of onion mixture; set aside.

2. Add mushrooms to skillet and cook about 5 minutes or until tender. Combine mushroom mixture, beans and sauce in 1½-quart casserole.

3. Spray medium skillet with nonstick cooking spray; heat over medium heat. Add bread crumbs to skillet; spray top of crumbs lightly with nonstick cooking spray. Cook 3 to 4 minutes or until crumbs are golden. Stir in reserved onion mixture and parsley. Sprinkle bread crumb mixture over casserole. Bake, uncovered, 20 to 30 minutes or until heated through. *Makes 6 servings*

Tip: There is no need to peel garlic if you are using a garlic press. The garlic gets passed through the press leaving the skin behind.

Prep Time: 10 minutes
Cook Time: 35 to 40 minutes

ranch-style white sauce

> **1½ tablespoons margarine**
> **3 tablespoons all-purpose flour**
> **1½ cups fat-free (skim) milk**
> **3 to 4 teaspoons dry ranch-style salad dressing mix**
> **¼ to ½ teaspoon white pepper**

Melt margarine in small saucepan over low heat. Stir in flour; cook 1 to 2 minutes, stirring constantly. Using wire whisk, stir in milk; bring to a boil. Cook, whisking constantly, 1 to 2 minutes or until thickened. Stir in dressing mix and pepper.

Makes 1½ cups

green bean casserole

nutrients per serving:

¼ of total recipe

Calories: 47

Carbohydrate: 9 g

Calories From Fat: 24%

Total Fat: 1 g

Saturated Fat: <1 g

Cholesterol: 0 mg

Sodium: 15 mg

Dietary Fiber: 2 g

Protein: 1 g

lemon and fennel marinated vegetables

1 cup water
2 medium carrots, cut diagonally into ½-inch-thick slices
1 cup small whole fresh mushrooms
1 small red or green bell pepper, cut into ¾-inch pieces
3 tablespoons lemon juice
1 tablespoon sugar
1 tablespoon olive oil
1 clove garlic, minced
½ teaspoon fennel seeds, crushed
½ teaspoon dried basil leaves, crushed
¼ teaspoon black pepper

Bring water to a boil over high heat in small saucepan. Add carrots. Return to a boil. Reduce heat to medium-low. Cover and simmer about 5 minutes or until carrots are crisp-tender. Drain and cool.

Place carrots, mushrooms and bell pepper in large resealable plastic food storage bag. Combine lemon juice, sugar, oil, garlic, fennel seeds, basil and black pepper in small bowl. Pour over vegetables. Close bag securely; turn to coat. Marinate in refrigerator 8 to 24 hours, turning occasionally.

Drain vegetables; discard marinade. Place vegetables in serving dish. Serve with toothpicks.   *Makes 4 servings*

lemon and fennel marinated vegetables

creamy spinach and brown rice

1½ cups sliced fresh mushrooms
½ cup thinly sliced leek, white part only
2 teaspoons reduced-fat margarine
2 cups fat-free (skim) milk
½ cup brown rice
⅓ cup shredded low-fat Swiss cheese
1 tablespoon chopped fresh thyme *or* 1 teaspoon dried
thyme leaves, crushed
⅛ teaspoon black pepper
2 cups chopped stemmed washed spinach

Cook and stir mushrooms and leek in margarine in medium saucepan over medium-high heat until leek is tender. Add milk and brown rice. Bring to a boil over medium-high heat. Reduce heat to medium-low. Cover; simmer 45 to 50 minutes or until rice is tender, stirring frequently. Remove from heat.

Add cheese, thyme and pepper. Cook and stir until cheese melts. Stir in spinach. Cover; let stand 5 minutes. *Makes 4 servings*

tip

All spinach should be well washed and rinsed to remove the sand and grit that adheres to the leaves. First, remove any roots or slimy leaves and soak the spinach leaves in a sinkful of cold water for a few minutes. Then swish the leaves gently to remove dirt and sand. Repeat this process several times with fresh water, if necessary.

creamy spinach and brown rice

lemon-tossed linguine

8 ounces uncooked linguine noodles
3 tablespoons fresh lemon juice
2 teaspoons reduced-fat margarine
2 tablespoons minced chives
⅓ cup fat-free (skim) milk
1 teaspoon cornstarch
1 tablespoon minced fresh dill *or* **1 teaspoon dried dill weed**
1 tablespoon minced fresh parsley *or* **1 teaspoon dried**
    parsley flakes
2 teaspoons grated lemon peel
¼ teaspoon white pepper
3 tablespoons grated Romano or Parmesan cheese
    Lemon slices (optional)
    Dill sprigs (optional)

Cook linguine according to package directions, omitting salt. Drain well. Place in medium bowl; sprinkle lemon juice over noodles.

Meanwhile, melt margarine in small saucepan over medium heat. Add chives; cook until chives are soft. Combine milk and cornstarch in small bowl; stir into saucepan. Cook and stir until thickened. Stir in dill, parsley, lemon peel and pepper.

Pour milk mixture over noodles. Sprinkle with cheese; toss to coat evenly. Garnish with lemon slices and dill sprigs, if desired. Serve immediately.   *Makes 3 servings*

lemon-tossed linguine

sesame honey vegetable casserole

**1 package (16 ounces) frozen mixed vegetables such as baby
    carrots, broccoli, onions and red peppers, thawed and drained**
3 tablespoons honey
1 tablespoon dark sesame oil
1 tablespoon reduced-sodium soy sauce
2 teaspoons sesame seeds

1. Heat oven to 350°F. Place mixed vegetables in shallow 1½-quart casserole dish or quiche dish.

2. Combine honey, oil, soy sauce and sesame seeds; mix well. Drizzle evenly over vegetables. Bake 20 to 25 minutes or until vegetables are hot, stirring after 15 minutes.

Makes 4 side-dish servings

nutrients per serving:

¼ of total recipe

Calories: 176
Carbohydrate: 28 g
Calories From Fat: 27%
Total Fat: 5 g
Saturated Fat: 1 g
Cholesterol: 0 mg
Sodium: 173 mg
Dietary Fiber: 3 g
Protein: 4 g

mediterranean baked potato topper

½ cup chopped red bell pepper
¼ cup part-skim ricotta cheese
¼ cup reduced-fat sour cream
1 large clove garlic, crushed
1 teaspoon dried basil leaves
¼ teaspoon salt
¼ teaspoon black pepper
½ cup chopped and seeded plum tomato
4 large hot baked potatoes, cut into halves

Combine bell pepper, cheese, sour cream, garlic, basil, salt and black pepper in small bowl. Mix well. Add tomatoes. Toss gently. Cover and refrigerate at least 2 hours. To serve, divide and spoon topping over potato halves.

Makes 8 servings

nutrients per serving:

1 Potato half

Calories: 98
Carbohydrate: 20 g
Calories From Fat: 12%
Total Fat: 1 g
Saturated Fat: 1 g
Cholesterol: 5 mg
Sodium: 93 mg
Dietary Fiber: 2 g
Protein: 3 g

sesame honey vegetable casserole

wild rice and lentil pilaf

4½ cups water, divided
¾ cup dried brown lentils, sorted, rinsed and drained
1 tablespoon plus 2 teaspoons extra-virgin olive oil, divided
2 cups finely chopped yellow onions
1 medium red bell pepper, chopped
1 cup thinly sliced celery
4 cloves garlic, minced
½ teaspoon dried oregano leaves
½ teaspoon salt
  Dash ground red pepper (optional)
1 box (6.2-ounce) quick-cooking white and wild rice with seasoning packet

1. Bring 4 cups water to a boil in medium saucepan. Stir in lentils and return to a boil. Reduce heat to low and simmer, uncovered, 10 minutes.

2. Meanwhile, heat large nonstick skillet over medium-high heat until hot. Coat skillet with nonstick cooking spray. Add 2 teaspoons oil and tilt skillet to coat bottom evenly. Add onions, bell pepper, celery, garlic and oregano; cook 12 minutes or until celery is crisp-tender, stirring frequently. Stir in remaining ½ cup water, salt and ground red pepper.

3. When lentils have cooked 10 minutes, stir in rice and seasoning packet. Cover tightly and simmer 5 minutes. Remove from heat. Stir in onion mixture and remaining 1 tablespoon oil; toss gently. *Makes 7 servings*

Variation: For a more decorative dish, coat a 6-cup mold with cooking spray. Place rice mixture in mold and press down gently but firmly to allow rice mixture to stick together. Place a dinner plate on top of mold and invert mold onto plate. Tap gently on side and top of mold to release rice mixture and slowly remove mold. Garnish with red bell pepper cutouts or strips.

wild rice and lentil pilaf

magnificent main meals

nutrients per serving:

1 Kabob with sauce

Calories: 286
Carbohydrate: 27 g
Calories From Fat: 23%
Total Fat: 8 g
Saturated Fat: 3 g
Cholesterol: 77 mg
Sodium: 1,273 mg
Dietary Fiber: 4 g
Protein: 31 g

southern style mustard bbq chicken kabobs

1½ cups catsup
1 cup prepared mustard
½ to ⅔ cup cider vinegar
½ cup EQUAL® SPOONFUL*
2 tablespoons stick butter or margarine
1 tablespoon Worcestershire sauce
½ teaspoon maple flavoring
½ teaspoon coarsely ground black pepper
1½ pounds skinless, boneless chicken breasts, cut into ¾-inch cubes
2 small yellow summer squash, cut crosswise into 1-inch slices
12 medium mushroom caps
1 large red or green bell pepper, cut into 1-inch pieces

May substitute 12 packets Equal® sweetener.

• Mix all ingredients, except chicken and vegetables, in medium saucepan. Cook over medium heat 3 to 4 minutes or until sauce is hot and butter is melted.

• Assemble chicken cubes and vegetables on skewers; grill over medium heat 10 to 15 minutes until chicken is no longer pink, turning occasionally and basting generously with sauce. Bring remaining sauce to a boil in small saucepan. Boil 5 minutes. Serve with kabobs.   *Makes 6 servings*

Tip: Kabobs can also be baked. Arrange kabobs in greased baking pan; spray with nonstick cooking spray. Bake, uncovered, in preheated 375°F oven until chicken is no longer pink and vegetables are tender, about 20 minutes. Turn kabobs and baste generously with sauce during last 10 minutes of baking time.

Tip: Kabobs can also be broiled. Broil 6 inches from heat source until chicken is no longer pink and vegetables are tender, 10 to 12 minutes, turning occasionally and basting generously with sauce. Do not baste during last 5 minutes of broiling.

southern style mustard bbq chicken kabobs

blackberry-glazed pork medallions

⅓ cup no-sugar-added seedless blackberry spread
1½ tablespoons red wine vinegar
1 tablespoon sugar
¼ teaspoon red pepper flakes
1 teaspoon vegetable oil
1 pound pork tenderloin, cut in ¼-inch slices
¼ teaspoon dried thyme leaves, divided
¼ teaspoon salt, divided

1. Whisk blackberry spread, vinegar, sugar and red pepper flakes in small bowl until blended; set aside.

2. Heat large nonstick skillet over medium-high heat until hot. Coat skillet with nonstick cooking spray; add oil and tilt skillet to coat bottom. Add half of pork slices; sprinkle with half of thyme and half of salt. Cook 2 minutes; turn and cook 1 minute on other side. Remove pork from skillet and set aside. Repeat with remaining pork, thyme and salt.

3. Add blackberry mixture to skillet; bring to a boil over high heat. Add reserved pork slices, discarding any accumulated juices. Cook about 4 minutes, turning constantly, until pork is richly glazed. *Makes 4 servings*

blackberry-glazed pork medallions

broiled caribbean sea bass

6 skinless sea bass or striped bass fillets (5 to 6 ounces each), about ½ inch thick
⅓ cup chopped fresh cilantro
2 tablespoons olive oil
2 tablespoons fresh lime juice
2 teaspoons hot pepper sauce
2 cloves garlic, minced
1 package (7 ounces) black bean and rice mix
Lime wedges

1. Place fish in shallow dish. Combine cilantro, oil, lime juice, pepper sauce and garlic in small bowl; pour over fish. Cover; marinate in refrigerator 30 minutes, but no longer than 2 hours.

2. Prepare black bean and rice mix according to package directions; keep warm.

3. Preheat broiler. Remove fish from marinade. Place fish on rack of broiler pan; drizzle with any remaining marinade in dish. Broil, 4 to 5 inches from heat, 8 to 10 minutes or until fish is opaque. Serve fish with black beans and rice and lime wedges.

Makes 6 servings

tip

Fish is generally separated into two categories, lean and fatty. Lean fish contain from 1 to 5 percent fat. Fatty fish contain from 5 to 35 percent fat, which makes their flesh darker, richer and stronger tasting than lean fish. The type of fish is an important factor when preparing and cooking it.

broiled caribbean sea bass

south-of-the-border lunch express

nutrients per serving:

total recipe (without cheese)

Calories: 345
Carbohydrate: 74 g
Calories From Fat: 7%
Total Fat: 3 g
Saturated Fat: <1 g
Cholesterol: 0 mg
Sodium: 610 mg
Dietary Fiber: 11 g
Protein: 14 g

½ **cup chopped tomato**
¼ **cup chunky salsa**
¼ **cup rinsed and drained black beans**
¼ **cup frozen whole kernel corn, thawed**
1 **teaspoon chopped fresh cilantro**
¼ **teaspoon bottled chopped garlic**
   Dash ground red pepper
1 **cup cooked brown rice**
   Reduced-fat Cheddar cheese (optional)

1. Combine tomato, salsa, beans, corn, cilantro, garlic and pepper in 1-quart microwavable bowl. Cover with vented plastic wrap. Microwave at HIGH (100%) 1 to 1½ minutes or until heated through; stir.

2. Microwave rice at HIGH 1 to 1½ minutes in 1-quart microwavable dish or until heated through. Top with tomato mixture and cheese, if desired.   *Makes 1 serving*

shrimp stir-fry

nutrients per serving:

⅙ of total recipe

Calories: 218
Carbohydrate: 34 g
Calories From Fat: 6%
Total Fat: 2 g
Saturated Fat: <1 g
Cholesterol: 111 mg
Sodium: 358 mg
Dietary Fiber: 4 g
Protein: 18 g

1 **bag SUCCESS® Brown Rice**
   Vegetable cooking spray
1 **tablespoon cornstarch**
2 **tablespoons reduced-sodium soy sauce**
3 **medium carrots, sliced**
1 **medium yellow bell pepper, cut into strips**
¾ **pound cleaned, cooked shrimp (or any other cooked meat)**
½ **pound snow pea pods, trimmed**
¾ **cup plain nonfat yogurt**

Prepare rice according to package directions.

Spray skillet or wok with cooking spray. Combine cornstarch and soy sauce in small bowl; mix well. Set aside. Add carrots and bell pepper to hot skillet; stir-fry until crisp-tender. Stir cornstarch mixture. Add to vegetable mixture; cook and stir until sauce is thickened. Remove from heat. Stir in shrimp, pea pods and yogurt; heat thoroughly, stirring occasionally, about 5 minutes. Serve over hot rice. Garnish, if desired.   *Makes 6 servings*

south-of-the-border lunch express

sausage & mushroom pasta

1 can (10¾ ounces) reduced-fat condensed tomato soup
¼ cup fat-free (skim) milk
½ cup chopped onion
½ cup chopped green bell pepper
2 cloves garlic, minced
1 teaspoon dried Italian seasoning
1 cup sliced mushrooms
½ teaspoon salt (optional)
1 (7-ounce package) reduced-fat smoked turkey sausage, cut into ⅛-inch slices
4 cups cooked bow tie pasta

Combine soup and milk in small bowl; mix well and set aside. Spray large nonstick skillet with nonstick cooking spray; heat over medium-high heat until hot. Add onion, pepper, garlic and Italian seasoning; cook and stir until onion and peppers are tender. Add mushrooms and salt; cook and stir 2 to 3 minutes. Add sausage; mix well. Reduce heat; cover and simmer an additional 2 minutes. Add pasta; toss until coated with sauce. *Makes 6 servings*

tip

Non-egg pastas contain no cholesterol. Noodles (pasta made with eggs) are low in cholesterol. Pasta is also an excellent source of complex carbohydrates. It also contains six essential amino acids, three B-complex vitamins and iron.

sausage & mushroom pasta

toasted ravioli with fresh tomato-basil salsa

1 package (9 ounces) refrigerated cheese ravioli
Nonstick olive oil cooking spray
¾ cup plain dry bread crumbs
2 tablespoons grated Parmesan cheese
1 teaspoon dried basil leaves
1 teaspoon dried oregano leaves
¼ teaspoon black pepper
2 egg whites
Fresh Tomato-Basil Salsa (recipe follows)

1. Cook ravioli according to package directions, omitting salt. Rinse under cold running water until ravioli are cool; drain well.

2. Preheat oven to 375°F. Spray large nonstick baking sheet with cooking spray.

3. Combine bread crumbs, cheese, basil, oregano and pepper in medium bowl.

4. Beat egg whites lightly in shallow dish. Add ravioli; toss lightly to coat. Transfer ravioli, a few at a time, to crumb mixture; toss to coat evenly. Arrange on prepared baking sheet. Repeat with remaining ravioli. Spray tops of ravioli with cooking spray.

5. Bake 12 to 14 minutes or until crisp. Meanwhile, prepare Fresh Tomato-Basil Salsa; serve with ravioli. Garnish, if desired.   *Makes 8 servings*

fresh tomato-basil salsa

1 pound fresh tomatoes, peeled and seeded
½ cup loosely packed fresh basil leaves
¼ small onion (about 2×1-inch piece)
1 teaspoon red wine vinegar
¼ teaspoon salt

Combine ingredients in food processor; process until finely chopped but not smooth.
Makes about 1 cup

toasted ravioli with fresh tomato-basil salsa

spiced turkey with fruit salsa

nutrients per serving:

½ of total recipe

Calories: 125
Carbohydrate: 11 g
Calories From Fat: 13%
Total Fat: 2 g
Saturated Fat: 1 g
Cholesterol: 34 mg
Sodium: 264 mg
Dietary Fiber: 2 g
Protein: 16 g

6 ounces turkey breast tenderloin
2 teaspoons lime juice
1 teaspoon mesquite seasoning blend or ground cumin
½ cup frozen pitted sweet cherries, thawed and cut into halves*
¼ cup chunky salsa

Drained canned sweet cherries can be substituted for frozen cherries.

1. Prepare grill for direct grilling. Brush both sides of turkey with lime juice. Sprinkle with mesquite seasoning.

2. Grill turkey over medium coals 15 to 20 minutes or until turkey is no longer pink in center and juices run clear, turning once.

3. Meanwhile, stir together cherries and salsa.

4. Thinly slice turkey. Spoon salsa mixture over turkey.   *Makes 2 servings*

vegetable-shrimp stir-fry

nutrients per serving:

¼ of total recipe

Calories: 199
Carbohydrate: 8 g
Calories From Fat: 28%
Total Fat: 6 g
Saturated Fat: 1 g
Cholesterol: 221 mg
Sodium: 721 mg
Dietary Fiber: 3 g
Protein: 27 g

1 tablespoon olive oil
6 ounces snow peas, trimmed
6 green onions, cut into 1-inch pieces
1 red bell pepper, cut into ½-inch strips
1 pound peeled, deveined medium shrimp
¼ pound large mushrooms, quartered
2 tablespoons soy sauce
1 tablespoon seasoned rice vinegar
1 teaspoon sesame oil

1. Heat olive oil in large skillet or wok over medium-high heat. Add snow peas, onions and bell pepper; stir-fry 2 minutes.

2. Add shrimp; stir-fry 2 minutes or until shrimp turn pink.

3. Add mushrooms; stir-fry until tender and most of liquid evaporates.

4. Add remaining ingredients; heat thoroughly, stirring constantly.

Makes 4 servings

spiced turkey with fruit salsa

healthy fettuccine primavera

nutrients per serving:

⅙ of total recipe

Calories: 178
Carbohydrate: 34 g
Calories From Fat: 13%
Total Fat: 3 g
Saturated Fat: 1 g
Cholesterol: 7 mg
Sodium: 616 mg
Dietary Fiber: 4 g
Protein: 7 g

1 can (10¾ ounces) reduced-fat condensed cream of chicken soup, undiluted
⅓ cup fat-free (skim) milk
2 cloves garlic, minced
½ teaspoon salt
½ teaspoon dried Italian seasoning
⅛ teaspoon fennel seeds, crushed
4 cups sliced fresh vegetables (peppers, zucchini, carrots, asparagus) or thawed frozen vegetables
1 cup coarsely chopped fresh plum tomatoes
4 cups hot cooked fettuccine

Combine soup, milk, garlic, salt, Italian seasoning and fennel in small bowl; set aside. Spray large nonstick skillet with vegetable cooking spray. Sauté vegetables over medium heat 4 to 5 minutes.* Stir in soup mixture; simmer 3 to 4 minutes. Add tomato; mix well. Serve over hot fettuccine. *Makes 6 servings*

½ pound cooked chicken, turkey sausage or shrimp may be added at this point.

healthy fettuccine primavera

washington apple turkey gyros

1 cup vertically sliced onion
1 cup thinly sliced red bell pepper
1 cup thinly sliced green bell pepper
2 tablespoons lemon juice
1 tablespoon vegetable oil
½ pound cooked turkey breast, cut into thin strips
1 medium Washington Golden Delicious or Winesap apple,
   cored and thinly sliced
8 pita rounds, lightly toasted
½ cup plain low fat yogurt

Cook and stir onion, bell peppers and lemon juice in oil in nonstick skillet until crisp-tender; stir in turkey and cook until heated through. Remove from heat; stir in apple. Fold pita in half and fill with apple mixture; drizzle with yogurt. Repeat with remaining ingredients. Serve warm. *Makes 8 servings*

Favorite recipe from **Washington Apple Commission**

tip

Today, turkey is no longer restricted to the Thanksgiving table. Because it is low in fat, it is masquerading as everything from bologna to hot dogs to ham. Ground turkey and fresh turkey pieces, now available year-round in supermarket meat cases, are finding their way to the dinner table with increasing frequency.

washington apple turkey gyro

chicken with orange almond sauce

nutrients per serving:

¼ of total recipe

Calories: 188
Carbohydrate: 21 g
Calories From Fat: 16%
Total Fat: 3 g
Saturated Fat: <1 g
Cholesterol: 43 mg
Sodium: 47 mg
Dietary Fiber: 1 g
Protein: 19 g

Butter-flavored cooking spray
4 (4 ounces each) skinless boneless chicken breast halves
1 cup orange juice
⅓ cup SPLENDA® Granular
2 tablespoons cornstarch
1 can (11 ounces) mandarin oranges, rinsed and drained
2 tablespoons slivered almonds
1 teaspoon dried onion flakes
1 teaspoon dried parsley flakes

1. In large skillet sprayed with cooking spray, brown chicken pieces for 4 to 5 minutes on each side.

2. Meanwhile, in covered jar, combine orange juice, SPLENDA® and cornstarch. Shake well to blend.

3. Pour sauce mixture into medium saucepan sprayed with cooking spray. Cook over medium heat until mixture thickens, stirring constantly. Remove from heat.

4. Stir mandarin oranges, almonds, onion flakes and parsley flakes into sauce. Spoon sauce evenly over browned chicken breasts.

5. Reduce heat and simmer for 5 minutes. When serving, evenly spoon sauce over chicken breasts.

Makes 4 servings

chicken with orange almond sauce

stanley sandwiches

nutrients per serving:
1 Sandwich

Calories: 236
Carbohydrate: 35 g
Calories From Fat: 12%
Total Fat: 3 g
Saturated Fat: 1 g
Cholesterol: 20 mg
Sodium: 815 mg
Dietary Fiber: 2 g
Protein: 16 g

½ cup shredded carrot
2 tablespoons bottled reduced-fat ranch salad dressing
½ (12-ounce) focaccia
3 lettuce leaves
6 ounces thinly sliced reduced-fat, reduced-sodium deli-style
    roast beef, roast chicken or roast turkey

1. Stir together carrot and salad dressing. Cut focaccia into 3 pieces. Split each piece horizontally. Place lettuce leaves on bottom halves. Top with meat. Spoon carrot mixture on top. Top with remaining focaccia halves. Wrap in plastic wrap.

2. Pack in insulated bag with ice pack, if desired.

Makes 3 servings

open-faced smoked turkey and asparagus sandwiches

nutrients per serving:
1 Sandwich

Calories: 161
Carbohydrate: 26 g
Calories From Fat: 17%
Total Fat: 4 g
Saturated Fat: 1 g
Cholesterol: 15 mg
Sodium: 810 mg
Dietary Fiber: 5 g
Protein: 18 g

1 box (10 ounces) BIRDS EYE® frozen Deluxe Asparagus Cuts
½ pound smoked turkey breast, cubed
2 tablespoons creamy mustard blend
1 teaspoon honey
4 thick slices whole grain bread, lightly toasted
    Lettuce leaves
1 large tomato, sliced

• In small saucepan, cook asparagus according to package directions; drain in colander and rinse under cold water to cool.

• In large bowl, combine asparagus, turkey, mustard and honey.

• To assemble sandwiches, line bread slices with lettuce. Top with tomato and turkey mixture, dividing evenly.

Makes 4 servings

Serving Suggestion: Serve sandwiches topped with ½ cup alfalfa sprouts.

Birds Eye Idea: When microwaving vegetables, do not salt them until they are cooked. Salting vegetables before cooking will leave dark spots.

Prep Time: 5 minutes
Cook Time: 15 minutes

stanley sandwich

crab and corn enchilada casserole

nutrients per
serving:

⅙ of total recipe
(without sour cream)

Calories: 366
Carbohydrate: 51 g
Calories From Fat: 20%
Total Fat: 9 g
Saturated Fat: 2 g
Cholesterol: 46 mg
Sodium: 343 mg
Dietary Fiber: 7 g
Protein: 27 g

Spicy Tomato Sauce (recipe follows), divided
10 to 12 ounces fresh crabmeat or flaked or chopped surimi crab
1 package (10 ounces) frozen corn, thawed and drained
**1½ cups (6 ounces) shredded reduced-fat Monterey Jack cheese,
    divided**
1 can (4 ounces) diced mild green chilies
12 (6-inch) corn tortillas
1 lime, cut into 6 wedges
Sour cream (optional)

1. Preheat oven to 350°F. Prepare Spicy Tomato Sauce.

2. Combine 2 cups Spicy Tomato Sauce, crabmeat, corn, 1 cup cheese and chilies in medium bowl. Cut each tortilla into 4 wedges. Place one-third of tortilla wedges in bottom of shallow 3- to 4-quart casserole, overlapping to make solid layer. Spread half of crab mixture on top. Repeat with another layer of tortilla wedges, remaining crab mixture and remaining tortillas. Spread remaining 1 cup Spicy Tomato Sauce over top; cover.

3. Bake 30 to 40 minutes or until heated through. Sprinkle with remaining ½ cup cheese; bake uncovered 5 minutes or until cheese melts. Squeeze lime over individual servings. Serve with sour cream, if desired.   *Makes 6 servings*

spicy tomato sauce

**2 cans (15 ounces each) no-salt-added stewed tomatoes, undrained
    or 6 medium tomatoes**
2 teaspoons olive oil
1 medium onion, chopped
1 tablespoon minced garlic
2 tablespoons chili powder
2 teaspoons ground cumin
2 teaspoons dried oregano leaves, crushed
1 teaspoon ground cinnamon
¼ teaspoon red pepper flakes
¼ teaspoon ground cloves

1. Place tomatoes with juice in food processor or blender; process until finely chopped. Set aside.

2. Heat oil over medium-high heat in large saucepan or Dutch oven. Add onion and garlic. Cook and stir 5 minutes or until onion is tender. Add chili powder, cumin, oregano, cinnamon, red pepper flakes and cloves. Cook and stir 1 minute. Add tomatoes; reduce heat to medium-low. Simmer, uncovered, 20 minutes or until sauce is reduced to 3 to 3¼ cups. *Makes about 3 cups sauce*

marinated steak with parslied rice

nutrients per serving:
⅛ of total recipe
Calories: 297
Carbohydrate: 30 g
Calories From Fat: 18%
Total Fat: 6 g
Saturated Fat: 2 g
Cholesterol: 64 mg
Sodium: 121 mg
Dietary Fiber: 1 g
Protein: 29 g

Oriental Marinade
½ cup CRISCO® Oil*
⅓ cup soy sauce
¾ teaspoon ginger
1 clove garlic, minced *or* ⅛ teaspoon garlic powder

Meat
1 beef top round steak, ¾ to 1 inch thick (about 2 pounds)

Rice
5⅓ cups hot cooked rice (cooked without salt or fat)
⅓ cup chopped fresh parsley

*Use your favorite Crisco Oil product.

1. Combine all marinade ingredients in shallow bowl. Add meat, turning to coat all surfaces. Refrigerate at least 30 minutes, turning meat after 15 minutes and spooning marinade over meat.

2. Heat broiler or prepare grill.

3. Remove meat from marinade; discard marinade. Broil or grill meat to desired doneness. Cut diagonally into very thin slices.

4. Toss hot rice with parsley. Serve with meat. Garnish, if desired.

Makes 8 servings

creole beans and rice

2 cans (14½ ounces *each*) peeled no salt added tomatoes, undrained
1 cup uncooked rice
2 tablespoons CRISCO® Oil*
½ cup chopped onion
4 cloves garlic, minced
1 cup chopped celery
1 cup chopped carrots
1 cup chopped green bell pepper
1 tablespoon ground cumin
1 tablespoon chili powder
1 teaspoon dried basil leaves
½ teaspoon cayenne pepper
2 cans (15½ ounces *each*) kidney beans, drained
1 can (6 ounces) no salt added tomato paste
3 tablespoons vinegar
1 tablespoon Worcestershire sauce
1 teaspoon sugar

*Use your favorite Crisco Oil product.

1. Drain tomatoes, reserving liquid. Add enough water to reserved liquid to measure 2 cups. Pour into medium saucepan. Add rice. Bring to a boil on medium-high heat. Reduce heat to low. Simmer 20 minutes or until rice is tender.

2. Heat oil in large saucepan on medium heat. Add onion and garlic. Cook and stir until tender. Add celery and carrots. Cook and stir until crisp-tender. Add green pepper, cumin, chili powder, basil and cayenne. Cook and stir until green pepper is tender.

3. Add tomatoes. Break up with spoon. Stir in rice, beans, tomato paste, vinegar, Worcestershire sauce and sugar. Reduce heat to low. Heat thoroughly, stirring occasionally. Garnish, if desired.

Makes 8 servings

creole beans and rice

moo shu pork

nutrients per serving:

2 tortillas, each filled with ⅛ of Pork mixture (without sauce or garnish)

Calories: 353
Carbohydrate: 48 g
Calories From Fat: 22%
Total Fat: 9 g
Saturated Fat: 2 g
Cholesterol: 37 mg
Sodium: 467 mg
Dietary Fiber: 3 g
Protein: 19 g

1 cup DOLE® Pineapple Juice
1 tablespoon low-sodium soy sauce
2 teaspoons sesame seed oil
2 teaspoons cornstarch
8 ounces pork tenderloin, cut into thin strips
1½ cups Oriental-style mixed vegetables
¼ cup hoisin sauce (optional)
8 (8-inch) flour tortillas, warmed
2 green onions, cut into thin strips

• **Stir** juice, soy sauce, sesame seed oil and cornstarch in shallow, nonmetallic dish until blended; remove ½ cup mixture for sauce.

• **Add** pork to remaining juice mixture in shallow dish. Cover and marinate 15 minutes in refrigerator. Drain pork; discard marinade.

• **Cook** and stir pork in large, nonstick skillet over medium-high heat 2 minutes or until pork is lightly browned. Add vegetables; cook and stir 3 to 4 minutes or until vegetables are tender-crisp. Stir in reserved ½ cup juice mixture; cook 1 minute or until sauce thickens.

• **Spread** hoisin sauce onto center of each tortilla, if desired; top with moo shu pork. Sprinkle with green onions. Fold opposite sides of tortilla over filling; fold remaining sides of tortilla over filling. Garnish with slivered green onions, kumquats and fresh herbs, if desired.

Makes 4 servings

Prep Time: 10 minutes
Marinate Time: 15 minutes
Cook Time: 10 minutes

moo shu pork

nutrients per
serving:
¼ of total recipe

Calories: 398
Carbohydrate: 52 g
Calories From Fat: 23%
Total Fat: 10 g
Saturated Fat: 2 g
Cholesterol: 100 mg
Sodium: 320 mg
Dietary Fiber: 4 g
Protein: 23 g

chicken & beans with pasta

½ pound boneless skinless chicken breasts, cut into bite-size strips
 1 small carrot, chopped
½ cup chopped onion
⅓ cup thinly sliced celery
 2 cloves garlic, finely chopped
 2 tablespoons FLEISCHMANN'S® Original Margarine
 1 (14-ounce) can whole peeled tomatoes, coarsely chopped
½ cup canned cannellini beans, drained
 8 ounces bow-tie pasta, cooked and drained
   Fresh chopped parsley and grated Parmesan cheese, optional

1. Cook and stir chicken, carrot, onion, celery and garlic in margarine in large skillet over medium-high heat until chicken is no longer pink and vegetables are tender.

2. Add tomatoes and beans; reduce heat and cook for 15 minutes.

3. Toss bean mixture with hot cooked pasta. Garnish with parsley and cheese if desired.

Makes 4 servings

Prep Time: 15 minutes
Cook Time: 25 minutes
Total Time: 40 minutes

chicken & beans with pasta

peppercorn beef kabobs

nutrients per serving:

1 Kabob (without tomato garnish)

Calories: 158
Carbohydrate: 3 g
Calories From Fat: 26%
Total Fat: 4 g
Saturated Fat: 2 g
Cholesterol: 54 mg
Sodium: 339 mg
Dietary Fiber: 1 g
Protein: 25 g

    1 boneless beef top sirloin steak (about 1 pound)
1 ½ teaspoons black peppercorns, crushed
    1 clove garlic, minced
    ½ teaspoon salt
    ½ teaspoon paprika
    1 medium onion, cut into 12 wedges

Cut beef into 1-inch pieces. Combine peppercorns, garlic, salt and paprika in shallow dish. Add beef; toss to coat. Thread an equal number of beef pieces onto each of four 12-inch skewers along with 3 onion wedges. (If using bamboo skewers, soak in water 20 to 30 minutes before using, to prevent them from burning.) Place kabobs on rack in broiler pan. Broil 3 to 4 inches from heat source 9 to 12 minutes, turning occasionally. Garnish with tomatoes, if desired. *Makes 4 servings*

light 'n' lean chicken breasts

nutrients per serving:

¼ of total recipe

Calories: 287
Carbohydrate: 26 g
Calories From Fat: 11%
Total Fat: 3 g
Saturated Fat: 1 g
Cholesterol: 70 mg
Sodium: 126 mg
Dietary Fiber: <1 g
Protein: 30 g

    4 chicken breast halves, skinned
      Vegetable cooking spray
    ½ teaspoon ground black pepper, divided
    2 cloves garlic, halved
    1 cup low-sodium chicken broth
    ½ cup dry white wine
    2 teaspoons cornstarch
    ⅔ cup skim milk
    1 teaspoon finely chopped fresh chives
    2 cups hot cooked rice (cooked without salt and fat)

Coat skillet with cooking spray; heat over medium heat until hot. Add chicken; sprinkle with ¼ teaspoon pepper. Cook 20 minutes or until brown, turning occasionally. Reduce heat to low; add garlic. Cook 10 minutes more or until fork can be inserted into chicken with ease and juices run clear, not pink. Remove chicken; keep warm. Add broth and wine to garlic. Bring to a boil over high heat; boil 5 minutes. Reduce heat to low. Stir cornstarch into milk and slowly add mixture to skillet. Sprinkle with remaining ¼ teaspoon pepper; cook and stir 2 minutes or until thickened. Return chicken to skillet. Spoon sauce over chicken; sprinkle with chives. Simmer 5 minutes or until thoroughly heated. Serve with hot rice. *Makes 4 servings*

Favorite recipe from **USA Rice Federation**

peppercorn beef kabobs

tex-mex tostadas

4 (8-inch) fat-free flour tortillas
   Nonstick cooking spray
1 green bell pepper, diced
¾ pound boneless skinless chicken breast, cut into strips
1½ teaspoons fresh or bottled minced garlic
1 teaspoon chili powder
1 teaspoon ground cumin
½ cup chunky salsa, divided
⅓ cup sliced green onions
1 cup canned fat-free refried beans
1 medium tomato, diced
¼ cup fat-free or reduced-fat sour cream (optional)

1. Preheat oven to 450°F. Place tortillas on baking sheet; coat both sides with cooking spray. Bake 5 minutes or until lightly browned and crisp. Remove; set aside.

2. Coat large nonstick skillet with cooking spray. Add bell pepper; cook and stir 4 minutes. Add chicken, garlic, chili powder and cumin; cook and stir 4 minutes or until chicken is no longer pink in center. Add ¼ cup salsa and green onions; cook and stir 1 minute. Remove skillet from heat; set aside.

3. Combine refried beans and remaining ¼ cup salsa in microwavable bowl. Cook uncovered at HIGH 1½ minutes or until beans are heated through.

4. Spread bean mixture evenly over tortillas. Spoon chicken mixture and tomato over bean mixture. Garnish with sour cream, if desired. *Makes 4 servings*

tex-mex tostada

hazelnut coated salmon steaks

¼ cup hazelnuts
4 salmon steaks, about 5 ounces each
1 tablespoon apple butter
1 tablespoon Dijon mustard
¼ teaspoon dry thyme leaves
⅛ teaspoon black pepper
2 cups cooked white rice

1. Preheat oven to 375°F. Place hazelnuts on baking sheet; bake 8 minutes or until lightly browned. Quickly transfer nuts to clean dry dish towel. Fold towel; rub vigorously to remove as much of the skins as possible. Finely chop hazelnuts using food processor, nut grinder or chef's knife.

2. Increase oven temperature to 450°F. Place salmon in baking dish. Combine apple butter, mustard, thyme and pepper in small bowl. Brush on salmon; top each with nuts. Bake, nut side up, 14 to 16 minutes or until fish flakes easily with fork. Serve with rice.

Makes 4 servings

tip

Although salmon has a higher fat content than most fish, it is still very nutritious. Salmon's fat content is made up primarily of omega-3 fatty acids. There is a wealth of research available today that links consumption of omega-3 fatty acids with the reduced risk of heart attack and heart disease.

hazelnut coated salmon steak

nutrients per serving:

¼ of total recipe
(without sesame oil)

Calories: 252
Carbohydrate: 22 g
Calories From Fat: 10%
Total Fat: 3 g
Saturated Fat: 1 g
Cholesterol: 66 mg
Sodium: 161 mg
Dietary Fiber: 2 g
Protein: 31 g

chicken chow mein

1 pound boneless skinless chicken breasts, cut into thin strips
2 cloves garlic, minced
1 teaspoon vegetable oil, divided
2 tablespoons reduced-sodium soy sauce
2 tablespoons dry sherry
6 ounces (2 cups) fresh snow peas, cut into halves *or* 1 package
    (6 ounces) frozen snow peas, thawed
3 large green onions, cut diagonally into 1-inch pieces
4 ounces uncooked Chinese egg noodles or vermicelli,
    cooked, drained
1 teaspoon dark sesame oil (optional)
    Cherry tomatoes (optional)
    Fresh herbs (optional)

1. Toss chicken with garlic in small bowl.

2. Heat ½ teaspoon vegetable oil in wok or large nonstick skillet over medium-high heat. Add chicken mixture; stir-fry 3 minutes or until chicken is no longer pink. Transfer to medium bowl; toss with soy sauce and sherry.

3. Heat remaining ½ teaspoon vegetable oil in wok. Add snow peas; stir-fry 2 minutes for fresh or 1 minute for frozen snow peas. Add green onions; stir-fry 30 seconds. Add chicken mixture; stir-fry 1 minute.

4. Add noodles to wok; stir-fry 2 minutes or until heated through. Stir in sesame oil, if desired. Garnish with cherry tomatoes and fresh herbs, if desired.

Makes 4 servings

shanghai steamed fish

**1 cleaned whole sea bass, red snapper, carp or grouper
(about 1½ pounds)**
¼ cup teriyaki sauce
2 teaspoons grated fresh ginger
2 green onions, cut into 4-inch pieces
1 teaspoon dark sesame oil (optional)
Bell pepper strips (optional)
Green onions (optional)

1. Sprinkle inside cavity of fish with teriyaki sauce and ginger. Place onions in cavity in single layer.

2. Place steaming rack in wok. Pour enough water into wok so that water is just below steaming rack. (Water should not touch rack.) Bring water to a boil in wok. Reduce heat to medium-low to maintain a simmer. Place fish on steaming rack in wok. Cover and steam fish about 10 minutes per inch of thickness measured at thickest part. Fish is done when it flakes easily when tested with fork.

3. Carefully remove fish; discard onions. Cut fish into 4 portions. Sprinkle with sesame oil and garnish with pepper strips and green onions, if desired.

Makes 4 servings

nutrients per serving:
¼ of total recipe

Calories: 174
Carbohydrate: 2 g
Calories From Fat: 19%
Total Fat: 3 g
Saturated Fat: 1 g
Cholesterol: 71 mg
Sodium: 416 mg
Dietary Fiber: <1 g
Protein: 32 g

nutrients per serving:
¼ of total recipe

Calories: 120
Carbohydrate: 6 g
Calories From Fat: 31%
Total Fat: 4 g
Saturated Fat: 1 g
Cholesterol: 54 mg
Sodium: 89 mg
Dietary Fiber: 1 g
Protein: 14 g

veal in gingered sweet bell pepper sauce

  1 teaspoon olive oil
¾ pound veal cutlets, thinly sliced
½ cup fat-free (skim) milk
  1 tablespoon finely chopped fresh tarragon
  2 teaspoons crushed capers
  1 jar (7 ounces) roasted red peppers, drained
  1 tablespoon lemon juice
½ teaspoon grated fresh ginger
½ teaspoon black pepper

1. Heat oil in medium saucepan over high heat. Add veal; lightly brown both sides. Reduce heat to medium. Add milk, chopped tarragon and capers. Cook, uncovered, 5 minutes or until veal is fork-tender and milk evaporates.

2. Place roasted peppers, lemon juice, ginger and black pepper in food processor or blender; process until smooth. Set aside.

3. Remove veal from pan with slotted spoon; place in serving dish. Spoon roasted pepper sauce over veal. Sprinkle with cooked capers and fresh tarragon, if desired.

Makes 4 servings

tip

Capers are the small, pea-sized bud of a flower from the caper bush. Found mostly in Central America and the Mediterranean, capers add pungency to sauces, dips and relishes. Usually these green buds are pickled and can be found in the condiment section of the supermarket. They taste very much like gherkin pickles.

veal in gingered sweet bell pepper sauce

nutrients per serving:

⅙ of total recipe

Calories: 345
Carbohydrate: 36 g
Calories From Fat: 24%
Total Fat: 9 g
Saturated Fat: 5 g
Cholesterol: 34 mg
Sodium: 628 mg
Dietary Fiber: 1 g
Protein: 30 g

three-cheese penne

2 cups uncooked penne pasta
   Nonstick cooking spray
2 slices whole wheat bread, cut into cubes
2 cups fat-free cottage cheese
2 cups (8 ounces) shredded reduced-fat Cheddar cheese
1 cup chopped Roma tomatoes, divided
⅓ cup sliced green onions
¼ cup grated Parmesan cheese
¼ cup reduced-fat (2%) milk

1. Cook pasta according to package directions, omitting salt. Drain and rinse well under cold water until pasta is cool; drain well.

2. Spray large nonstick skillet with cooking spray; heat over medium heat until hot. Place bread cubes in skillet; spray bread cubes lightly with cooking spray. Cook and stir 5 minutes or until bread cubes are browned and crisp.

3. Preheat oven to 350°F. Combine pasta, cottage cheese, Cheddar cheese, ¾ cup tomatoes, green onions, Parmesan cheese and milk in medium bowl. Spray 2-quart casserole with nonstick cooking spray. Place pasta mixture in casserole. Top with remaining ¼ cup tomatoes and cooled bread cubes.

4. Bake 20 minutes or until heated through. Garnish, if desired.

Makes 6 servings

three-cheese penne

nutrients per serving:

1 Chicken Breast half

Calories: 206
Carbohydrate: 3 g
Calories From Fat: 25%
Total Fat: 6 g
Saturated Fat: 1 g
Cholesterol: 91 mg
Sodium: 113 mg
Dietary Fiber: <1 g
Protein: 34 g

chicken breasts with orange basil pesto

½ cup fresh basil leaves
2 tablespoons grated orange peel
2 cloves garlic
2 teaspoons olive oil
3 tablespoons Florida orange juice
1 tablespoon Dijon-style mustard
   Salt and pepper to taste
6 chicken breast halves

Preheat broiler. Add basil, orange peel and garlic to food processor; process until finely chopped. Add oil, orange juice, mustard, salt and pepper; process a few seconds or until paste forms. Spread equal amounts mixture under skin and on bone side of each chicken breast. Place chicken skin-side down on broiler pan and place 4 inches from heat. Broil 10 minutes. Turn chicken over and broil 10 to 12 minutes or until chicken is no longer pink in center. If chicken browns too quickly, cover with foil. Remove skin from chicken before serving.   *Makes 6 servings*

Favorite recipe from **Florida Department of Citrus**

tip

Chicken breasts, the white meat of the chicken, are a popular cut and one of the more costly. Breasts are available whole, with both skin and bone intact. They can also be purchased with the bone removed but the skin intact or with the skin and bone both removed. The breast is often split. Recipe references to a chicken breast usually mean a chicken breast half. The convenience of split skinless and boneless breasts is obvious, but those that are cooked on the bone often result in a juicier and more flavorful dish. Studies have shown that the breast is juicier if cooked with the skin attached. After removing and discarding the skin, the chicken does not have any more fat than chicken cooked without the skin.

chicken breast with orange basil pesto

tandoori-spiced game hens

nutrients per serving:

1 Game Hen half

Calories: 179
Carbohydrate: 6 g
Calories From Fat: 23%
Total Fat: 4 g
Saturated Fat: 1 g
Cholesterol: 110 mg
Sodium: 130 mg
Dietary Fiber: <1 g
Protein: 28 g

4 cups (32 ounces) plain nonfat yogurt
1 tablespoon curry powder
1 tablespoon sweet paprika
1 teaspoon bottled puréed ginger
1 teaspoon bottled puréed garlic
4 fresh Cornish game hens, all visible fat removed

1. Combine yogurt with curry powder, paprika, ginger and garlic in large bowl; mix well.

2. Cut game hens in half by cutting through breast bone. Remove triangular breast bone; discard. Rinse hens.

3. Place hens in resealable plastic food storage bags. Divide yogurt mixture among hens; seal bags. Marinate in refrigerator 2 to 3 hours or overnight, turning bags once or twice.

4. Preheat oven to 500°F. Remove hens from bags; discard marinade. Place hens, skin side down, on cutting board; brush off excess marinade. Place hens on racks lightly sprayed with nonstick cooking spray. Place racks in shallow baking pans. Bake 30 to 35 minutes or until no longer pink in center and juices run clear. Garnish, if desired, with fresh celery leaves. *Makes 8 servings*

Note: Remove the skin before serving to keep the fat at 4 grams per serving. With skin, the fat is 24 grams per serving, 7 of it saturated.

tandoori-spiced game hen

sneaky snacks

s'more gorp

nutrients per serving:

about ½ cup Gorp

Calories: 137
Carbohydrate: 28 g
Calories From Fat: 17%
Total Fat: 3 g
Saturated Fat: <1 g
Cholesterol: <1 mg
Sodium: 138 mg
Dietary Fiber: 1 g
Protein: 3 g

2 cups honey graham cereal
2 cups low-fat granola cereal
2 cups crispy multi-bran cereal squares
2 tablespoons reduced-fat margarine
1 tablespoon honey
¼ teaspoon ground cinnamon
¾ cup miniature marshmallows
½ cup dried fruit bits or raisins
¼ cup mini semisweet chocolate chips

1. Preheat oven to 275°F.

2. Combine cereals in nonstick 15×10×1-inch jelly-roll pan. Melt margarine in small saucepan; stir in honey and cinnamon. Pour margarine mixture evenly over cereal mixture; toss until cereal is well coated. Spread mixture evenly in bottom of prepared pan.

3. Bake 35 to 40 minutes or until crisp, stirring after 20 minutes. Cool completely.

4. Add marshmallows, fruit bits and chocolate chips; toss to mix.

Makes 16 servings

frozen fudge pops

nutrients per serving:

1 Pop

Calories: 92
Carbohydrate: 17 g
Calories From Fat: 1%
Total Fat: <1 g
Saturated Fat: <1 g
Cholesterol: 2 mg
Sodium: 70 mg
Dietary Fiber: 0 g
Protein: 5 g

½ cup nonfat sweetened condensed milk
¼ cup unsweetened cocoa powder
1¼ cups nonfat evaporated milk
1 teaspoon vanilla

1. Beat together sweetened condensed milk and cocoa in medium bowl. Add evaporated milk and vanilla; beat until smooth.

2. Pour mixture into 8 small paper cups or 8 popsicle molds. Freeze about 2 hours or until beginning to set. Insert wooden popsicle sticks; freeze until solid.

Makes 8 pops

s'more gorp

nutrients per serving:

3 Quesadilla wedges with about ¼ cup Salsa Cruda

Calories: 167
Carbohydrate: 25 g
Calories From Fat: 21%
Total Fat: 4 g
Saturated Fat: 1 g
Cholesterol: 7 mg
Sodium: 172 mg
Dietary Fiber: 3 g
Protein: 10 g

chili-cheese quesadillas with salsa cruda

2 tablespoons part-skim ricotta cheese
6 (6-inch) corn tortillas
½ cup (2 ounces) shredded reduced-fat Monterey Jack cheese
2 tablespoons diced mild green chilies
   Salsa Cruda (recipe follows)

1. To make 1 quesadilla, spread 2 teaspoons ricotta over tortilla. Sprinkle with heaping tablespoonful Monterey Jack cheese and 2 teaspoons diced chilies. Top with another tortilla. Repeat to make 2 more quesadillas.

2. Spray small nonstick skillet with nonstick cooking spray. Heat over medium-high heat. Add 1 quesadilla; cook 2 minutes or until bottom is golden. Turn quesadilla over; cook 2 minutes. Remove from heat. Cut into 4 wedges. Repeat with remaining quesadillas. Serve warm with Salsa Cruda. *Makes 4 servings*

salsa cruda

1 cup chopped tomato
2 tablespoons minced onion
2 tablespoons minced fresh cilantro (optional)
2 tablespoons lime juice
½ jalapeño pepper,* seeded and minced
1 clove garlic, minced

*Jalapeño peppers can sting and irritate the skin; wear rubber gloves when handling peppers and do not touch eyes. Wash hands after handling.

Combine tomato, onion, cilantro, lime juice, jalapeño and garlic in small bowl. Stir to combine. *Makes 4 servings*

chile-cheese quesadillas with salsa cruda

bananas & cheesecake dipping sauce

½ **cup fat-free sour cream**
2 **ounces reduced-fat cream cheese**
2 **tablespoons plus 1 teaspoon fat-free (skim) milk**
3 **packages sugar substitute** *or* **equivalent of 2 tablespoons sugar**
½ **teaspoon vanilla**
   Nutmeg (optional)
6 **medium bananas, unpeeled and cut crosswise into halves**
   or **6 red bananas**

Place all ingredients except bananas in blender and blend until smooth. Pour 2 tablespoons sauce into each of 6 small plastic containers; sprinkle with nutmeg, if desired. Cover tightly. Refrigerate until needed or place containers in small cooler with ice.

To serve, partially peel banana and dip directly into sauce; continue to peel and dip.
Makes 6 (2 tablespoons sauce plus ½ banana) servings

Tropical Coconut Cream Dipping Sauce: Substitute coconut extract for vanilla.

green pea mockamole

1 **package (16 ounces) frozen petit peas**
4 **green onions**
½ **cup lightly packed fresh cilantro**
2 **tablespoons lemon juice**
½ **cup GUILTLESS GOURMET® Salsa (Roasted Red Pepper
   or Southwestern Grill)**
   Fresh cilantro sprigs (optional)
1 **large bag (7 ounces) GUILTLESS GOURMET® Baked Tortilla Chips
   (yellow, red or blue corn)**

Cook peas according to package directions; drain. Place peas, onions, ½ cup cilantro and juice in food processor or blender; process until smooth. Transfer to serving bowl; gently stir in salsa to combine. Garnish with cilantro sprigs, if desired. Serve warm with tortilla chips or cover and refrigerate until ready to serve.   *Makes 12 servings*

banana & cheesecake dipping sauce

oven "fries"

2 small baking potatoes (10 ounces)
2 teaspoons olive oil
¼ teaspoon salt or onion salt

1. Place potatoes in refrigerator for 1 to 2 days.

2. Preheat oven to 450°F. Peel potatoes and cut lengthwise into ¼-inch square strips. Place in colander. Rinse potato strips under cold running water 2 minutes. Drain. Pat dry with paper towels. Place potatoes in small resealable plastic food storage bag. Drizzle with oil. Seal bag; shake to coat potatoes with oil.

3. Arrange potatoes in single layer on baking sheet. Bake 20 to 25 minutes or until light brown and crisp. Sprinkle with salt or onion salt. *Makes 2 servings*

nutrients per serving:

½ of total recipe

Calories: 237
Carbohydrate: 41 g
Calories From Fat: 26%
Total Fat: 7 g
Saturated Fat: 1 g
Cholesterol: 0 mg
Sodium: 300 mg
Dietary Fiber: 3 g
Protein: 4 g

pineapple-scallop bites

½ cup *French's*® Napa Valley Style Dijon Mustard
¼ cup orange marmalade
1 cup canned pineapple cubes (24 pieces)
12 sea scallops (8 ounces), cut in half crosswise
12 strips (6 ounces) uncooked turkey bacon, cut in half crosswise*

*Or substitute regular bacon for turkey bacon. Simmer 5 minutes in enough boiling water to cover; drain well before wrapping scallops.

1. Soak 12 (6-inch) bamboo skewers in hot water 20 minutes. Combine mustard and marmalade in small bowl. Reserve ½ cup mixture for dipping sauce.

2. Hold 1 pineapple cube and 1 scallop half together. Wrap with 1 bacon strip. Thread onto skewer. Repeat with remaining pineapple, scallops and bacon.

3. Place skewers on oiled grid. Grill over medium heat 6 minutes, turning frequently and brushing with remaining mustard mixture. Serve hot with reserved dipping sauce. *Makes 6 servings*

Prep Time: 25 minutes
Cook Time: 6 minutes

nutrients per serving:

2 skewers (made with turkey bacon) with about 1 tablespoon plus 1 teaspoon dipping sauce

Calories: 179
Carbohydrate: 16 g
Calories From Fat: 35%
Total Fat: 6 g
Saturated Fat: 1 g
Cholesterol: 32 mg
Sodium: 1,015 mg
Dietary Fiber: <1 g
Protein: 10 g

oven "fries"

crabmeat crostini

nutrients per serving:

1 Crostini
(1/12 of total recipe)

Calories: 202
Carbohydrate: 20 g
Calories From Fat: 33%
Total Fat: 7 g
Saturated Fat: 2 g
Cholesterol: 40 mg
Sodium: 516 mg
Dietary Fiber: 2 g
Protein: 15 g

  1 pound Florida blue crab or stone crab meat
1½ cups shredded low-fat mozzarella cheese
  ½ cup Florida pecan pieces, toasted and chopped
  2 Florida datil peppers, seeded and chopped (or other hot peppers)
  2 teaspoons chopped fresh Florida rosemary leaves
  2 teaspoons chopped fresh Florida thyme leaves
  1 (3-ounce) package sun dried tomatoes, rehydrated and chopped
 12 (1-inch-thick) slices French bread, sliced diagonally

Remove any remaining shell particles from crab meat. Combine all ingredients except bread, mix well, cover and refrigerate for one hour. Arrange bread slices on baking sheet and place equal portions of crab mixture on each slice. Broil 4 to 6 inches from source of heat for 6 to 8 minutes or until cheese melts or begins to brown.

Makes 12 servings

Favorite recipe from **Florida Department of Agriculture and Consumer Services, Bureau of Seafood and Aquaculture**

papaya pops

nutrients per serving:

1 Pop

Calories: 150
Carbohydrate: 34 g
Calories From Fat: 4%
Total Fat: 1 g
Saturated Fat: <1 g
Cholesterol: 3 mg
Sodium: 40 mg
Dietary Fiber: 2 g
Protein: 3 g

  1 very ripe papaya
  1 cup peach or vanilla nonfat yogurt
  2 tablespoons honey
  1 teaspoon lime juice
  ¾ teaspoon grated lime peel

Cut papaya lengthwise into halves; discard seeds. Scrape out flesh with spoon; discard skin. Combine papaya, yogurt, honey, lime juice and lime peel in blender or food processor. Process until smooth.

Fill four 5-ounce paper or pliable plastic cups with papaya mixture. Freeze 20 minutes. Insert wooden ice cream stick or plastic spoon in center of each cup. Freeze 8 hours or overnight until firm.

To serve, peel away paper cup or gently twist and ease frozen pop out of plastic cup.

Makes 4 servings

roasted garlic hummus

2 tablespoons Roasted Garlic (recipe follows)
1 can (15 ounces) chick-peas (garbanzo beans), rinsed and drained
¼ cup fresh parsley, stems removed
2 tablespoons lemon juice
2 tablespoons water
½ teaspoon curry powder
3 drops dark sesame oil
Dash hot pepper sauce

Prepare Roasted Garlic. Place chick-peas, parsley, 2 tablespoons Roasted Garlic, lemon juice, water, curry powder, sesame oil and hot pepper sauce in food processor or blender; process until smooth, scraping down side of bowl once.

Makes 6 servings

Roasted Garlic: Cut off top third of 1 large garlic head (not the root end) to expose cloves; discard top. Place head of garlic, trimmed end up, on 10-inch square of foil. Rub garlic generously with olive oil and sprinkle with salt. Gather foil ends together and close tightly. Roast in preheated 350°F oven 45 minutes or until cloves are golden and soft. When cool enough to handle, squeeze roasted garlic cloves from skins; discard skins.

nutrients per serving:
¼ cup Hummus (without pita bread)

Calories: 85
Carbohydrate: 15 g
Calories From Fat: 15%
Total Fat: 1 g
Saturated Fat: <1 g
Cholesterol: 0 mg
Sodium: 303 mg
Dietary Fiber: 4 g
Protein: 4 g

mini cheese burritos

2 (8-inch) fat-free flour tortillas
¼ cup canned fat-free refried beans
¼ cup chunky salsa
4 (¾-ounce) reduced-fat Cheddar cheese sticks*

*Reduced-fat Cheddar cheese block can be substituted. Cut cheese into 2×¼×¼-inch sticks.

1. Cut tortillas in half. Spread beans over tortilla halves leaving ½-inch border around all edges. Spoon salsa over beans.

2. Cut cheese sticks crosswise in half; arrange on one side of tortilla. Fold rounded edge of tortilla over cheese; roll up, burrito fashion. Place burritos seam side down on microwavable plate.

3. Microwave at HIGH power 1 to 2 minutes or until cheese is melted. Let stand 1 to 2 minutes before serving.

Makes 4 servings

nutrients per serving:
1 Burrito

Calories: 109
Carbohydrate: 11 g
Calories From Fat: 31%
Total Fat: 4 g
Saturated Fat: 3 g
Cholesterol: 10 mg
Sodium: 435 mg
Dietary Fiber: 4 g
Protein: 9 g

nachos

nutrients per
serving:

6 chips with ⅛
of topping

Calories: 202
Carbohydrate: 29 g
Calories From Fat: 21%
Total Fat: 5 g
Saturated Fat: 1 g
Cholesterol: 6 mg
Sodium: 455 mg
Dietary Fiber: 6 g
Protein: 13 g

8 (6-inch) corn tortillas
1 cup chopped onion
1 tablespoon chili powder
2 teaspoons dried oregano leaves, crushed
1 can (15 ounces) pinto beans or black beans, rinsed and drained
1¼ cups (5 ounces) shredded reduced-fat Monterey Jack cheese
¾ cup frozen whole kernel corn, thawed, drained
1 jar (2 ounces) pimientos, drained
3 tablespoons ripe olive slices
2 to 3 tablespoons pickled jalapeño pepper slices,* drained
   Nonstick cooking spray

*Jalapeño peppers can sting and irritate the skin; wear rubber gloves when handling peppers and do not touch eyes. Wash hands after handling.

1. Preheat oven to 375°F. Sprinkle 1 tortilla with water to dampen; shake off excess water. Repeat with remaining tortillas. Cut each tortilla into 6 wedges. Arrange wedges in single layer on baking sheet or in two 9-inch pie plates. Bake 4 minutes. Rotate sheet. Bake another 2 to 4 minutes or until chips are firm; do not let brown. Remove chips to plate to cool. Set aside.

2. Spray bottom of medium saucepan with cooking spray. Cook and stir onion over medium-high heat 8 to 10 minutes or until onion is tender and beginning to brown. Add chili powder and oregano; stir 1 minute more.

3. Remove from heat. Add beans and 2 tablespoons water; mash with fork or potato masher until blended yet chunky. Return to heat. Cover; cook beans, stirring occasionally, 6 to 8 minutes or until bubbly. Stir in additional water if beans become dry. Remove from heat. Set beans aside.

4. Sprinkle cheese evenly over chips. Spoon beans over chips.

5. Combine corn and pimientos; spoon over beans. Bake about 8 minutes or until cheese melts. Sprinkle olives and jalapeños over top.   *Makes 8 servings*

nachos

honey crunch popcorn

nutrients per serving:

1 cup Popcorn

Calories: 133
Carbohydrate: 26 g
Calories From Fat: 20%
Total Fat: 3 g
Saturated Fat: <1 g
Cholesterol: 0 mg
Sodium: 4 mg
Dietary Fiber: 1 g
Protein: 1 g

    Nonstick cooking spray
  3 quarts (12 cups) hot air-popped popcorn
  ½ cup chopped pecans
  ½ cup packed brown sugar
  ½ cup honey

1. Preheat oven to 300°F. Spray large nonstick baking sheet with nonstick cooking spray.

2. Combine popcorn and pecans in large bowl; mix lightly. Set aside.

3. Combine brown sugar and honey in small saucepan. Cook over medium heat just until brown sugar is dissolved and mixture comes to a boil, stirring occasionally. Pour over popcorn mixture; toss lightly to coat evenly. Transfer to prepared baking sheet.

4. Bake 30 minutes, stirring after 15 minutes. Spray large sheet of waxed paper with nonstick cooking spray. Transfer popcorn to prepared waxed paper to cool. Store in airtight containers. *Makes 12 servings*

Variation: Add 1 cup chopped, mixed dried fruit immediately after removing popcorn from oven.

ginger snap sandwiches

nutrients per serving:

1 Ginger Snap Sandwich

Calories: 76
Carbohydrate: 15 g
Calories From Fat: 17%
Total Fat: 1 g
Saturated Fat: <1 g
Cholesterol: <1 mg
Sodium: 110 mg
Dietary Fiber: <1 g
Protein: 1 g

  ¼ cup 1% low-fat cottage cheese
  ¼ cup vanilla nonfat yogurt
    1 McIntosh apple, peeled, cored and grated
    2 tablespoons sugar
  30 ginger snaps

Add cottage cheese and yogurt to food processor or blender; process until smooth. Blend in apple and sugar. Using rubber spatula, spread apple filling onto flat side of ginger snap; top with another ginger snap to make sandwich. Repeat with remaining ingredients. *Makes 15 servings*

Favorite recipe from **The Sugar Association, Inc.**

honey crunch popcorn

savory pita chips

2 whole wheat or white pita bread rounds
Nonstick olive oil cooking spray
3 tablespoons grated Parmesan cheese
1 teaspoon dried basil leaves
¼ teaspoon garlic powder

1. Preheat oven to 350°F. Line baking sheet with foil; set aside.

2. Using small scissors, carefully split each pita bread round around edges; separate to form 2 rounds. Cut each round into 6 wedges.

3. Place wedges, rough side down, on prepared baking sheet; coat lightly with cooking spray. Turn wedges over; spray again.

4. Combine Parmesan cheese, basil and garlic powder in small bowl; sprinkle evenly over pita wedges.

5. Bake 12 to 14 minutes or until golden brown. Cool completely.

Makes 4 servings

Cinnamon Crisps: Substitute butter-flavored cooking spray for olive oil-flavored cooking spray and 1 tablespoon sugar mixed with ¼ teaspoon ground cinnamon for Parmesan cheese, basil and garlic powder.

nutrients per serving:

6 Chips

Calories: 108
Carbohydrate: 18 g
Calories From Fat: 18%
Total Fat: 2 g
Saturated Fat: 1 g
Cholesterol: 4 mg
Sodium: 257 mg
Dietary Fiber: 0 g
Protein: 5 g

today's slim line dip

1 cup dry curd cottage cheese
½ cup buttermilk
¼ teaspoon lemon juice
1 package dry onion soup mix

Add cottage cheese, buttermilk, lemon juice and onion soup mix to food processor or blender. Process until smooth. Refrigerate. Serve with raw vegetables.

Makes 16 servings (about 2 cups)

Favorite recipe from **Wisconsin Milk Marketing Board**

nutrients per serving:

2 tablespoons Dip (without vegetables)

Calories: 40
Carbohydrate: 6 g
Calories From Fat: 15%
Total Fat: 1 g
Saturated Fat: <1 g
Cholesterol: 1 mg
Sodium: 883 mg
Dietary Fiber: 1 g
Protein: 3 g

savory pita chips

new age candy apple

nutrients per serving:

total recipe

Calories: 102
Carbohydrate: 23 g
Calories From Fat: 17%
Total Fat: 2 g
Saturated Fat: 1 g
Cholesterol: 0 mg
Sodium: 1 mg
Dietary Fiber: 4 g
Protein: <1 g

1 Granny Smith apple, peeled
¼ teaspoon sugar-free cherry-flavored gelatin
2 tablespoons diet cherry cola
2 tablespoons thawed frozen reduced-fat nondairy whipped topping

1. Slice apple crosswise into ¼-inch-thick slices; remove seeds. Place stack of apple slices in small microwavable bowl; sprinkle with gelatin. Pour cola over slices.

2. Cover loosely with waxed paper. Microwave at HIGH (100% power) 2 minutes or until liquid is boiling. Allow to stand, covered, 5 minutes. Arrange rings on dessert plate. Serve warm with whipped topping. *Makes 1 serving*

Note: This recipe can be doubled or tripled easily. To cook 2 apples at a time, increase cooking time to 3½ minutes. To cook 3 apples at a time, increase cooking time to 5 minutes.

Tip: This recipe works great with any crisp apple. A Jonathan apple will give a tart flavor, a Cortland apple will give a sweet-tart flavor and a Red Delicious apple will give a sweet flavor. Choose your favorite apple and enjoy!

tuna schooners

nutrients per serving:

1 Tuna Schooner

Calories: 204
Carbohydrate: 23 g
Calories From Fat: 28%
Total Fat: 6 g
Saturated Fat: 1 g
Cholesterol: 13 mg
Sodium: 607 mg
Dietary Fiber: 2 g
Protein: 14 g

2 (3-ounce) cans water-packed light tuna, drained
½ cup finely chopped apple
¼ cup shredded carrot
⅓ cup reduced-fat ranch salad dressing
2 English muffins, split and lightly toasted
8 triangular-shaped baked whole wheat crackers or triangular-shaped tortilla chips

1. Combine tuna, apple and carrot in medium bowl. Add salad dressing; stir to combine.

2. Spread ¼ of tuna mixture over top of each muffin half. Stand 2 crackers and press firmly into tuna mixture on each muffin half to form 'sails.' *Makes 4 servings*

new age candy apple

nutrients per serving:

⅛ of total recipe (without tortilla chips)

Calories: 100
Carbohydrate: 15 g
Calories From Fat: 28%
Total Fat: 3 g
Saturated Fat: 1 g
Cholesterol: 0 mg
Sodium: 141 mg
Dietary Fiber: 4 g
Protein: 5 g

green pea guacamole with avocado and tomato

½ cup diced ripe California avocado*
3 tablespoons lemon juice, divided
1 package (16 ounces) frozen petit peas, thawed
4 green onions
½ cup lightly packed fresh cilantro
1 jalapeño pepper, seeded
1 medium tomato, diced
Baked Tortilla Chips (recipe follows, optional)

To lower fat content, omit avocado.

**Jalapeño peppers can sting and irritate the skin; wear rubber gloves when handling peppers and do not touch eyes. Wash hands after handling.*

1. Combine avocado and 1 tablespoon lemon juice in medium bowl.

2. Combine peas, onions, cilantro, remaining 2 tablespoons lemon juice and jalapeño in food processor or blender; process until smooth. Add avocado and tomato; gently stir to combine. Garnish with cilantro or tomato wedges, if desired. Serve with Baked Tortilla Chips, if desired. *Makes 8 servings*

nutrients per serving:

8 Chips

Calories: 67
Carbohydrate: 13 g
Calories From Fat: 15%
Total Fat: 1 g
Saturated Fat: <1 g
Cholesterol: 0 mg
Sodium: 53 mg
Dietary Fiber: 2 g
Protein: 2 g

baked tortilla chips

6 (7- or 8-inch) flour tortillas or (6-inch) corn tortillas
Paprika, chili powder or ground red pepper

1. Preheat oven to 375°F. Sprinkle 1 tortilla with water to dampen; shake off excess water. Lightly sprinkle top with paprika. Repeat with remaining tortillas. Cut each flour tortilla into 8 wedges, or each corn tortilla into 6 wedges.

2. Arrange as many wedges as fit in single layer on baking sheet (edges may overlap slightly). Bake 4 minutes. Rotate sheet. Bake another 2 to 4 minutes or until chips are firm and flour tortillas are spotted with light golden color. Do not let corn tortillas brown. Remove chips to plate to cool. Repeat with remaining wedges. *Makes 6 servings*

green pea guacamole with avocado and tomato

successful sweets

nutrients per serving:

1 Cheesecake

Calories: 214
Carbohydrate: 29 g
Calories From Fat: 29%
Total Fat: 7 g
Saturated Fat: 4 g
Cholesterol: 16 mg
Sodium: 387 mg
Dietary Fiber: 1 g
Protein: 9 g

cherry bowl cheesecakes

1 package (8 ounces) fat-free cream cheese, softened
1 package (8 ounces) reduced-fat cream cheese, softened
2 tablespoons fat-free (skim) milk
4 packets sugar substitute *or* equivalent of 8 teaspoons sugar
¼ teaspoon almond extract
40 reduced-fat vanilla wafers
1 can (16 ounces) light cherry pie filling

1. Beat cream cheese, milk, sugar substitute and almond extract in medium bowl with electric mixer at high speed until well blended.

2. Place one vanilla wafer on bottom of 4-ounce ramekin.* Arrange four additional vanilla wafers around side of ramekin. Repeat with remaining wafers. Fill each ramekin with ¼ cup cream cheese mixture; top each with ¼ cup cherry pie filling. Cover with plastic wrap; refrigerate 8 hours or overnight.   *Makes 8 servings*

*Note: If ramekins are not available, you may substitute with custard dishes or line 8 muffin cups with paper liners and fill according to above directions.

Cheesecake Parfaits: Crush 32 wafers. Prepare cream cheese mixture as directed above. Layer ½ crushed wafers, ½ cream cheese mixture and ½ pie filling in 8 small dessert glasses. Repeat layers. Garnish with remaining wafers and thawed fat-free nondairy frozen topping, if desired.

cherry bowl cheesecake

dessert nachos

nutrients per serving:

6 tortilla wedges plus ½ cup berries plus ¼ cup yogurt mixture plus 1 teaspoon chocolate chips

Calories: 160
Carbohydrate: 28 g
Calories From Fat: 19%
Total Fat: 3 g
Saturated Fat: 1 g
Cholesterol: 2 mg
Sodium: 146 mg
Dietary Fiber: 3 g
Protein: 4 g

3 (6- to 7-inch) flour tortillas
    Nonstick cooking spray
1 tablespoon sugar
⅛ teaspoon ground cinnamon
    Dash ground allspice
1 (6- or 8-ounce) container fat-free sugar-free vanilla yogurt
1 teaspoon grated orange peel
1½ cups strawberries
½ cup blueberries
4 teaspoons miniature semisweet chocolate chips

1. Preheat oven to 375°F.

2. Cut each flour tortilla into 8 wedges. Place on ungreased baking sheet. Generously spray tortilla wedges with cooking spray. Stir together sugar, cinnamon and allspice. Sprinkle over tortilla wedges. Bake 7 to 9 minutes or until lightly browned; cool completely.

3. Meanwhile, stir together yogurt and orange peel. Stem strawberries; cut lengthwise into fourths.

4. Place 6 tortilla wedges on each of 4 small plates. Top with strawberries and blueberries. Drizzle yogurt mixture on top. Sprinkle with chocolate chips. Serve immediately.   *Makes 4 servings*

dessert nachos

polenta apricot pudding cake

¼ **cup chopped dried apricots**
2 **cups orange juice**
1 **cup part-skim ricotta cheese**
3 **tablespoons honey**
¾ **cup sugar**
½ **cup cornmeal**
½ **cup all-purpose flour**
¼ **teaspoon grated nutmeg**
¼ **cup slivered almonds**
   Powdered sugar (optional)

1. Preheat oven to 300°F. Soak apricots in ¼ cup water in small bowl 15 minutes. Drain and discard water. Pat apricots dry with paper towels; set aside.

2. Combine orange juice, ricotta cheese and honey in medium bowl. Mix on medium speed of electric mixer 5 minutes or until smooth. Combine sugar, cornmeal, flour and nutmeg in small bowl. Gradually add sugar mixture to orange juice mixture; blend well. Slowly stir in apricots.

3. Spray 10-inch nonstick springform pan with nonstick cooking spray. Pour batter into prepared pan. Sprinkle with almonds. Bake 60 to 70 minutes or until center is firm and cake is golden brown. Garnish with powdered sugar, if desired. Serve warm.

Makes 8 servings

tip

Dried apricots are an excellent source of beta-carotene, which is converted to Vitamin A in the body. Vitamin A helps with vision, growth and bone development. Other fruit sources of beta-carotene include cantaloupe, peaches, oranges and apples.

polenta apricot pudding cake

nutrients per serving:

⅛ of total recipe

Calories: 130
Carbohydrate: 23 g
Calories From Fat: 26%
Total Fat: 4 g
Saturated Fat: 2 g
Cholesterol: 11 mg
Sodium: 13 mg
Dietary Fiber: 1 g
Protein: 2 g

refreshing cocoa-fruit sherbet

1 ripe medium banana
1½ cups orange juice
1 cup (½ pint) half-and-half
½ cup sugar
¼ cup HERSHEY'S Cocoa

1. Slice banana into blender container. Add orange juice; cover and blend until smooth. Add remaining ingredients; cover and blend well. Pour into 8- or 9-inch square pan. Cover; freeze until hard around edges.

2. Spoon partially frozen mixture into blender container. Cover; blend until smooth but not melted. Pour into 1-quart mold. Cover; freeze until firm. Unmold onto cold plate and slice. Garnish as desired.
Makes 8 servings

nutrients per serving:

1 Cupcake

Calories: 102
Carbohydrate: 19 g
Calories From Fat: 19%
Total Fat: 2 g
Saturated Fat: <1 g
Cholesterol: 1 mg
Sodium: 130 mg
Dietary Fiber: 1 g
Protein: 2 g

chocolate cupcakes

6 tablespoons lower fat margarine (40% oil)
1 cup sugar
1¼ cups all-purpose flour
⅓ cup HERSHEY'S Cocoa
1 teaspoon baking soda
Dash salt
1 cup lowfat buttermilk
½ teaspoon vanilla extract
1 teaspoon powdered sugar

1. Heat oven to 350°F. Line 18 muffin cups with paper bake cups.

2. Melt margarine in large saucepan over low heat. Remove from heat; stir in sugar.

3. Stir together flour, cocoa, baking soda and salt in small bowl; add alternately with buttermilk and vanilla to mixture in saucepan. Stir with whisk until well blended. Fill muffin cups ⅔ full with batter.

4. Bake 18 to 20 minutes or until wooden pick inserted in centers comes out clean. Remove from pans to wire racks. Cool completely.

5. Sift powdered sugar over tops of cupcakes. Store, covered, at room temperature.
Makes 18 cupcakes

refreshing cocoa-fruit sherbet

nutrients per serving:

½ of total recipe

Calories: 155

Carbohydrate: 27 g

Calories From Fat: 11%

Total Fat: 2 g

Saturated Fat: 1 g

Cholesterol: 7 mg

Sodium: 249 mg

Dietary Fiber: 1 g

Protein: 7 g

blueberry custard supreme

½ **cup fresh blueberries**
 2 **tablespoons all-purpose flour**
1½ **tablespoons granulated sugar**
⅛ **teaspoon salt**
¼ **teaspoon ground cardamom**
¼ **cup cholesterol-free egg substitute**
 1 **teaspoon grated lemon peel**
½ **teaspoon vanilla**
¾ **cup reduced-fat (2%) milk**
 1 **teaspoon powdered sugar**

1. Preheat oven to 350°F. Spray 1-quart soufflé or casserole dish with nonstick cooking spray. Distribute blueberries over bottom of prepared dish.

2. Whisk flour, granulated sugar, salt and cardamom in small bowl. Add egg substitute, lemon peel and vanilla; whisk until smooth and well blended. Whisk in milk. Pour over blueberries.

3. Bake 30 minutes or until puffed, lightly browned and center is set. Cool on wire rack. Serve warm or at room temperature. Sprinkle with powdered sugar just before serving. *Makes 2 servings*

Blackberry Custard Supreme: Substitute fresh blackberries for blueberries; proceed as directed.

blueberry custard supreme

pineapple-coconut upside-down cake

nutrients per serving:

1 slice Cake
(¹⁄₁₀ of total recipe)

Calories: 272
Carbohydrate: 47 g
Calories From Fat: 27%
Total Fat: 8 g
Saturated Fat: 2 g
Cholesterol: 22 mg
Sodium: 224 mg
Dietary Fiber: 1 g
Protein: 3 g

2 tablespoons light corn syrup
6 tablespoons margarine, softened and divided
½ cup packed light brown sugar
2 tablespoons flaked coconut
1 can (8 ounces) sliced pineapple in light syrup, drained
1⅓ cups all-purpose flour
2 teaspoons baking powder
¼ teaspoon salt
¾ cup granulated sugar
1 egg
1 teaspoon vanilla
⅔ cup fat-free (skim) milk
10 tablespoons thawed frozen light nondairy whipped topping

1. Heat corn syrup and 1 tablespoon margarine until melted in small skillet over medium heat. Stir in brown sugar; cook over medium heat until mixture is bubbly. Pour mixture into ungreased 9-inch round cake pan; sprinkle coconut evenly over top. Arrange whole pineapple slices on top of coconut.

2. Preheat oven to 350°F. Combine flour, baking powder and salt in medium bowl. Set aside. Beat remaining 5 tablespoons margarine in large bowl until fluffy; beat in granulated sugar, egg and vanilla. Add flour mixture to margarine mixture alternately with milk, beginning and ending with flour mixture. Pour batter into cake pan with prepared topping.

3. Bake about 40 minutes or until cake springs back when touched lightly. Cool in pan on wire rack 2 to 3 minutes; loosen side of cake with knife and invert onto serving plate. Cut cake into wedges. Serve warm or cool, topped with whipped topping. Garnish with pineapple slices, if desired.

Makes 10 servings

pineapple-coconut upside-down cake

blackberry sorbet

1 (8-fluid-ounce) can chilled Vanilla GLUCERNA® Shake
1 cup frozen whole blackberries, unsweetened
½ teaspoon cinnamon
¼ teaspoon nutmeg
   Sugar substitute to taste

1. Combine all ingredients in blender. Blend until thick.

2. Serve immediately or freeze 10 to 15 minutes.

Makes 2 servings

nutrients per serving:

¾ cup Sorbet

Calories: 161
Carbohydrate: 23 g
Calories From Fat: 31%
Total Fat: 6 g
Saturated Fat: 1 g
Cholesterol: 1 mg
Sodium: 106 mg
Dietary Fiber: 5 g
Protein: 6 g

angelic cupcakes

1 box (16 ounces) angel food cake mix
1¼ cups cold water
¼ teaspoon peppermint extract (optional)
   Red food coloring
4½ cups thawed frozen light whipped topping
   Green food coloring (optional)

1. Preheat oven to 375°F. Line 36 medium muffin cups with paper liners; set aside.

2. Beat cake mix, water and peppermint extract, if desired, in large bowl with electric mixer at low speed 30 seconds. Increase speed to medium and beat 1 minute.

3. Pour half of batter into medium bowl; carefully stir in 9 drops red food coloring. In each muffin cup, alternate spoonfuls of white and pink batter, filling baking cups ¾ full.

4. Bake 11 minutes or until cupcakes are golden with deep cracks on top. Remove to wire rack. Cool completely.

5. Divide whipped topping between three small bowls. Add 2 drops green food coloring to one bowl of whipped topping; stir gently to combine. Add 2 drops red food coloring to one bowl of whipped topping; stir gently to combine. Frost cupcakes with red, green and white whipped topping as desired. Refrigerate leftovers.

Makes 3 dozen cupcakes

nutrients per serving:

1 Cupcake

Calories: 68
Carbohydrate: 13 g
Calories From Fat: 14%
Total Fat: 1 g
Saturated Fat: 1 g
Cholesterol: 0 mg
Sodium: 113 mg
Dietary Fiber: 0 g
Protein: 1 g

blackberry sorbet

nutrients per serving:

⅙ of total recipe

Calories: 337

Carbohydrate: 64 g

Calories From Fat: 23%

Total Fat: 9 g

Saturated Fat: 5 g

Cholesterol: 22 mg

Sodium: 196 mg

Dietary Fiber: 4 g

Protein: 3 g

apple-raisin crisp

1 cup plus 3 tablespoons thawed frozen unsweetened apple juice concentrate, divided
¼ cup uncooked old-fashioned oats
4 large cooking apples,* peeled, cored and sliced (about 6 cups sliced)
¾ cup raisins
2 tablespoons cornstarch
2 teaspoons ground cinnamon, divided
½ teaspoon ground nutmeg
¼ teaspoon salt
½ cup all-purpose flour
¼ cup cold butter or margarine
½ cup chopped walnuts *or* pecans (optional)

Use Jonathan, Rome Beauty, Courtland or McIntosh apples.

Preheat oven to 375°F. Combine 3 tablespoons apple juice concentrate and oats; mix lightly. Set aside. Combine apples and raisins in large bowl; set aside. Combine cornstarch, 1½ teaspoons cinnamon, nutmeg and salt in medium bowl; mix well. Blend in remaining 1 cup apple juice concentrate. Add to apple mixture; mix lightly to coat. Spoon into shallow 1½-quart or 8-inch square baking dish. Combine flour and remaining ½ teaspoon cinnamon; cut in butter with pastry blender or two knives until mixture resembles coarse crumbs. Add oat mixture; mix lightly. Stir in walnuts, if desired; sprinkle evenly over apple mixture. Bake 35 minutes or until apples are tender. Serve warm, at room temperature or chilled. *Makes 6 servings*

apple-raisin crisp

apple-cheddar turnovers

nutrients per serving:

1 Turnover

Calories: 189
Carbohydrate: 33 g
Calories From Fat: 20%
Total Fat: 4 g
Saturated Fat: 1 g
Cholesterol: 19 mg
Sodium: 196 mg
Dietary Fiber: 1 g
Protein: 4 g

2 packages active dry yeast
¼ cup warm water (110° to 115°F)
⅓ cup reduced calorie margarine
⅓ cup granulated sugar
1 teaspoon salt
1 container (8 ounces) low fat sour cream
1 egg, slightly beaten
3½ to 4 cups all-purpose flour
⅓ cup (2 ounces) shredded aged Wisconsin Cheddar cheese
1¼ cups apple pie filling
1 cup powdered sugar
½ teaspoon vanilla
1 to 2 teaspoons 2% low-fat milk

Sprinkle yeast over warm water in small bowl. Heat margarine in large saucepan over medium heat; add sugar and salt. Heat until just warm (115° to 120°F) and margarine is almost melted, stirring constantly. Pour into large bowl. Add sour cream and egg; mix well. Stir in 1½ cups flour and cheese; beat well. Add yeast mixture; stir until smooth. Stir in enough remaining flour to make soft dough. Place on floured surface; knead 2 minutes. Cover; let rest 10 minutes.

Roll half of dough into 12-inch square. Cut into nine 4-inch squares. Place about 1 tablespoon apple pie filling in center of each square. Fold dough over to form triangle; seal edges well. Repeat with remaining half of dough. Preheat oven to 350°F. Spray baking sheet with nonstick cooking spray. Place pastries on prepared baking sheets; cover and let rise in warm place until doubled in bulk (about 20 minutes). Bake 10 to 15 minutes or until lightly browned. Remove from baking sheets to wire rack.

For frosting, combine powdered sugar and vanilla in small bowl. Stir in enough milk for spreading consistency. Spread on top of warm pastries. Serve warm or cooled.

Makes 18 pastries

Favorite recipe from **Wisconsin Milk Marketing Board**

apple-cheddar turnovers

pumpkin cheesecake

nutrients per serving:

1 slice Cheesecake (1/16 of total recipe) without garnish

Calories: 121
Carbohydrate: 22 g
Calories From Fat: 15%
Total Fat: 2 g
Saturated Fat: 0 g
Cholesterol: 4 mg
Sodium: 56 mg
Dietary Fiber: 1 g
Protein: 4 g

⅓ cup graham cracker crumbs
1 can (16 ounces) solid pack pumpkin
2 cups reduced-fat ricotta cheese
1 cup sugar
3 tablespoons all-purpose flour
1 tablespoon nonfat dry milk powder
1 tablespoon ground cinnamon
1 teaspoon ground allspice
1 egg white
¾ cup canned evaporated skimmed milk
1 tablespoon vegetable oil
1 tablespoon vanilla

1. Preheat oven to 400°F. Spray 9-inch springform pan with nonstick cooking spray. Add graham cracker crumbs; shake to coat pan evenly. Set aside.

2. Combine pumpkin and ricotta cheese in food processor or blender; process until smooth. Add sugar, flour, milk powder, cinnamon, allspice, egg white, evaporated skimmed milk, oil and vanilla; process until smooth.

3. Pour mixture into prepared pan. Bake 15 minutes. *Reduce oven temperature to 275°F;* bake 1 hour and 15 minutes. Turn off oven; leave cheesecake in oven with door closed 1 hour. Remove from oven; cool completely on wire rack. Remove springform pan side. Cover cheesecake with plastic wrap; refrigerate at least 4 hours or up to 2 days. Garnish with fresh fruit, if desired. *Makes 16 servings*

tip

Ricotta resembles cottage cheese but is smoother, richer and creamier. It is made from whey left over from mozzarella cheese production. This cheese is inexpensive and readily available.

raspberry rice pudding with vanilla sauce

1 bag SUCCESS® Rice
2 tablespoons sugar
1 cup skim milk
1 cup vanilla nonfat yogurt
1 teaspoon vanilla
Vanilla Sauce (recipe follows)
1 cup fresh raspberries

Prepare rice according to package directions.

Combine rice, sugar and milk in medium saucepan. Cook over medium heat, stirring frequently, until thick and creamy, 12 to 15 minutes. Remove from heat. Stir in yogurt and vanilla. Spoon into individual dessert dishes; top with Vanilla Sauce and raspberries. Garnish, if desired. *Makes 4 servings*

vanilla sauce

1 cup skim milk
5 egg whites
½ cup sugar
¼ cup vanilla nonfat yogurt

Bring milk just to a boil over medium heat. Remove from heat; cool to room temperature. Beat egg whites with sugar until soft peaks form; gradually whisk in milk. Transfer mixture to top of double boiler; cook over hot water, stirring frequently, until thick, 25 to 30 minutes. Remove from heat. Cool. Blend in yogurt. Chill.

nutrients per serving:
¼ of Pudding with Vanilla Sauce

Calories: 398
Carbohydrate: 84 g
Calories From Fat: 1%
Total Fat: <1 g
Saturated Fat: <1 g
Cholesterol: 2 mg
Sodium: 179 mg
Dietary Fiber: 3 g
Protein: 15 g

METRIC CONVERSION CHART

VOLUME MEASUREMENTS (dry)

1/8 teaspoon = 0.5 mL
1/4 teaspoon = 1 mL
1/2 teaspoon = 2 mL
3/4 teaspoon = 4 mL
1 teaspoon = 5 mL
1 tablespoon = 15 mL
2 tablespoons = 30 mL
1/4 cup = 60 mL
1/3 cup = 75 mL
1/2 cup = 125 mL
2/3 cup = 150 mL
3/4 cup = 175 mL
1 cup = 250 mL
2 cups = 1 pint = 500 mL
3 cups = 750 mL
4 cups = 1 quart = 1 L

VOLUME MEASUREMENTS (fluid)

1 fluid ounce (2 tablespoons) = 30 mL
4 fluid ounces (1/2 cup) = 125 mL
8 fluid ounces (1 cup) = 250 mL
12 fluid ounces (1 1/2 cups) = 375 mL
16 fluid ounces (2 cups) = 500 mL

WEIGHTS (mass)

1/2 ounce = 15 g
1 ounce = 30 g
3 ounces = 90 g
4 ounces = 120 g
8 ounces = 225 g
10 ounces = 285 g
12 ounces = 360 g
16 ounces = 1 pound = 450 g

DIMENSIONS

1/16 inch = 2 mm
1/8 inch = 3 mm
1/4 inch = 6 mm
1/2 inch = 1.5 cm
3/4 inch = 2 cm
1 inch = 2.5 cm

OVEN TEMPERATURES

250°F = 120°C
275°F = 140°C
300°F = 150°C
325°F = 160°C
350°F = 180°C
375°F = 190°C
400°F = 200°C
425°F = 220°C
450°F = 230°C

BAKING PAN SIZES

Utensil	Size in Inches/Quarts	Metric Volume	Size in Centimeters
Baking or	8×8×2	2 L	20×20×5
Cake Pan	9×9×2	2.5 L	23×23×5
(square or	12×8×2	3 L	30×20×5
rectangular)	13×9×2	3.5 L	33×23×5
Loaf Pan	8×4×3	1.5 L	20×10×7
	9×5×3	2 L	23×13×7
Round Layer	8×1½	1.2 L	20×4
Cake Pan	9×1½	1.5 L	23×4
Pie Plate	8×1¼	750 mL	20×3
	9×1¼	1 L	23×3
Baking Dish	1 quart	1 L	—
or Casserole	1½ quart	1.5 L	—
	2 quart	2 L	—

acknowledgments

The publisher would like to thank the companies and organizations listed below for the use of their recipes and photographs in this publication.

Birds Eye®
California Tree Fruit Agreement
ConAgra Foods®
Delmarva Poultry Industry, Inc.
Dole Food Company, Inc.
Equal® sweetener
Filippo Berio® Olive Oil
Fleischmann's® Margarines and Spreads
Florida Department of Agriculture and Consumer Services,
Bureau of Seafood and Aquaculture
Florida's Citrus Growers
Glucerna® is a registered trademark of Abbott Laboratories
Guiltless Gourmet®
Hershey Foods Corporation
National Honey Board
Nestlé USA
Reckitt Benckiser Inc.
Riviana Foods Inc.
The J.M. Smucker Company
Splenda® is a registered trademark of McNeil Nutritionals
The Sugar Association, Inc.
Reprinted with permission of Sunkist Growers, Inc.
Uncle Ben's Inc.
USA Rice
Washington Apple Commission
Wisconsin Milk Marketing Board

recipe index

general index